Care and Repair of Furniture
Including Refinishing and Upholstering

Care and Repair of Furniture
Including Refinishing and Upholstering
Desmond Gaston

Doubleday & Company, Inc.
Garden City, New York
1978

Published in the United States
by Doubleday & Company, Inc.
First published 1977
by William Collins Sons and Company Limited,
Glasgow and London, Great Britain
© 1977 Desmond Gaston
Designed and edited by Youé and Spooner Limited
Drawings by Malcolm Ward
from references supplied by Desmond Gaston

Printed in Great Britain
ISBN 0-385-14466-0
Library of Congress Catalog Number 78-55622

Contents

Foreword

As someone closely associated with the do-it-yourself world I recognise that although tremendous strides have been made as far as materials and techniques are concerned, little is being done to encourage individual craftsmanship. Everything leans towards a pre-packed mass market, and we've reached the point where perfectly functional furniture can be constructed with little more than saw and screwdriver. Surfaces come ready-finished, hinges and catches pre-positioned, so there is little to tax skill or imagination.

Because of these trends, I am delighted to have had the opportunity to make a detailed study of Desmond Gaston's text prior to publication and to discover that here is a man, every inch a craftsman, who takes pride in producing beautiful things – even if they do consume more time and energy. And I believe that there are tens of thousands of people who, despite the pre-processed age in which we live, have a yearning to satisfy the craftsman within; people who appreciate the beauty of well finished timber, elegant lines and immaculate upholstery – although these things may seem an age away from their own experience.

I have found great reluctance among many who would like to try their hand at renovation work, because of the real danger of spoiling things and thus affecting the value of furniture by adding inferior repair work. We must accept it is a danger, and I would join Desmond Gaston in discouraging anyone from tackling this kind of work unless he or she is willing to devote long hours to practising and improving techniques before turning to valuable pieces of furniture.

Desmond Gaston has produced a delightful book, for in it he conveys something of his love and enthusiasm for traditional furniture making. And he has combined this enthusiasm with very clear, concise instructions and first class illustrations. And I have no hesitation in recommending his book to the cautious, for in it they can learn the skills of the furniture-maker, wood finisher and upholsterer from a man with a lifetime of experience behind him.

I would recommend the book is used in two ways. First, relax and read it from cover to cover to get a feel for the subject and the man who has introduced it to you. Then use it more slowly as a textbook from which to learn and practise new skills. Concentrate on the chapters on tools, for upon these will depend the quality of your work.

May you find here hours of enjoyment and satisfaction. And I hope you will be inspired to keep alive something of our national heritage – a quality of craftsmanship for which this country has been noted for hundreds of years.

Tony Wilkins
Editor, *Do it yourself* magazine

Introduction

I have tried, in the following pages, to give not only instruction in repairing and re-furbishing good furniture but also to capture something of the romance of tackling this kind of work.

To me there is both enjoyment and fulfilment in bringing a wrecked piece of furniture back to life and usefulness. It may be a chair or a settee destined to be dumped, perhaps with little more left than a good timber frame. Or perhaps it's a chest of drawers or a cabinet which has long been relegated to the garage or shed.

An old friend of mine, a builder by trade, has often said to me: 'We often have to listen to information we already know, but keep listening because every now and then a little gem of new knowledge comes to light.'

Perhaps you will find a few gems here – if you can stomach the rest!

I'm aware that I have covered only a fraction of the jobs that can come under the headings of repair and re-furbishing, but the methods described for those I have included can be applied to many similar tasks.

When re-making or re-building, one is mindful of the craftmanship, the skill and pride of the tradesman who originally brought this piece into being. And at times I become so engrossed when copying the ways and methods of these craftsmen that I can almost sense the atmosphere filtering through from the time when the piece was being made.

The first section of the book deals with repairing and restoring woodwork, and I have written it assuming that the reader already has a knowledge of basic woodwork. If this is not so, I would advise taking a course at an evening or day institute to gain sufficient knowledge before attempting difficult jobs involving repair or restoration. This section also includes methods of finishing and polishing and a short piece on furniture metalwork.

I must confess I was hesitant about writing the first section, as I have seen so many lovely pieces of furniture ruined by enthusiastic do-it-yourselfers who really hadn't a clue. Their abilities may well lie in other directions, for even if such people read a thousand books of instructions they should never be let loose to repair quality furniture.

This is not you, however, for the people I refer to would never bother to read an introduction such as this!

But even to you, a person patently willing to learn, I would give a strong word of caution. Never attempt any repair or restoration to a valuable piece of furniture until you are absolutely confident of your ability. If there is an atom of doubt about this, take the job to an expert.

I have spent considerable time on basic instruction in the section on upholstery, assuming that you are just starting and know very little about this trade. Many of you may already have a considerable knowledge of cabinet-making and upholstery, but even so I hope that this book may still be of value.

Desmond Gaston.

Part I: Woodwork and Metalwork

Woodworking tools

A workshop, be it garden shed, a bench in a space at the end of the garage or even an unused room upstairs, is the first essential; a place to work unhindered, where you can arrange and lay out tools and equipment so that everything is to hand.

Your work bench should be stout, immovable and high. Just under elbow height is ideal, for this will save a lot of unnecessary backache that you get with a conventional lower bench. Attach to the bench a carpenter's vice of a good size. Quick-release jaws save a lot of time winding in and out. Make some smooth,

Fig 1 The workbench - showing the vice, bench stop and the well in the centre. Length 6ft (1.83m), width 2ft (609mm), height 3ft (915mm).

even, softwood blocks to attach to the inside of the vice plates. These will protect work when held in the vice.

You need a bench stop at the end of the bench, against which timber to be planed can be held. This can be a simple piece of 50mm × 50mm × 460mm (2in × 2in × 18in) long softwood let into the end of the bench so that it can be raised or lowered according to need. And, in the edge facing you, it is a good idea to fix and sharpen a row of spikes *(see fig.1)*.

In the top of the bench should be a dip, or well, usually formed by the space between two straight and true boards – used as working surfaces. Why a well? How many times I've nearly cut my hand on a sharp chisel left carelessly with edge towards me or, when planing, missed seeing the chisel lying on the blind side of the plane until it has grazed my fingertips! So, into the well, below your working surface, go all your sharp tools that are in use, well out of harm's way.

Tools are fascinating things. I remember starting work apprenticed to a joiner and marvelling at the sight of the old fellow's tools, tools he had used, cleaned and cherished for years and years. His set of wooden planes was a sight to behold, the handles and heads worn to the exact shape of his hand, fingers, thumb and palm of his left hand where they gripped the planes. It was the same with the handles of his saws, mallets, chisels and screwdrivers. And all the wood had that unmistakable colour, smoothness and polish which indicated years of deep impregnation with linseed oil, everyday use, cleaning and being cared for with pride.

To help you decide which tools and accessories to collect, let me introduce you to my workshop, to see what there is and how everything is arranged. My layout has evolved over many years and is now in a state where I can immediately put my hand to anything. Well, almost anything!

I have my bench under the window, with its back to a wall and with light from windows left and right. On the wall behind the bench I've arranged racks, hooks and fixings for all the tools in use. I also have drawers and drawers of duplicates, strange tools, old tools, 'once in a blue moon tools' which hardly ever see the light of day. But you never know what you might need sooner or later.

So let us have a look at the tools you will need *(see figs.2 and 3)*.

Mallet Forget the socking great ones you usually see in tool shops, and remember that the cabinet-maker's tools are usually smaller and finer than the joiner's or carpenter's. The mallet can be small; its head should be about 100mm × 76mm × 63mm (4in × 3in × 2½in).

Hammer Here again all you need is a small brad hammer with about a 12-15mm (½-⅝in) face, but with a fairly long handle.

Chisels I have two sets, one of old ordinary square-edged chisels used for cleaning out joints, scraping off old glue and so on and a set of best bevel-edged ones which I keep sharp and clean. The sizes of my chisels in the racks are from 3-38mm (⅛-1½in), but looking at them hanging there I can see which I use most by the varying lengths of blade. So I would say a set comprising 3mm (⅛in), 6mm (¼in), 12mm (½in) and 19mm (¾in) should be adequate to start with. They can be added to later.

Carving tools While I am on the subject of sharp-edged tools, a few carving tools are very useful. I have a couple of boxes full but generally use only about half a dozen of these. The most useful ones I find are gouges, 3mm (⅛in), 6mm (¼in), 9mm (⅜in), 12mm (½in); a fine veiner and a 12mm (½in) double bevelled tool. These and a sharp knife will get you over most difficulties.

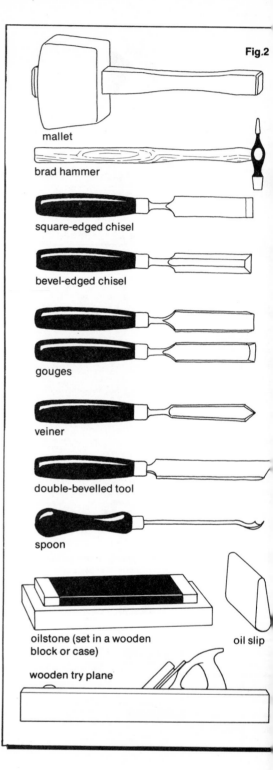

Fig.2

mallet

brad hammer

square-edged chisel

bevel-edged chisel

gouges

veiner

double-bevelled tool

spoon

oilstone (set in a wooden block or case)

oil slip

wooden try plane

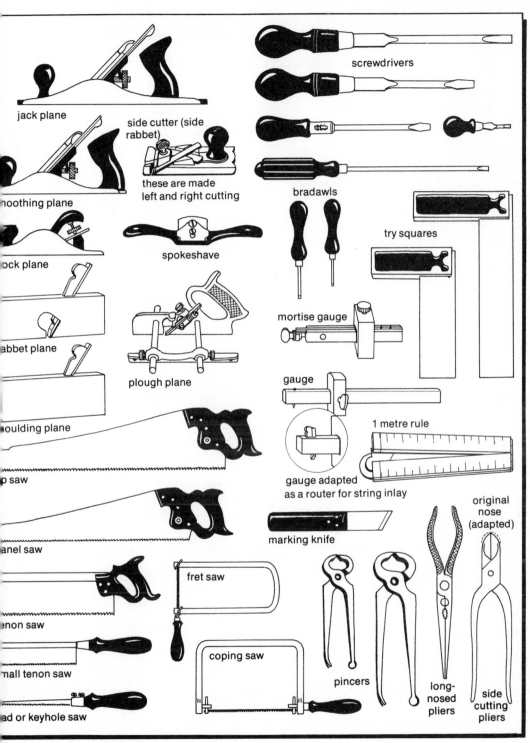

jack plane

side cutter (side rabbet)

these are made left and right cutting

smoothing plane

spokeshave

block plane

rabbet plane

plough plane

moulding plane

rip saw

panel saw

tenon saw

small tenon saw

pad or keyhole saw

screwdrivers

bradawls

mortise gauge

gauge

gauge adapted as a router for string inlay

marking knife

fret saw

coping saw

try squares

1 metre rule

original nose (adapted)

pincers

long-nosed pliers

side cutting pliers

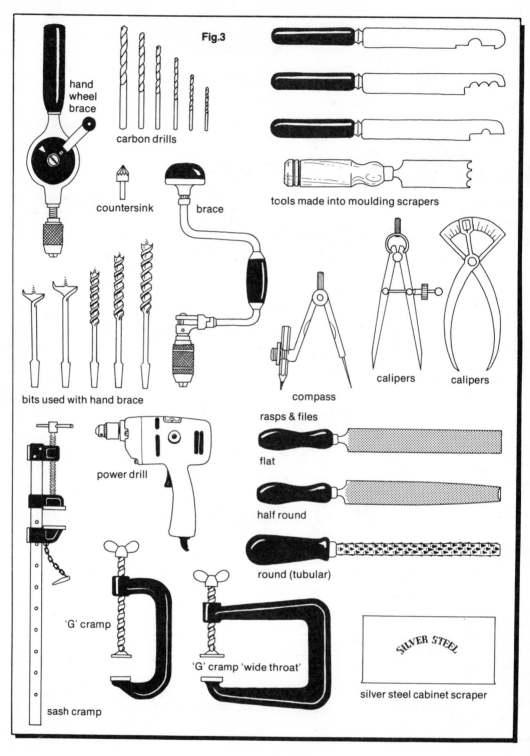

Fig.3

hand wheel brace

carbon drills

countersink

brace

tools made into moulding scrapers

bits used with hand brace

compass

calipers   calipers

power drill

rasps & files

flat

half round

round (tubular)

'G' cramp

'G' cramp 'wide throat'

sash cramp

SILVER STEEL

silver steel cabinet scraper

Planes On top of my bench I always keep four planes: my old wooden tryer, steel jack and smoothing planes and a small block plane. Also, in a drawer I have a very useful side cutter plane, a couple of spokeshaves, a good old wooden rabbet plane and a very useful tool called a combination plane or plough plane which has sets of irons for making grooves and mouldings.

I also have a specially adapted bookcase full of various old moulding planes which I've collected over the years. Many of my chisels, carving tools, planes and other tools I've come across while browsing around the numerous junk shops, antique shops and jumble sales in nearby towns. Keep an eye open for bargains in these places, for many old tools are of a much finer quality steel than the new tools on sale today. With a good clean-up, grind and sharpen, they will serve you well – despite their age.

Oilstones and oil slips To sharpen these tools, you need oilstones and oil slips (shaped stones for sharpening gouges and moulding plane irons).

Saws Looking up, I see hanging over my bench a rip saw (seldom used when a circular saw bench is at hand); a panel saw; a 300mm (12in) tenon saw; two small, round-handled tenon saws, one 200mm (8in) the other 125mm (5in); a most useful coping saw (small frame saw); a pad or keyhole saw and a fret saw. Of these, I suppose to begin with the panel saw, tenon and coping saw are the most essential. A fine fret saw is occasionally needed.

Screwdrivers About four sizes of these are necessary. The largest should be good and long – say 460-508mm (18-20in) – for it's surprising what extra purchase and control a long-handled screwdriver has over the short-handled one, even though their blades are the same width.

Small tools A variety of small tools will be required: bradawls, in about three sizes; rules and straight edges; a 300mm (12in) flexible ruler which is very handy for scribing straight lines on, say, a curved chair leg. A 220mm (9in) try square, a wooden gauge, a mortise gauge and a marking knife will also be useful.

Scraper or router I have adapted one old wooden gauge as a scraper or router for making very fine grooves – usually for stringing (fine line inlay) or parts of mouldings. Instead of the usual spiked scriber you get in the end of most gauges, I have used a very fine chisel-shaped piece of steel. This is made from a sewing needle broken off and shaped square across the end, then bevelled from each side. A number of these cutters of different sizes can be inserted tightly through the gauge bar and pushed out to the depth and width of the groove required. You'll be surprised what a neat channel you can make with this scraping tool, even in the softer woods.

Pincers and pliers Pincers and a pair of long-nosed pliers are a must, and I have some old wire side cutters ground to a point at the end which are very useful for removing panel pins and nails hammered by misguided people through joints.

Drills You will need a hand wheel brace and a good selection of carbon drills or high-speed drills. A countersinking bit will help you sink screws below the wood. For boring larger holes, use a brace, with bits sized from 10-31mm (⅜-1¼in).

There are many advantages in owning a power drill; I wouldn't be without mine. There are times when a small piece of furniture cannot be held in a vice, and it is a great advantage to be able to hold the piece with one hand and use your power drill with the other.

Cramps I have a goodly collection of sash cramps and you will need at least four, about 760mm (30in) long, as well as 'G' cramps of all sizes. There are other types of cramp and improvisations that you can make which I will deal with later on.

Other tools I have one rack on the wall in which I keep all sorts of odd things, including an old stainless steel table knife (very useful for mixing and spreading glue) and an old spoon for measuring small quantities. Then there are a number of thick-bladed knives which I have cut off and filed out as profiles for forming small mouldings and beads. These work very well as scrapers. There are knives of all sorts – most of them old, steel kitchen ones of excellent quality. These take a really keen edge. The rack also holds calipers and compasses, but I think I've said enough to show you that many useful tools can be made from all sorts of seeming junk.

Rasps and files The rasp, looked down upon by many a joiner, is nevertheless a very useful item for the furniture-maker and repairer. It will quickly get rid of surplus wood on legs, carvings and so on. I have several different shapes: a flat, two-sided one, coarse and fine-toothed; a half-round or convex; and a round, hollow Surform rasp – or shaper.

Cabinet scraper This is usually a strip of steel, about 100-125mm (4-5in) long by 50mm (2in) wide and about 1mm ($^1/_{32}$in) thick. Very little skill is required in using a scraper, but much practice is needed before you can sharpen and prepare it so that it scrapes.

This list of tools makes a formidable array and, of course, were you to go immediately to your nearest tool shop and purchase all these, you would find yourself parting with a large sum of money! However, as I have suggested before, many tools can be bought and collected from jumble sales, junk shops and at auction sales, and this way you can enjoy building up your collection gradually, piece by piece.

Looking after your tools

When you have a reasonable tool kit, it is important to keep tools in good condition – and in the main that means with keen edges and free from rust.

Rust is the enemy of all metal tools, especially those with cutting edges. And a small rust pit in the back of a chisel, for example, can cause a nasty gap in the chisel edge when the sharpened bevel reaches it. Keep a jar handy in which you can store a pad of oil-soaked felt, and after you finish with tools give them a light rub with oil before storing them away. This will prevent rusting. A light wipe with a clean rag is all that is needed on the next occasion you want to use the tools.

Small tools can be stored in a drawer or box in which is placed a piece of rust-inhibiting paper. This will protect the metal chemically – but such paper must be used in a confined space, otherwise the fumes given off are just dissipated. Store all edge tools in such a way that edges cannot be blunted. You can buy plastic caps for chisels, and most saws are now provided with a plastic protecting strip to slip over the teeth when the saw is not in use.

The next point to note is that all edge tools

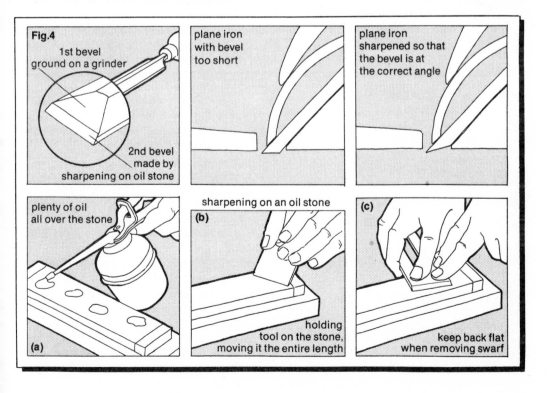

Fig.4
1st bevel ground on a grinder
2nd bevel made by sharpening on oil stone

plane iron with bevel too short

plane iron sharpened so that the bevel is at the correct angle

plenty of oil all over the stone

(a)

sharpening on an oil stone
(b)
holding tool on the stone, moving it the entire length

(c)
keep back flat when removing swarf

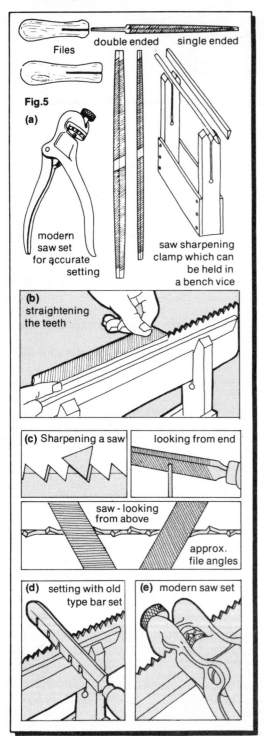

Files

double ended   single ended

Fig.5
(a)

modern
saw set
for accurate
setting

saw sharpening
clamp which can
be held in
a bench vice

(b)
straightening
the teeth

(c) Sharpening a saw   looking from end

saw - looking
from above

approx.
file angles

(d) setting with old
type bar set   **(e)** modern saw set

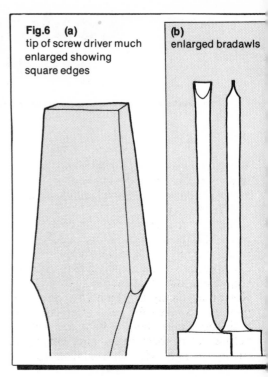

Fig.6 (a)
tip of screw driver much
enlarged showing
square edges

(b)
enlarged bradawls

should be kept sharp, for it is the blunt tool
which is dangerous. It is far more likely to
slip than bite into the wood. Most wood-
workers favour a long bevel on chisels and
gouges. Then, when sharpening on an
oilstone, a shorter bevel can be formed. But
I am in favour of keeping to just one bevel. I
know it takes longer to sharpen, but you will
never need to grind, and you always have a
good thin edge on the tool. The same is true
of plane irons, but ensure that the bevel
doesn't become too short or the back edge
will come into contact with the wood before
the cutting edge *(see fig.4)*.

It is difficult to describe sharpening
chisels and irons in words, so perhaps the
illustrations will help. It is a good idea to set
your stone in a block of wood, especially if a
honing guide is used as an aid. It ensures
even wear of the stone and avoids a hollow
in the middle.

(a) Put plenty of oil all over the stone.

(b) Hold the tool on the stone. Move it
using the whole length of the stone.

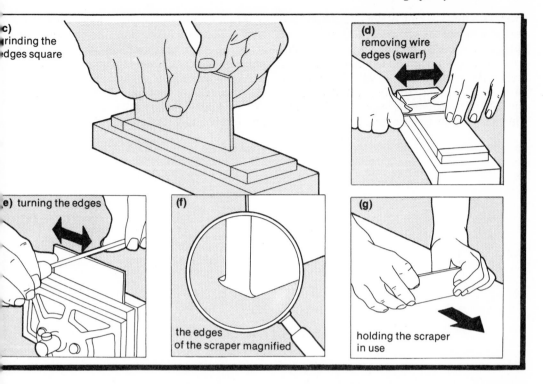

(c) Remove the swarf or wire edge.

To get the cutting edge really keen, use a strip of leather as a hone or strop in the way barbers used to strop a cut-throat razor.

Sharpening and setting a saw is a skilled operation *(see fig.5)*, and if you wish to try it I suggest you buy a saw-sharpening guide – then follow the instructions very carefully. Merely sharpening the teeth with a file can do more harm than good. Once you have mastered the guide, you will find that even a new saw blade will benefit from a little sharpening. You also need a saw set which sets the teeth at the correct angle – each alternate tooth is set the opposite way and ensures clearance for the saw blade. The method is shown in diagrams *(a)* to *(e)*.

Screwdrivers will also benefit from a little regular attention *(see fig.6)*, for the tip should be nice and square with clearly-defined edges *(a)*. You will never get a driver with rounded edges to stay in a slot when pressure is applied. It is best not to use a file on a driver tip as it tends to soften the blade. Grind it carefully on your oil stone, finally squaring off the tip.

Sharpen a bradawl in a similar manner *(b)*, though it can come to a sharp point rather than have a squared end.

The best cabinet scrapers are made from silver steel, and it does pay to buy the best, for a cheap one will not hold its edge. And there is a knack to sharpening.

First square off each long edge on an oil stone *(c)*, and remove the swarf edge from each side *(d)*. Place the scraper in a vice, protecting the vice jaws with wood blocks.

Now you need a bar of very hard, smooth steel. I use a chrome vanadium screwdriver blade about 6mm (¼in) in diameter. Rub the blade along the edge of the scraper blade, holding it at an angle *(e)*. Apply a hard, even pressure, and come right off the end of the scraper each time. The object of the exercise is to turn the square edge over to form a burr – which acts rather like a hook when in use. Enlarged it will resemble *(f)*.

When sharpened correctly, the scraper

will take a thin shaving off any hardwood for the full width of the scraper *(g)*. Quite a lot of practice is needed before you get a really good edge, but once you have mastered the technique you will have a valuable tool for putting the finishing touches to flat surfaces and for finishing woods such as mahogany. This very often has opposing grain which makes it impossible to plane to a finish.

It is also, in my opinion, the best tool for stripping polished surfaces – even hard polishes such as cellulose and polyurethane.

Apply the same care and maintenance to all your cutting tools, whether twist drills, bits or knife blades. They will work more efficiently and with far less effort.

Structural repairs

EXAMINATION AND PLANNING THE SEQUENCE OF WORK

Before starting work, make a thorough examination of the piece of furniture to be repaired. Let us imagine you have some-thing simple – say a small stool or maybe its modern equivalent, a dressing-table stool with bars or rails low down between the legs *(see fig.7)*.

You probably owned such a stool for many years, never really taking much notice of it until it suddenly collapsed. Ever since, it has been gathering dust in the corner of the garage.

Examine it carefully, making mental notes of the work to be done. First see what the damage is. One leg is split from the middle of a joint to half way down its length. One of the stretchers (rails) is broken, and all the other joints are loose *(a)*.

Luckily the seat, a drop-in trap type, is undamaged, so you can put that to one side. The joints are loose, but note that they all have pegs through the mortise and tenons, so before you can knock the joints apart you will have to remove them. Some go right through to the inside, so tap them out, using a smaller diameter hardwood peg or a large

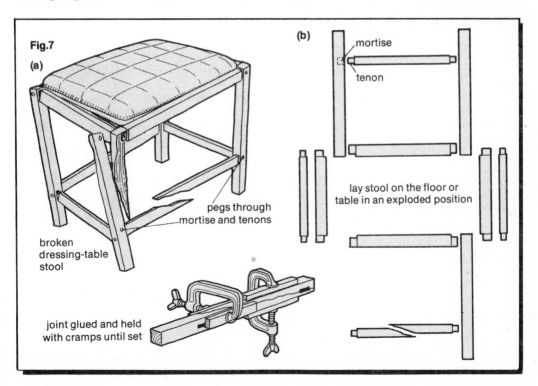

Fig.7

(a)

pegs through
mortise and tenons

broken
dressing-table
stool

joint glued and held
with cramps until set

(b)

mortise

tenon

lay stool on the floor or
table in an exploded position

nail with its point cut off as a punch. Pegs that don't go through will have to be drilled out, using a twist drill equal in diameter to that of the peg.

It is important that before you start to take the stool to pieces you make sure that when you re-assemble you know which piece goes where – and which tenon goes into which mortise! So number all joints with a wax pencil or crayon, or something that won't leave a permanent mark or damage the polish. To make doubly sure, it helps to lay your stool on the floor or table in a sort of exploded position *(7b)*.

Remember that at this stage you are just examining and assessing the work to be done. In the long run, it pays to spend some time doing this rather than to rush in and maybe cause more damage.

Before starting to re-assemble the stool, you must repair the split leg and broken rail. Luckily there is no wood missing and the splits are long and tapering, so glue and cramps should be all that's necessary.

Now for somthing a little larger. Let us assume you have a bureau in the boxroom. It came from old Uncle George, and it's in pieces *(see fig.8)*. Uncle George believed it to be Sheraton, but an antique dealer confirmed that although very well made it dated no earlier than 1910. Let's have it out and see what's wrong with it.

Remember, in this chapter we are dealing with major structural repairs, so we must ignore, for the present, scratches, dents, missing banding and stringing and concentrate on getting the carcase into a firm and strong state. With a bureau in this condition, it's obviously going to be a fairly long job, so it will be wise to write a list of things you will have to do. By thinking the job through, you will get an idea of the correct sequence. For instance, a gaping joint from top to bottom of the side of the bureau will have to be attended to before you re-glue and replace the drawer runners.

Examine every part thoroughly. Underneath the bottom there may well be glue blocks missing. And the bracket feet will probably need corner posts and glue blocks

Fig.8   Uncle George's bureau

replaced. The joints between the partition rails (between the drawers) and the sides are gaping and the dust liners (under the drawers) are dropping down. Also, the back boards are loose. Looking at the drawers, inside, you will see that many of the panels have shrunk and no longer reach the back. The drawer runners are badly worn, and drawer stops are missing, allowing the drawers to tilt back and slide in too far. Although I have drawn an imaginary picture of a wreck of a bureau, when you get to work and break the work into sections, things are usually not as bad as they look.

You may well come across jobs where you just can't see how to cope with them or how to effect a repair. I'm very often faced with this problem and I remember the old fellow to whom I was apprenticed saying: 'There's no such word as Can't!' So bear this in mind when you can't see how to do it. Put it to one side and 'sleep on it', or seek expert advice. I have a friend, a very clever and practical fellow, who has a workshop very near mine. We talk over problems together and it's surprising how, suddenly, a solution appears, and you say: 'Why didn't I think of that before?'

WOODWORM AND DECAY

When you come to repair old furniture you will invariably find signs of woodworm. The woodworm is the enemy of all furniture, and its taste is for woods such as birch and beech, which are used for most seat rails and frames in upholstered chairs. They love to get their teeth into walnut, and with oak they prefer the sapwood, though when hungry they will go for the heartwood as well.

There are hardwoods which resist attack. Mahogany usually escapes, though I have seen woodworm in some types. And teak is an oily, naturally preserved wood. Nothing seems sacred to the woodworm. I've seen a badly infected piano with holes that have been eaten right through the lead balancing weights in the keys! I don't know how the worm must have felt when he emerged from the lead, but it just goes to show that they will stop at nothing.

After finding signs of infestation, you must decide whether it is possible to cure by treatment or whether the infected wood must be removed.

If the plywood back of a piece of furniture is badly holed, it is usually best to remove and burn it, replacing it with a new back. If the damage is in the leg of a table or chair, try to find out how much wood has been eaten away inside by probing with a needle. I've had black lacquered chairs in the workshop with broken legs where practically the whole of the inside of the legs has been honeycombed, yet barely half a dozen holes have shown through the surface lacquer.

In the case of antique furniture, the rule is to cut out and replace as little as possible, but with a modern piece of furniture the emphasis is, of course, on making it strong and sound once again.

How does it start? Well, adult beetles can fly – but you may have a breeding ground indoors. Perhaps you've found a yellowish dust, or frass, under a fireside chair – or by a large wicker log basket. The whole basket may be full of activity, indicated by holes. Woodworm love wicker-work! How did they get there? Take out a log and remove a piece of the bark. See the holes in the sapwood inside the bark? This is how it came into your house: from the log into your wicker basket, basket to fireside chair – where to next?

Let us consider the method of treatment. There are many good preparations on the market and most have clear, written instructions on the can or bottle. I find the best way to effect a cure is to inject liquid into at least one hole every square inch with a good pump. I have an oil can with a pump action which I've fitted with a special nozzle and shield to prevent worm killer squirting back in my face. With this you can really get some pressure, and you can see the liquid travelling along the grain as you pump. Alternatively, you can buy insecticide in an aerosol can, which is also effective.

The next stage is to give all the affected areas a good soaking with a brush. Afterwards, when they are dry, fill all the holes with a wax polish similar in colour to the wood, applying it with a putty knife or palette knife. Examine the wood after a few months to see if there are any new holes. If there are, repeat the process, but if the first treatment is done thoroughly this should not be necessary. All the grubs will have died inside.

When treating a piece of furniture that has to be repaired – for example, a chair that requires all the joints to be re-glued and on which the woodworm has attacked near or in the joints – treat each piece after you have dismantled the chair, then leave for a week or two so that the solution dries out. Otherwise the bond between wood and glue will be very poor.

Prevention is better than cure, and there are several things we can bear in mind. First, keep a watchful eye open for first signs: new holes near the bottom of legs, in birch seat rails and chair seats. Look at the backs of large pieces of furniture, and watch for light-coloured dust on the floor under-

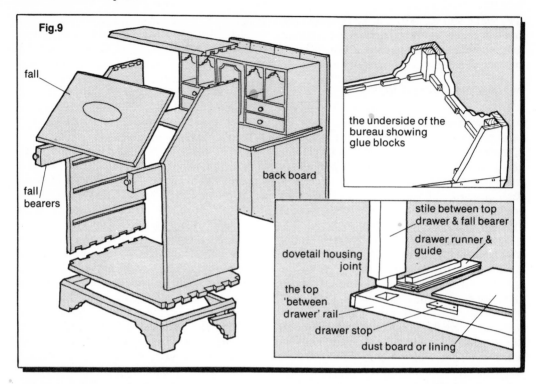

Fig.9

fall

fall bearers

back board

the underside of the bureau showing glue blocks

stile between top drawer & fall bearer

drawer runner & guide

dovetail housing joint

the top 'between drawer' rail

drawer stop

dust board or lining

neath. Second, you can buy insecticidal furniture polish that will kill off any beetles which try to lay eggs.

Other forms of decay are much more rare and are usually found only in very old wood. They take various forms, usually following the grain in bands, where the wood appears soft and crumbling. A good soak with clear wood preservative will check this.

STARTING WORK

I think I will concentrate on describing methods of repairing one specific piece of furniture, and then you can relate this to other pieces of similar construction. Later we can deal with repairs peculiar to other furniture. So let's concentrate on the bureau already described.

Move the bureau down to the workshop, having examined it and decided upon the best way to repair it. Take off everything that can easily be removed – drawers, the fall, fall bearers, the loose back boards *(see fig.9)*. And don't forget your crayon for

marking the position of all these pieces!

It will be as well to get the interior fitments (pigeon holes) and small drawers out too. These should come out in one piece if you can ease the glue top and bottom. You cannot do this with a bureau of an earlier period (pre-Victorian), as in most cases the partitions forming the pigeon holes were made and grooved into the actual timber of the carcase.

Your bureau, now stripped of all bracing support, may be very rocky, so go the whole hog and take everything apart. Remove the bracket feet – or what's left of them – and mark them. A gentle tap with a wide chisel and mallet under the glue blocks will shift them. Then carefully remove the plinth moulding around the base on each side.

Now remove the top and the bottom – the top first. As in all good cabinet work, the top is secured with concealed dovetail joints so, holding a block of wood the width of the top under it, gently knock the top upwards a little at a time at each end. As it comes up you will see where the dovetails are situated. With the top off, tackle the bottom. Turn the carcase upside down and you will see that the dovetails come right through. Gently knock the bottom off in the same way, taking care not to bruise the wood.

Remember to lay each section in an exploded fashion on the floor as you dismantle, as suggested earlier. The rest is easy, and everything should practically fall apart. Be cautious with the drawer division rails; they are either mortised into the sides, or they may be slid in from the front with a one-sided dovetail on the top edge. Have a look at the joints that are already gaping, and you should be able to determine whether to knock them out towards the front or sideways. Avoid brute force!

You will probably find that pieces of wood keep falling out from somewhere inside. Try to keep track of where they come from. If the drawer runners drop out, you will see that they are grooved into the sides and that they also have a small tongue that fits into the backs of the division rails. The division rails and runners will be grooved on the insides to take the dust liners. Mark all of these pieces carefully if you can.

There may be various pieces missing from the inside such as the guides between the top drawer and fall bearers. These may have fallen out and got lost at some time. And items such as drawer stops – those small pieces glued to the top of the division rails – may also be missing.

Next, take every piece in turn and scrape off the old glue. Clean out the dovetails, mortises and grooves so that when re-assembled they will fit neatly, the joints will close up tight and the new glue will hold really fast.

Now, check your notes and see what you've put down for the first step. Yes, that split side, now in two pieces. It is actually a glued joint that has come apart, so it's perfectly straight and clean, apart from the old glue and dirt that has accumulated.

Clean up the surfaces of the two edges to be joined, carefully scraping the dirt and glue off with a cabinet scraper or a

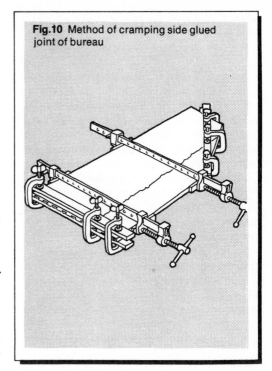

Fig.10 Method of cramping side glued joint of bureau

straight-bladed knife. Be especially careful not to remove any wood and to preserve the sharp edges. Put the two edges together and see if they fit without any daylight showing between them. If they don't match up, they will have to be trimmed with a try plane – but I will deal with this in the next section when we will study joints in more detail.

You will need two or three sash cramps, four pieces of wood about 50mm × 25mm (2in × 1in) and about the width of your bureau side, as well as six 100mm (4in) or 125mm (5in) 'G' cramps.

Mix up your glue and spread along the two edges to be joined. Take your pieces of wood and rub wax polish, linseed oil or paraffin wax on one side of each to prevent glue sticking where it shouldn't. Lay two of your pieces of wood down on a flat surface (*see fig.10*) and place the side of your bureau on top of them. Put the other pieces on top, immediately above the pieces underneath, and apply the 'G' cramps lightly, one in the middle and one at each end. The sash cramps can now be put across to pull the joint together.

Always use scrap material as softening between cramp and furniture, otherwise bad bruising will occur. Sometimes when I go to our local timber merchant I rummage about on his rubbish heap picking out pieces of soft insulation board. This I cut into small blocks about 38mm × 50mm (1½in × 2in) in size, keeping a box full ready for use when cramping joints.

Tighten the cramps on the bureau side and make sure the joint is flush in the centre. If it is uneven, place more cross pieces with 'G' cramps across the centre, then use thin wedges between the joint and the batten to get the wood flush. Don't forget to wax these to prevent adhesion.

If you are using the simple waterproof resin glue, don't wipe away glue that has squeezed from the joint. It will easily peel away from the polished outside surface when dry. On the inside it may need persuading with a chisel, but it's better than

Fig.11 Fitting new runners to drawer

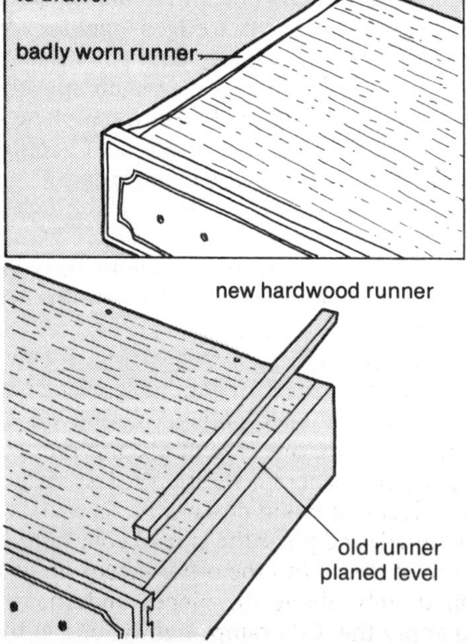

badly worn runner

new hardwood runner

old runner planed level

spreading it about so that everything is covered by a thin film of glue! Put the repaired side somewhere in the warm to set. Then sit down and have another look at that list you made out.

Yes, the drawers can be seen to, using up the glue you have left to fix the bottom panels and loose dovetails in the sides. You also have to plane down those worn drawer runners and fit new wood to bring the drawer side to the right width *(see fig.11)*.

If you finish the drawers and still have time, you can make up those missing parts of the bracket feet. For these, you'll need some mahogany to match the existing wood.

All repairs to panels may not be so simple. On occasions you may have to replace pieces completely, so be on the lookout for pieces of hardwood furniture. Most antique shops have a yard where they keep all the old broken pieces, and occasionally you'll come across some beautiful pieces of timber in the shape of leaves of tables, drawer fronts and sides of wardrobes, in mahogany, walnut, oak, ash or satin walnut.

Watch out too for pieces that have been veneered, such as doors, drawer fronts, table tops and parts of chests of drawers. Although the wood underneath is only yellow pine, the veneer, after soaking, is easily removed for re-use in repair work.

There are plenty of huge Edwardian wardrobes made of ash, satin walnut and even satinwood to be found – but beware, for I believe even these are becoming valuable and shouldn't be broken up just for the wood unless badly damaged. You can collect legs, chair rails and stretchers, but you'll find that wood in the square or plank form is the most useful.

For making up the missing parts of your bureau feet, you need to find a piece of mahogany that matches the existing wood, so plane a shaving from underneath or behind the foot to check the raw colour of the wood – then see what you have available in your collection.

There are a number of different kinds of mahogany, from the very heavy, dark Cuban and Spanish to the light, soft, open-grained mahogany used a lot in the last century for drawer sides and bottoms and to this day for cigar boxes.

To make up any missing brackets, draw a template on a piece of cardboard, using one of the feet that is still whole as a guide. Cut out your template and mark out a new bracket on a suitable piece of wood. Holding this in your vice, cut it out with a coping saw. Note that the brackets forming the front legs are mitred at the corners, so you will have to make two mitres. For this you need a mitre box and, as this must be set out and cut extremely accurately, you may prefer to buy one rather than improvise.

Your bureau side has now been in the cramps for a whole day, so it should be well and truly set. Remove the cramps and clean off the dry surplus glue, being careful not to scratch the outside polished surface. Now the way is clear for you to start re-assembling, and you need to put the sides, rails, top shelf (part of writing surface behind the fall), top and bottom sections together in one go. So make sure you have sufficient sash cramps and that they are long enough. And mix up enough glue.

You won't have any problem deciding which piece goes together first or last, because you'll remember the order in which you took the bureau apart. And of course, you have all the pieces laid out in position, haven't you?

When positioning a cramp, make sure before you tighten it that it is exactly at right angles to the front and back edges – or parallel with the top or the bottom in the case of our bureau. If this detail is not attended to, the work could be drawn out of square or made to wind (twist) when you tighten the cramps.

When you have the main body assembled and cramped up, all the joints flush to the front, the dovetailed joints top and bottom well and truly down, and all surplus glue squeezed out, make sure the carcase is square and that it keeps in that state. Use your try square for this job. The obvious way to hold it would be to fix the back on, but you will need to get inside to glue the

runners and guides. So, instead, find a piece of batten about 25mm × 25mm (1in × 1in), and use it to brace the carcase by nailing it diagonally across the back. But before you nail it, check again to ensure all is square, as follows.

Take a long, straight-edge rule, place it diagonally from top corner to bottom corner and mark the length on the stick. Then place it across the opposite way and mark again. You now have two marks and they could be up to 25mm (1in) apart. Make a mark half way between the two; again, place your measuring stick diagonally across the back of the bureau and move the carcase gently until it corresponds with this central mark. Nail on your bracing piece, and there you are, all square. Don't drive the nails home, as you will have to remove them later.

Leave this for a day at the very least so that the glue sets thoroughly. Then, after taking off the cramps, turn the whole unit upside down and re-fix the plinth moulding.

In cabinet work, nails are used as little as

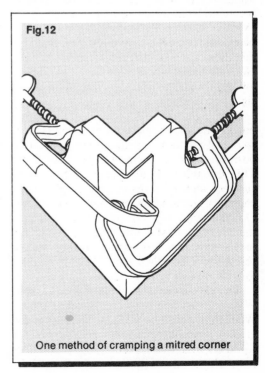

Fig.12

One method of cramping a mitred corner

possible, but you will probably need a few fine panel pins (or veneer pins, as the finer ones are called) as well as glue to fix the moulding and leg brackets in place. Pins should be punched well below the surface with a fine punch, no bigger than the head of the pin used.

The better way, if you have time, is to use only glue to fix the mouldings. Strap them on tightly with adhesive tape. I always keep a large roll of self-adhesive tape handy for this purpose. Then there won't be any nasty little pin holes, which nearly always show even when filled.

The bracket feet are then applied flush or nearly flush with the outside edge of the moulding. Glue them on and hold the mitres of the front feet by strapping around with tape or by cramping both ways with a metal angle strip held over the corner *(see fig.12)*. Each end of the brackets can be secured with a fairly long panel pin.

The corner posts and glue blocks come next. The method of fixing is as follows. Make sure that the face side and face edge of the wood from which you cut your blocks is exactly square. Plane and clean up your blocks nicely, even across the end grain, so that there are no rough edges from saw cuts. Nothing looks worse than wood put into a job in a rough sawn state – even if it is out of sight, underneath.

Spread glue on both surfaces of the corner posts to be joined; place them 25mm (1in) or so out of position and slide them down into position, pressing them firmly as they slide. This excludes all air between the wood surfaces and squeezes out the surplus glue, causing a suction between the two surfaces. Do the same with the glue blocks. Press them home and slide them along a little and they'll stay put. You don't need to nail or screw them, and they are all that is required to hold the feet firm.

Why do we use a lot of short glue blocks? Why not just one long one glued in place? Well, that would be all right so long as the grain of your block ran the same way as the wood on which you were fixing it. But note that, where we are fitting blocks behind the side brackets, the grain of the wood forming the base of our bureau is running the opposite way.

Now, wood expands and shrinks most in the width of the plank, and it does this continuously, according to the varying humidity of the atmosphere. Perhaps the worst offender is oak – but movement happens to most woods. In the length of the grain the dimension is practically constant.

If short blocks are placed across the grain, the space between the blocks allows for expansion and contraction. If a long, unbroken block were used, as soon as the wood underneath expanded – bang would go the glue joint and off it would come. If the wood shrank, the wood underneath would probably split.

When the feet are well and truly set you can turn your bureau the right way up – but just before you do so, fit some fairly large domes of silence (those plated steel domes with the spikes) to the feet. I find they make the piece of furniture easier to move, and they also protect the feet, for it is when the furniture is pushed about – especially on carpet – that the brackets catch and are forced off.

With the bureau on its feet you can tackle the inside jobs. The runners are all badly worn and need replacing, so take the best of the old ones to copy and make new runners from a hardwood such as oak or mahogany. Don't forget to use your plough plane to cut out the groove for the dust linings between the drawers. A lot of dust forms under drawers. Many times I have been asked to look at a chest of drawers because owners have found wood dust under the drawers. Usually this is dust from wood worn away by constant rubbing of dry wood surfaces – runner on runner. It is not caused by woodworm, as they have feared.

You will have noticed, of course that the runners for the top drawer are wider because they have to take the fall bearer. There is also a guide piece to glue on, which lies between the bearer and the top drawer.

When you have made your new runners, glue them into the grooves in the sides, then slide the dust linings in from the back. You can now trim your drawer runners to fit, for I expect you left them a little on the large side when you made them up.

Put the fall bearers in place and stick in the pegs which prevent them from coming right out. A little wax polish on the sliding surfaces will work wonders.

Tackle the drawer stops next. Make up the number you require: set your gauge to the thickness of the drawer front and scribe lines on the top surface of the partition rail in the places where you will put the stops. These are usually about 100-125mm (4-5in) from each side. Glue the stops up to the scribed lines and try the drawer. If everything fits, hammer a couple of panel pins through the stop.

It may be as well to clean and polish the pigeon hole assembly before putting it back, as you will find it easier to get into the nooks and crannies. The fall can be screwed on next, and here you may encounter another problem if the screws won't hold. It is no use

putting longer screws in because they will probably come through the front.

The best way is to drill out the holes to about 3mm (⅛in) diameter. Go very carefully with your drill – you don't want a hole right through to the outside! Glue well-fitting plugs or pegs into the holes and chisel off flush. Then lay in your flap hinges, make small holes (half the size of the screws) with a bradawl. Now put in your screws and all will be well.

All that remains is to fix the back boards. There will be no problem here as there has been only a little shrinkage which can be made good by gluing a strip of wood on to one of the boards before you put them in. Glue all the joints in the back boards as you place them, and make sure they are all flush. Fix with panel pins top, bottom and sides.

You have now finished all the major repairs, and your bureau, although still looking pretty sorry for itself, is at least strong and sound.

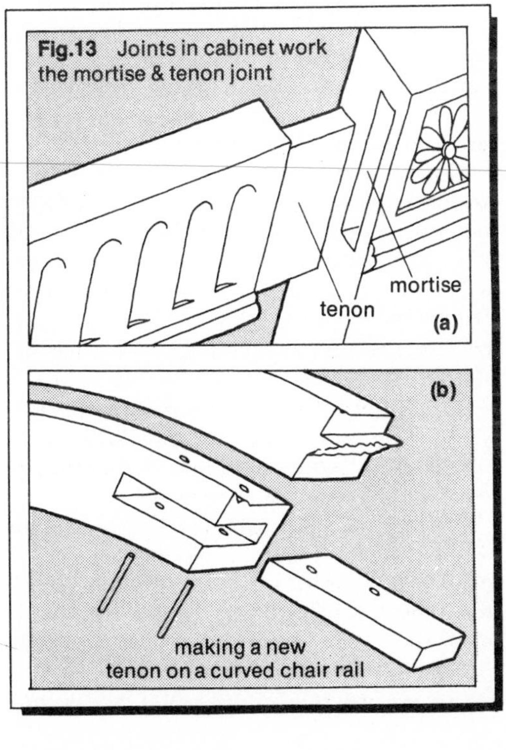

JOINTS AND GLUES

Before we go on to repair other items of furniture I would like to record a few thoughts on joints and glue. What makes a good joint? To take the most common, the mortise and tenon *(see fig.13)*, as an example, the tenon should be a tight fit in the mortise, but not so tight that the stile splits when it's driven in and not loose enough to allow you to pull it in and out easily *(a)*.

The faces of the wood surrounding the tenon, the shoulders as they are called, should be square and even, so that they fit with no gap against the stile.

When gluing a joint like this, make sure you have covered all meeting surfaces with glue, then cramp well. When you come across a very loose joint, where the tenon fairly rattles about in the mortise, don't think that by filling the mortise with glue you will make it into a good joint. When drying or hardening most glues tend to shrink, and the greater the amount of glue the more shrinkage there is, so in no time your joint will be apart again! In cases such as this it is best to make up the size of the tenon with

Fig.13 Joints in cabinet work the mortise & tenon joint

mortise

tenon

(a)

(b)

making a new tenon on a curved chair rail

thin pieces of wood, gluing them on and leaving to dry before trimming the stile to fit the joint.

On occasions you will find a tenon that has broken right off *(13b)*. In this case you will have to form a new tenon on the rail by slotting in a new piece of wood and pegging it in place. Make sure it's a really good fit and that the wood is of the same strength and nature as the original. Again, do this in two stages, leaving the new tenon to set before fitting and completing the joint.

The next most common joint you will encounter is the dowelled joint *(see fig.14)*. You will find that most frames of upholstered furniture (settees and easy chairs) are secured this way. There's a lot to be said for a well-made dowelled joint, although it's been condemned as a lazy man's way and is scorned by many joiners. There are many shapes of upholstered chair frames that are made much stronger with dowels than with other types of joint. I'm thinking particularly of the tub easy chair with the seat rails shaped in a semi-circle. If these rails were mortised and tenoned with the back legs (as some are), consider the tenon cut on the side rail. How short the grain will be *(a)* – not much strength there!

For making dowelled joints you can buy all sorts of guides and jigs. Some are very good and ensure an accurate fit, but if you don't possess one of these gadgets there is a simple way of doing the job. Let us assume, for example, that you want to make a replacement drop-in seat frame for a stool and that you have prepared your pieces of wood and cut them accurately to size *(b)*. In the end of each rail, knock in two panel pins, leaving 3mm (⅛in) proud. Cut off the heads. Lay your frame on a flat surface and press rails and stiles together, and the panel pins will mark the stiles. Then you can accentuate the marks with a pointed awl and all is ready to bore the holes. The most commonly used dowel rods are 9mm (⅜in), and 12mm (½in) for use with heavier frames and legs.

When drilling the holes, make sure your bit is perfectly upright, thus boring at right

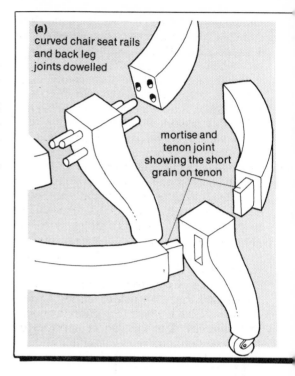

(a) curved chair seat rails and back leg joints dowelled

mortise and tenon joint showing the short grain on tenon

angles to the wood face. Cut dowel rod off to the correct lengths, making sure they are not too long. And before gluing, chisel a groove down the length of each dowel. This makes for easier cramping, as all the air and surplus glue can escape along the groove *(c)*.

Dowels can also be used to make plank-to-plank glued joints. There are several ways of making a joint of this description. The usual way is with glue only *(d)*, but sometimes it's done with dowels about 228mm (9in) apart *(e)*. Very often the boards are tongued and grooved *(f)*, while another method is called screwed and slotted *(g)*. With all these methods the most important factor is to ensure that the two faces to be joined are straight and square so that they fit together with no spaces between.

Perhaps the strongest of all these methods is the tongued and grooved joint *(f)*. A groove is made in the edge of each board, and then a tongue, which should be made with the grain running in the opposite direction, is inserted in the grooves.

The screwed and slotted joint is a method

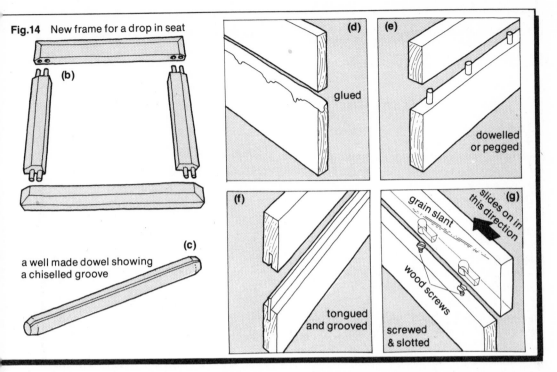

Fig.14 New frame for a drop in seat

(b)

(c)

a well made dowel showing
a chiselled groove

(d) glued

(e) dowelled
or pegged

(f) tongued
and grooved

(g) grain slant · slides on in this direction · wood screws · screwed
& slotted

that requires no cramping (*g*). The faces to
be joined are set out so that in one face you
have keyway shaped slots at intervals of
150-200mm (6-8in). On the other face steel
countersunk screws usually size 1½in × 8 or
10 are placed and left protruding 9-12mm
(⅜-½in). The screws are placed so that they
reach the end of the slot when the boards are
flush at each end.

An important point to remember before
setting out is that the grain of the board into
which you will cut the slots should descend
from the hole to the end of the slot. The
reason for this is that the edge of the screws
will follow the direction of the grain, thus
closing the joint as they progress along the
slots.

The dovetail joint appears in furniture in
several forms, three of which we have
already mentioned: the dovetail drawer
joint; the one-sided dovetail joining shelves
and division rails; and the dovetails forming
the joints of top and bottom to sides. If you
remember, the top of the bureau had
concealed or secret dovetails.

You will find many ways in which this
joint is used. Turn the tripod wine table
upside down (*see fig.15*), and, since it is a
well-made piece, you will see that each leg is
secured by a dovetailed tenon which slides
up into the base of the central pillar (*a*). If
you could take the top off your Pembroke
table, you would find that the rail over the
drawer is dovetailed into the leg tops (*b*).

There is one encouraging thing with
furniture repairing – you will seldom find
you have to make a completely new joint.
There will usually be something left for you
to set out to or to copy. The mortise is still
sound although the tenon has gone – or *vice
versa*; or the dovetails are still intact from
which you can mark out your new wood.

The joints I have mentioned are the main
ones in cabinet work. You will discover
many variations of these, but by going
carefully and being observant you will learn
to cope with them.

I have referred briefly to glues before, and
to my mind all the well-known makes seem
as good as each other if applied correctly.

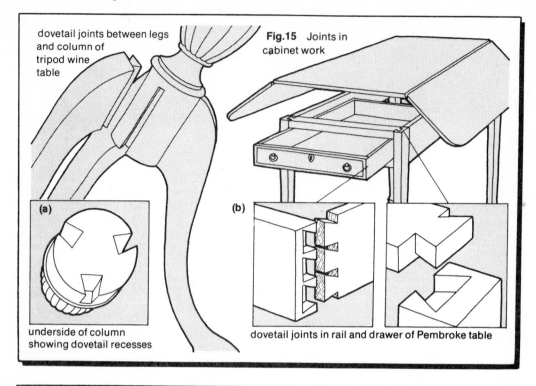

dovetail joints between legs and column of tripod wine table

Fig.15   Joints in cabinet work

(a)

underside of column showing dovetail recesses

(b)

dovetail joints in rail and drawer of Pembroke table

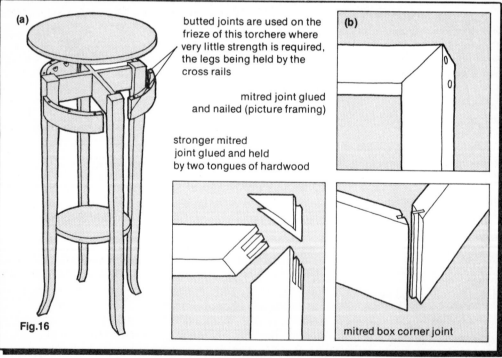

(a)

butted joints are used on the frieze of this torchere where very little strength is required, the legs being held by the cross rails

(b)

mitred joint glued and nailed (picture framing)

stronger mitred joint glued and held by two tongues of hardwood

Fig.16

mitred box corner joint

There are some that, when dry, retain a certain amount of elasticity, which is an advantage with some types of joint *(see fig.16)*, such as the uncomplicated butted joint *(a)*, mitred joints used for picture frames *(b)*, and simple joints that may have to take a lot of punishment and knocks. In these cases a hard-setting glue would shatter and break with a hard knock.

An advantage with the simple cold water resin glue is that a small amount of colouring matter can be added (ordinary powdered pigment). Although this weakens the glue to a small degree, it does prevent that thin white line in a joint that can't be disguised with stain. I use a little burnt sienna when working on mahogany and burnt umber for oak, varying the shade by the amount of pigment added. These two pigments seem to be safe. I don't advise using any other colouring matter; I've tried several and some have strange effects on the glue, such as retarding the setting.

REPAIRS TO OTHER FURNITURE

Now let us look at some other pieces of furniture and study repairs which are peculiar to each.

Chairs These are perhaps the most used pieces of furniture, and we'll start with dining chairs. There is an enormous variety of these around, some of which are of good design and of consequently strong construction. Others tend to be gimmicky in design and were probably never meant to last any longer than the period of fashion in which they were made. But let us take for our examples a few classic and basic styles in chairs.

The complaint suffered by most chairs, especially those without stretcher rails underneath, is loose joints between the back uprights and the seat rails. This is caused, in most cases, by those visitors who insist on sitting down on a chair and tilting back on the back legs!

The remedy for loose joints on dining chairs with loose seats is fairly simple. It entails removing the seat and then taking apart the joints; cleaning out mortises and tenons, or dowels, then re-gluing and cramping. Most back joints have a corner glue block screwed in. This should also be cleaned off and re-glued.

If the joints are dowelled, you will find, when you take the joint apart, that the dowels will stay in either the rail end or the back upright. Check that they are well secured in whichever part they are retained, and remember the slogan – 'When in doubt, drill out – and put in a new dowel.'

Dining chairs with upholstered, stuffed seats present more of a problem, as you will most likely have to remove the upholstery before you can get to the joints. If the seat is in good condition, you may need only to untack the upholstery from the back rail. Then, before knocking the joints apart, wedge a piece of scrap wood between the two side rails to keep them apart and in this way prevent the tension of the cross webbing and springs (if the seat is sprung) pulling the side rails together.

With Edwardian, Victorian and Regency chairs, you may have trouble with front leg tops where the wood has become dry and brittle. Countless tacks have been hammered in by innumerable upholsterers over the years, and you find that the mortises have split so much that nothing is left to hold onto. A splice is necessary in this case *(see fig.17)*. First study the leg to determine what would give the greatest strength – remembering that the longer the spliced joint, the stronger it will be. Try to keep the long slanting joint to the sides of the leg where it will be less noticeable. Also, if the front of the leg is moulded, or has inlaid stringing, it is possible to retain most of the decoration.

A method of splicing is shown at *(a)*. It is most important to match the new wood to the original as nearly as possible, in grain as well as colour.

First cut your wood for the new leg top, then lay it on the leg and mark with a scriber or marking knife. Try to position your wood so that the grain follows the direction of that of the original. You will see that the splice at the bottom does not follow through to feather off at the surface but stops and is cut up in a shallow V. This makes the line of the join on the front much finer – and it is easier

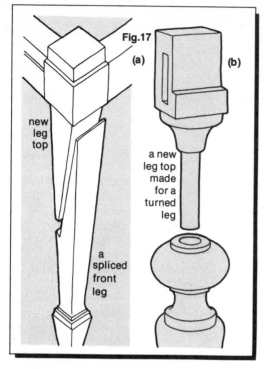

Fig.17

(a)

(b)

new leg top

a new leg top made for a turned leg

a spliced front leg

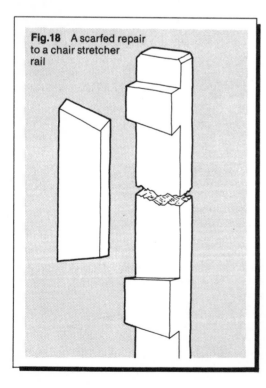

Fig.18 A scarfed repair to a chair stretcher rail

to cramp. Use one sash cramp from top to bottom and two 'G' cramps across the sides.

When the leg has set, plane off the surplus wood after marking to ensure you don't take off too much. Then you are ready to set out and cut the new mortises. Note the angle of the tenons, for the side rail tenons do not fit square into the leg.

When fitting a leg top to a turned front leg (*17b*), cut the leg off and bore it to take the new piece. You need to shape the new leg top to fit the hole, and the peg should be at least half the diameter of the leg. A wood-turning lathe is a great asset for re-turning the new part of the leg. But if you have no lathe, with care you can carve and rasp it into shape.

Understretchers often get broken, and with modern chairs it is generally best to cut new stretchers rather than repair old ones. With antique chairs you will want to keep as much of the original wood as possible. This is done by inserting a scarf piece into the broken understretcher. The wood is cut away to half the thickness of the stretcher bar (*see fig.18*) and several centimetres each side of the break and a piece of wood inserted to bridge or scarf the break.

Many chairs come into my workshop with pieces of ironwork inserted: steel brackets screwed on to try to strengthen legs that are loose; metal plates screwed across breaks; brass wire bound round and round chair legs that were split. All sorts of foreign bodies are used by those so-called handymen who have had a go at mending the chairs at some time or other.

Mind you, I have seen beautiful repairs done to chairs with metal – probably by a village blacksmith. For instance, there is an old ladder-back chair in my workshop with one leg beautifully splinted with shaped metal plates riveted right through to make a very strong repair. While we may admire the ingenuity of this old blacksmith, who must now have been dead many years, we must blame the then-owner of the chair, for he obviously took it to the wrong craftsman.

Most good repairs to chairs need no support from metal plates or brackets. Only a very few screws are needed – and no nails.

There is, however, one exception that comes to mind. Perhaps the most difficult repair is to the sugar stick back upright of high-backed chairs, the type descended from the early Charles II chairs. Many chairs of this type are made with the back upright far too slender, and there is never much strength in a sugar twist. Sometimes only the equivalent of 12mm (½in) of rod is left between the spirals. It's no wonder they snap so easily.

If all the joints in the back show signs of coming apart and the caned panel (if it has one) is in need of repair anyway, it is best to make and fit a new sugar twist. This is a very exacting task, involving an enormous amount of work – and at the end the job is still no stronger than the original.

On occasions such as this, I take a steel bar about 6mm (¼in) thick and about 19mm (¾in) wide and, ploughing a groove right down the length in the back of the twist, I let the bar in as deep as possible. The bar is then marked and drilled so that it can be screwed and secured.

The screws are placed so that they go into the thicker parts of the twist. The groove still left showing after the bar is secured can be made good with pieces of wood glued in, then carved to shape.

Another weak part of a chair is the top or cresting rail *(see fig.19)*. This does not apply with the type of chair where the rail is mortised into the back uprights, however, but only in the earlier chairs such as Regency or early Victorian, or in reproductions of these, where the cresting rail is jointed to the tops of the back uprights, usually extending each side. I suppose the weakest of all are the cresting rails on Victorian balloon back chairs.

This kind of damage is often caused by people lifting the chair incorrectly. Using one hand only, they pick it up by the centre of the rail, and in no time off it comes – usually splitting the wood. The grain is very short on the curves that meet the back uprights *(a)*. The correct way is to use both hands holding only the back uprights.

If you are lucky, the top of the balloon back will be loose only in the joints. Be very

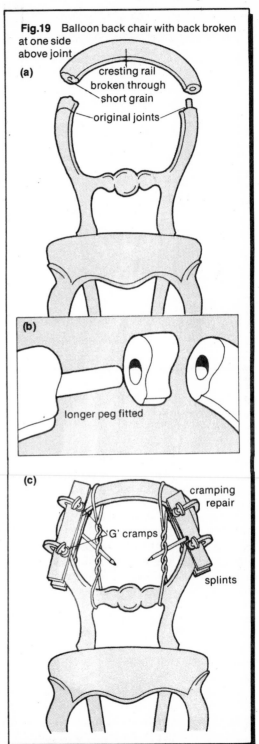

Fig.19 Balloon back chair with back broken at one side above joint

(a) cresting rail
broken through
short grain
original joints

(b) longer peg fitted

(c) cramping repair
'G' cramps
splints

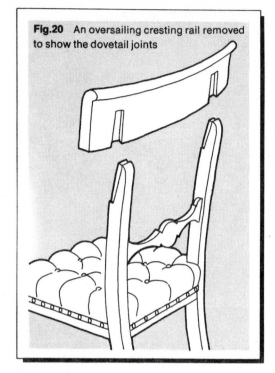

Fig.20 An oversailing cresting rail removed to show the dovetail joints

careful when you tap the rail off, for if you hit it too hard you will probably break the fragile, short cross grain that I spoke of. Once free, it is a simple matter to clean the dowels and holes and re-glue.

More often than not, the dowels on one side, or even on both, will have broken above the joint. This is then a tricky job, for if you try to make a new dowel hole you will probably cut through the old dowel and ruin the original joint when drilling down into the upright. I find the best remedy is to break the original joints, even if you have to saw through with a very thin tenon saw. Glue these pieces back to the top rail and leave to set. When they have set, you can then drill out the dowels, making sure that you bore the holes in the top rail quite a bit deeper, going well beyond the repaired splits. Make new dowel pegs and glue up *(19b)*.

Cramping this type of back while the glue sets is rather difficult. First, lightly cramp some scrap pieces over the joints as splints. Then apply a couple of cord 'tourniquets' at each end of the rail and tighten *(19c)*.

You will very often find that earlier chairs which have curved, oversailing, cresting rails have been very badly repaired with screws through the back uprights; these sometimes come through and make a mess of the front of the rail. If we examine these joints we find another species of dovetail *(see fig.20)*. To make a good job of these, make up all the missing pieces on the sides of the grooves in the rail, and make sure that the dovetailed ends of the back uprights are in good shape. Re-fit very carefully, first applying glue and then sliding on.

What about those nasty holes where the screws came through? They will need to be filled with pegs made so that the grain runs in the same direction as the grain in the wood into which you are plugging. Bore out the screw holes – not very deep – with a bit large enough to take away any countersinking of the screw holes. Now find a similar piece of wood at least the width of the hole and cut off a strip, so that you have a piece a few inches long and square in section, with the grain running widthways. With a sharp chisel, pare this piece into a round plug, working until it is a tight fit in the hole. If this is done with care, the plug will be hard to see when it has been glued in place.

In some chairs, fixing screws are disguised in this manner, and you will have to take out the plugs to get at the screws securing arms, seat backs and other parts.

Upholstered easy chairs are easy to repair when stripped of all upholstery. There is not a lot you can do unless they are stripped, and very often breaks in frame joints don't become apparent until the hessian, webbing and stuffing is taken away. I have known chairs where the upholstery was all that was holding them together!

You can test the frame of any easy chair by taking one corner of the back and the opposite corner of the front arm and pulling diagonally. If the joints are bad, there will be a lot of give here. Test the arms by pulling them in towards each other. You will find the front arm joints are often the first to go. I will deal with this type of chair more thoroughly in the upholstery section.

Tables First let's look at dining tables. On most modern ones, problem repairs are rare. The treatment of the odd loose joint is common, and remedies have already been covered in the previous section on chairs. The tops are often of laminated construction – plywood or blockboard – and these seldom give trouble. So let's deal with older tables.

The tops of old gate-leg tables with drop leaves very often come apart at the glued joints because of shrinkage. The tops of many of them are secured by screws through the top frame and may at some time have been nailed through from the top. The leaves must be removed, and the centre top carefully taken off. You may have to cut through old rusty nails with a hacksaw blade. Once it is free, you can deal with the joint in the way we have already described for joining boards.

There is one problem, however. Before you re-make the joint, check that when it is closed up there is still enough width across the top to allow the leaves to fold down. I have known gate-leg and Pembroke table tops shrink enough to prevent the leaves dropping, putting a considerable strain on flap hinges and top. If this is so in your table, the top will have to be made to the correct width by inserting a piece of wood with similar grain pattern between the joint.

The leaves often come apart in the same way; this is usually because a gate has not been extended properly. Support is given only a few centimetres away from the hinges, then someone comes along and leans on it, and, bang, it goes! The joints of a leaf need more strength than a plain glued joint can give, and one popular way of providing it is by butterfly cleat *(see fig.21)*.

Three pieces of wood about 76mm (3in) long and shaped as shown are let into the back of the leaf, bridging the joint. The butterfly cleat is also useful in order to arrest a shake or split caused by shrinkage in the end of the table top *(a)*. This is set in after the split has been filled with a narrow wedge of matching wood.

Club-foot tables, Sutherland tables and

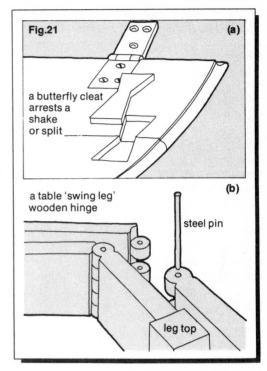

Fig.21 (a)

a butterfly cleat arrests a shake or split

(b)

a table 'swing leg' wooden hinge

steel pin

leg top

small tea-tables with drop leaves, all similar in principle to the gate-leg table, have wooden hinges for the extending legs, and these often need attention *(b)*. They are usually made of birch, beach or elm, and it is common to find that woodworm has weakened the flanges of the hinge; sooner or later they will break. Making one of these hinges is a good exercise in accuracy. It is more than likely that only one half will be damaged, so you will be able to copy or fit it to the good half.

These hinges also occur in sofa and Pembroke tables on the brackets that support the leaves. With constant use the hinge sections become loose on the pin, and it is best to find a larger steel pin and re-bore to give a nice tight fit.

Split tops are also common with the round tip-up tables such as the beautiful large ones with the central hollow pillar or those supported on a cluster of smaller pillars. To get a split top closed up you will have to remove the ring frieze *(see fig.22)* and most of the cleating from the back. See how beautifully the screws have been capped with pegs with little turned mushroom heads. Try if you can to get these out without breaking them.

You may find that the central pillar is loose and wobbly. This is secured through the centre from top to bottom with a very long bolt, so to repair this you will need to tighten it from underneath the base. Make sure that the washer under the nut is large enough to prevent it being pulled into the wood when it is tightened.

With the smaller, tripod leg tip-up tables *(see fig.23)*, the wooden pins on which the top hinges often wear and cause the top to become unsteady *(a)*. To remedy this, a new piece must be fixed to the top support, well secured by pegs or by screws countersunk well in and plugged. Pegs to fit the holes in the cleats can then be worked on the new wood *(b)*.

The square top support may also come loose from the central pillar. This needs

careful examination, for although loose most likely it will not come off the pillar. If you look closely you will see that this is because the post, a part of the pillar which extends through the square, has two wedges driven into the end. So to free the support you must remove as much of the wedges as possible. Drill into the wedge, then chop out with a small mortise chisel and mallet.

Hold the pillar secure in a vice while you chop, then you won't loosen the leg joints. Protect the pillar from the vice jaws by wrapping something soft around it. I keep pieces of 25mm (1in) thick foam for this purpose. Once the bulk of the wedges is removed, the square can be tapped free. Carefully re-cut the clefts for the wedges and make new wedges from hardwood.

Glue them, making sure you have the square in the right direction to the legs *(a)*. It is also vital that the grain of the wedges should run in the opposite direction from the grain of the square. Having checked all these points, tap home your new wedges, keeping the square well down on the shoulder of the pillar while you drive.

The smallest of the round tables is the tripod wine table, the best of which have the top secured with a wooden thread. This is not glued and can be easily taken off. You will find the legs are dovetailed into the bottom of the centre pillar, but cheaper tables have legs secured by dowels or by just one dowel screw (a metal screw with screw thread both ends).

The legs are the most vulnerable part of these tables and break across the narrow part just above the foot. This is a particularly difficult part to repair and whether one can scarf underneath the break depends on the thickness of the wood. In many cases, for a strong job, it is best to replace the whole leg.

The base of the centre pillar often comes to grief, for a blow to the legs can fracture it, the leg coming away with part of the centre still attached *(see fig.24)*. Try to detach the pillar from the leg, and glue it back to the centre pillar first. Then re-fit the leg.

The threaded peg retaining the top is

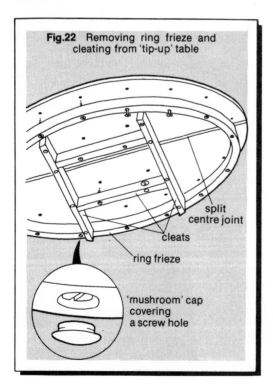

Fig.22 Removing ring frieze and cleating from 'tip-up' table

split centre joint

cleats

ring frieze

'mushroom' cap covering a screw hole

another weak spot. The thread can strip through being over-tightened or left too loose, then off comes the top. To make another thread would be a test of your craftsmanship – but it can be done without complicated machinery. Like me, you may be lucky enough to find a wooden thread cutting tool, but, if you don't, try to find a thread from a scrap table.

The types of damage I have dealt with occur in other pieces of furniture, and repairs can follow similar methods. You will find that every repair job is different to a lesser or greater degree, but there is always a way to mend it – although a lot of thought may be needed before a solution is found. Always try to work out the strongest way to do a repair. After a time you get a 'feel' for the job, and you begin to know just how much strength there is in the various methods of joining; you know when glue alone is strong enough and when and where pegs or screws need to be added. As with everything, practice makes perfect!

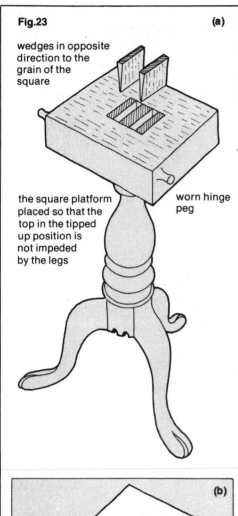

Fig.23 (a)

wedges in opposite direction to the grain of the square

the square platform placed so that the top in the tipped up position is not impeded by the legs

worn hinge peg

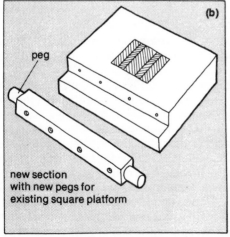

(b)

peg

new section with new pegs for existing square platform

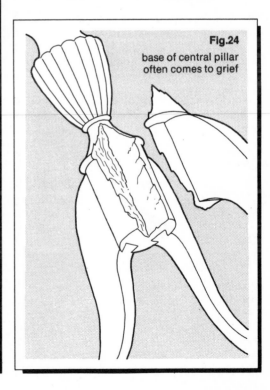

Fig.24
base of central pillar often comes to grief

Repairs to surfaces

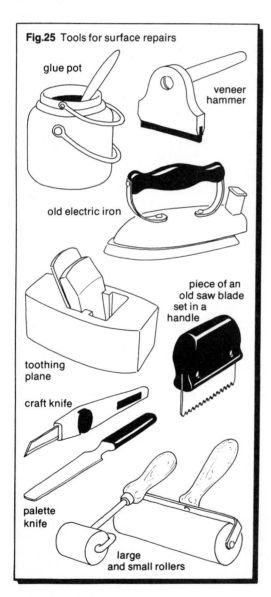

Fig.25 Tools for surface repairs

glue pot

veneer hammer

old electric iron

piece of an old saw blade set in a handle

toothing plane

craft knife

palette knife

large and small rollers

Now let's go back to the bureau you repaired so well. As I said at the time, although it is now sound in construction it still looks as if it has seen better days, with all those dents and scratches and the veneer and inlay missing.

Your task is now to repair these surfaces, but first you need to add a few more tools to your collection *(see fig.25)*: a glue pot, hide glue, a veneer hammer, which is not a hammer really but more of a squeegee type of tool, an old electric iron, a toothing plane or piece of old saw blade set in a handle, a thin-bladed knife or craft knife and a palette knife. A large and small roller will also be required.

Let us examine the bureau once again, this time noting all the surface defects. As I mentioned before, keep in mind the rule that you must leave as much of the original surface as possible. This applies not only to antiques but also to any well-made pieces such as our bureau. It'll last a long time and one day will be quite valuable.

Uncle George was a smoker, judging by the bad cigarette burn on the inside of the fall or flap – and a careless fellow too, as I gathered from the ink spilled over the writing surface. In addition the veneer on the top has split and bubbled up. This may well have been caused by Aunt Alice placing one of her flower arrangements for all to see on top of the bureau. Little did she know that the bowl had a leak, and when it was eventually moved – calamity! The veneer was sodden, blistered and ruined. After that, I guess that not another word was heard from her about Uncle George's careless habits.

There are several other surface repairs you may have to make. The motif in the centre of the fall has a segment missing. They get that amazing '3D' effect by what is known as sand shading, and I'll tell you how to do that a little later. Then there is a piece of the overlapping beading missing on the fall. I expect someone tried to open the flap with their fingernails instead of using the key in the proper way.

Pieces of the thin line of yellow-coloured wood running around the fall, called stringing, are also missing. And if we look at the drawer, we see that pieces of the cross-banded borders have gone – probably flicked off by Auntie Alice's duster, never to be seen again.

If you do find little pieces of veneer or chips of wood lying on the floor, don't throw them away. They've obviously come off somewhere, and how much easier it is to glue these back than to make up new ones.

In some of the houses where I work, the owners religiously save all the bits and pieces as they fall off, keeping them in a special box or drawer. It is then my task periodically to empty the drawer and go round finding the correct homes for all the pieces!

You will also have to do something about the large dent in the bottom drawer; it looks as if something with a very sharp corner has bumped into it *(see fig.26)*.

Having assessed the surface damage, let's get to work, starting with the deep cigarette burn in the fall and the dent in the bottom drawer *(a)*. In both of these areas the carcase wood has to be built up before we are able to lay veneer on top to produce an even surface once more. Chisel out the damaged areas nice and square, removing all the burnt wood in the case of the cigarette damage. Then fit in new pieces similar to the carcase wood, finishing just below the surface to allow for the thickness of veneer you will eventually put in *(b)*.

There are several points to note when inserting a piece of veneer if you are to make it as inconspicuous as possible. First, avoid cross-grained joints by cutting your new

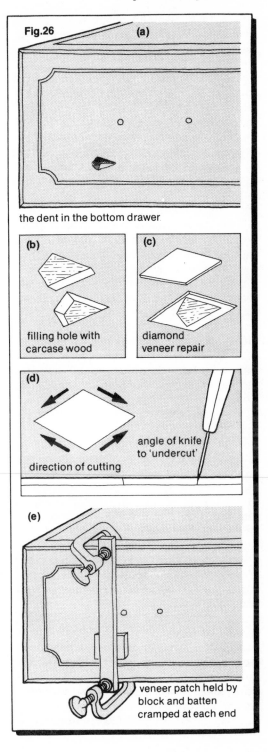

Fig.26 (a)

the dent in the bottom drawer

(b) filling hole with carcase wood

(c) diamond veneer repair

(d) direction of cutting / angle of knife to 'undercut'

(e) veneer patch held by block and batten cramped at each end

veneer to a diamond shape *(c)*. Second, match the colour and texture of the grain as near as possible to that of the original. And third, study the shading of the grain. By this I mean that light falling on the veneer from one angle will cause it to appear lighter, from the opposite angle, darker. So try your veneer this way and that to ensure that the shading corresponds with the original.

Having selected your piece of veneer, cut it as suggested into a diamond shape, undercutting the edges by holding your knife at an angle *(26d)*. Always cut away from your fingers holding the veneer!

Next place your diamond-shaped piece over the hole to be repaired and with your craft knife or very thin-bladed knife gently mark around the shape just deep enough to make a cut to guide your blade. Make a light pencil mark on the diamond to indicate the way it is to be placed. Take it away and very gently cut along the lines made in the surface, keeping the knife upright this time, until you are through the veneer.

With a fine chisel or double-bevelled carving chisel remove the unwanted veneer. Your diamond patch should now fit perfectly. Use resin glue to fix and press the shape well in with a roller.

If the veneer lies flat, one or two pieces of tape will hold it down. Very often, however, the veneer tends to curl when glue is applied. You will have to hold it down either with a weight or a block and 'G' cramp if near the edge. If away from the edge, like the dent in the drawer, use a slightly curved batten, cramped at each end *(26e)*.

When weighting the veneer, place a piece of greaseproof paper between the block and veneer, or rub wax polish on the block to prevent adhesion between the two surfaces. When the glue has set, remove blocks, cramps or tapes, then clean down to the level of the surrounding veneer by cutting back with fine glasspaper. Use No.1½ English and No.320 wet or dry carborundum paper. Wrap a small piece around a very small cork block about 25mm × 38mm (1in × 1½in). The idea, naturally, is to do as little damage as possible to the surrounding surface.

If the veneer projects quite a way, you will have to take off the surplus carefully with the cabinet scraper, using only the edge at the corner of the scraper. Be very careful when doing this, particularly when repairing antiques, because you must leave as much as possible of the surface and patina intact and undamaged.

Let us now deal with the missing overlapping beading on the fall. It will be best to take off the flap so that it can be held upright in a vice. First find some matching mahogany, then cut the existing beading each side of the gap to a slight dovetail *(see fig.27)*. Cut a piece to fit, apply glue, and gently slide in from the front.

If you find a piece is missing from a corner, glue and fit a replacement piece and strap it well with tape. Don't bother to shape it before you glue the piece in. This can be done after the glue has set, using a small block, rabbet, or moulding plane, if you have one.

Next, make up the missing stringing around the border of the fall. You will first have to find some yellow wood to match. A good tip is to collect and save old, broken boxwood rulers. Schools often throw these away when the edges are damaged. Or you can collect, for the future, long logs of holly, or, if you want a really bright yellow, berberis wood. I'm very lucky in having a brother-in-law who is a landscape gardener and he is always on the look-out for local exotic woods for me. As you probably know, you can't use such woods for many years until they have thoroughly dried out and seasoned. But it's a good investment to cut it up into small planks and store it away somewhere dry for use in future years.

You will need to make a small scraping tool to clean the dirt and old glue from the grooves where the stringing is missing. Then you need to make new stringing. This is a bit tricky by hand, but here are a couple of methods. Prepare your piece of yellow wood, giving it a square face and edge. Then, with a gauge fitted with a knife scriber as at *(a)* in *fig.27*, cut your stringing, taking

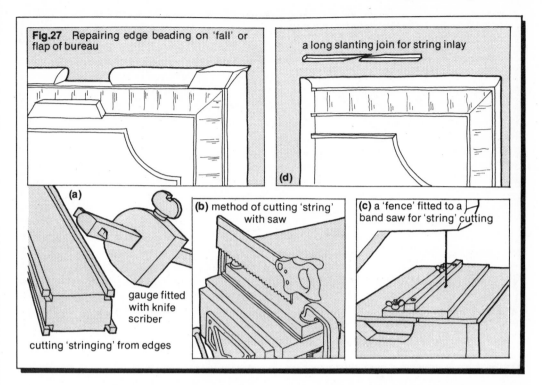

Fig.27 Repairing edge beading on 'fall' or flap of bureau

a long slanting join for string inlay

(d)

(a)

gauge fitted with knife scriber

cutting 'stringing' from edges

(b) method of cutting 'string' with saw

(c) a 'fence' fitted to a band saw for 'string' cutting

one piece from each corner of the prepared piece of wood. The gauge must be set to the exact size that you require.

The other way, if you are using thin pieces of wood such as old rulers, is first to plane away all the graduated marks, then reduce them to the thickness required for the width of the stringing. Clamp them between two pieces of wood (b), leaving the required amount protruding from under the top board, allowing for the width of the saw cut.

Strips can then be cut off with a fine tenon saw. Try the first piece in a groove to see if it's the correct size. It should be a tight fit.

If you have a small bandsaw for which you can make a jig or guide, you will be able to cut your stringing extremely accurately and quickly (c).

With the stringing prepared and the grooves cleaned out, apply glue to the groove and insert the new pieces, pressing them in with a smooth hammer face, working from one end to the other. The surplus glue will be squeezed along the

groove and out at the end. It is best to leave the inlay slightly proud, and then to scrape smooth after the glue has set.

When you come to corners, mitre them neatly. And when joining lengths of stringing a long diagonal joint is neater than cutting square across (d).

We will tackle the drawer fronts next. You will remember that you have to make up the missing pieces of the cross-banded borders. It's not too difficult. Let's examine the piece closely and see how it is made up. You will see it consists of a cross-grained 10mm (⅜in) wide ribbon of satinwood veneer with a very thin string of ebony each side and with a thicker string of yellow wood forming the outside edges.

Many kinds of exotic wood are used for this type of work, and they are sometimes very difficult to match. Rather than cutting all those fiddling pieces of string and veneer and fitting them in side by side, here is an easier method.

You need some ebony veneer, boxwood

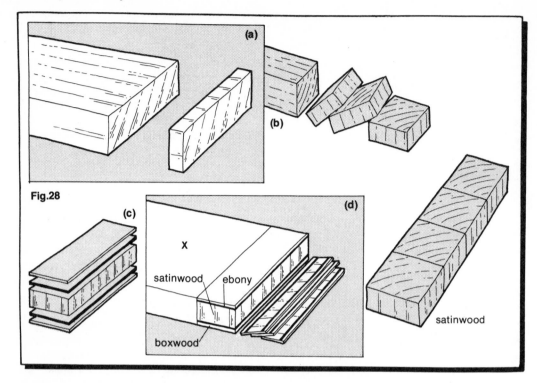

Fig.28

or other yellow wood and as thick a piece of satinwood as possible. For the ebony, look out for old parallel rules or even round rulers and walking sticks – you can get a lot of strips from the centres of such items. The yellow wood I have already mentioned, but satinwood is much more rare in plank form. You may find suitable pieces in old bedroom chairs, but for making cross-banding you need something wider, such as a drawer front or the bottom rail of a wardrobe door.

If you fail to find wood you need in the junk shop yards, don't give up hope. There are a number of firms which deal in exotic hardwoods and they advertise in the usual crafts, hobbies and woodworking magazines.

Once you have the ingredients for your border, cut the pieces of boxwood and ebony veneer to the exact thickness or width of the original in the border by planing or using a cabinet scraper. Cut a piece off the end of your plank of satinwood *(see fig.28)* across the grain and to the same width as

that of the border *(a)*.

If your satinwood is thin, cut two or three pieces and glue side by side. If you have only small wood such as a chair back or seat rail, cut more pieces so that they can be joined to make length and depth *(b)*. Now glue the layers together, sandwich form *(c)*. Cramp well and leave to set.

Your sandwich may only measure 19mm (¾in) in depth, this being the maximum width of your cross-grained centre. So for easy handling, glue it on to a wider piece of wood marked X at *(d)*. This can then be planed to the same thickness and length. Now all you have to do is cut 'rashers' off your sandwich and you will have enough borders to make up all the pieces missing on the drawers.

To ensure a good clean cut, cramp the sandwich on to a cutting board with a straight and square 25mm × 50mm (1in × 2in) batten on the top to act as a guide. Extend the sandwich beyond the top batten to the thickness required (allowing for the

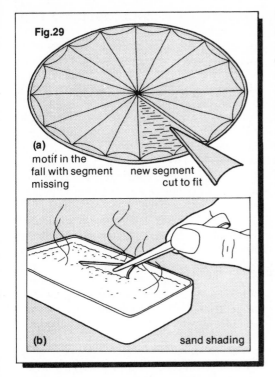

Fig.29

(a)
motif in the
fall with segment   new segment
missing   cut to fit

(b)   sand shading

saw cut), and cut off with a fine tenon saw.

Clean out the old glue and dirt from the spaces where the border is missing and trim square the original border to one side of the gap. Cut off the required length of new material, plus a fraction, with a fine, thin chisel and fit up tight to the newly trimmed original. Mark the original at the other end of the gap with your craft knife, guided by the edge of the new piece. Take away the new piece and remove the surplus up to the mark made by your craft knife. Apply a little glue, press in, tape it down and that's all there is to it!

It's best to cut square all the joints you have to make in your border — except corners, which should be mitred. Most of the wood comprising the satinwood centre of the border is cross-grained. Clean off in the same manner as you did after repairing the veneer. Use carborundum paper or, if there's a lot to come off, the cabinet scraper, as long as you handle it gently.

Now for that missing segment of motif in the centre of the fall *(see fig.29)*. You've probably got a piece of boxwood ruler left, and, if it's a good match, cut a piece from it *(a)*. Clean out the space where the piece is missing, then take a small square of brown paper, or a piece of gummed paper strip, place it over the area and with a soft pencil scribble over the paper, as if you were brass rubbing. The outline of the shape will be reproduced on the paper. Wet the paper and stick it on your piece of boxwood, then cut the shape out very carefully with a craft knife. Remove the paper and fit the piece.

You will probably find that it needs slight trimming as the paper template expands a fraction when wet. Now that it fits perfectly, here comes the crafty bit. You have to shade one edge to give it a scalloped look – and this is how to do it, by the method called sand shading *(b)*.

Find a shallow tin – an oblong tobacco tin will do fine. Fill this with fine, dry sand and level off to the top. Place the tin over a very low gas and leave until it's quite hot. You can test the temperature with slivers of spare wood. Hold a piece with flat-nosed pliers or large tweezers, and slowly push it edge first into the hot sand, timing operation by counting. Withdraw and examine the piece of wood.

If the colour has hardly changed, either the sand is not hot enough or the wood needs longer in the hot sand. On the other hand, the wood must not become too scorched or it will char and you will lose the edges. Keep experimenting until you are satisfied that the intensity of shading matches that of the original. Then use the same heat and timing for the piece you have prepared for fitting. Make sure which is the correct edge to be shaded, then push it into the sand for no more than half its width. The rest is easy. Simply glue it in place and strap down with tape as necessary.

Finally, we come to the job you may not be looking forward to: repairing the blistered veneer on the top. It may look an awful mess, but don't despair. First try to clean out all dirt, loose glue and bits from the cracks and from under the blisters. You can make yourself a tool or two for this operation from fine nails flattened and slightly bent. Alternatively, a thin palette knife will do the job. Damp the veneer with a wet rag or sponge so that it becomes supple before you start cleaning out.

There are two ways in which you can tackle this job. The simpler is with a 'caul' or flat and true board. For this method you need either hide or resin glue, a flat laminated board a little larger than the area to be repaired and a sheet of waxed paper. Hide glue needs to be heated in a glue pot. Resin glue can be used cold. In the case of the bureau, you will need two 900mm (3ft) sash cramps, two 200mm (8in) 'G' cramps and two 50mm × 50mm (2in × 2in) pieces of wood cut to the same length as the width of the top of the bureau. It will help if these pieces are slightly curved.

Place the caul over the damaged area, then put the two pieces of wood on top, convex side down, and try on the cramps, the smaller 'G' cramps on the front and the sash cramps at the back. Adjust the cramps so that when all is ready they can be quickly placed and tightened. If you choose hide glue, heat it and also warm the caul.

A useful gadget for a job like this is a glue injector with which you can squeeze glue under the veneer, through cracks. There are several kinds of plastic bottle from which you can make one – shampoo bottles, for instance, which can easily be squeezed. Make sure your bottle is made of a plastic which will stand up to boiling water, for after filling it you have to stand it in hot water.

This kind of squeezable bottle is also good for the ready-mixed type of resin glue. Bore a hole through the top and use a piece of fine plastic tubing to make a handy nozzle through which to dispense the glue. With everything prepared and to hand, damp the veneer again, then inject glue into the cracks and under the veneer. Do not use too much, but enough to satisfy yourself that all the under-surfaces will be covered.

If you use hot glue, it must be fairly thin, so work fast to get your waxed paper and warmed caul on top. Position your two pieces of wood on the caul and cramp down before the glue gels. If you use ready-mixed resin glue, the process is more leisurely. After injecting one or other of the glues, give the surface a gentle roll with a small seam roller to spread the glue underneath and to squeeze out any surplus.

After a day or two, when you remove the caul, you will find a pretty awful mess underneath. Whichever glue you have used, it will have oozed out and gone all over the place. This doesn't matter, and you can leave it until you clean off to re-polish. In any case, it won't be half as bad as the mess you will make if you try the ironing method!

For this you need a wider roller, a veneer hammer, greaseproof or waxed paper, hot glue and an old electric iron. I do mean old, so, in the interest of domestic harmony, don't borrow your wife's favourite iron. The temperature of the iron is crucial, for if it's too hot you will scorch the veneer, and if it isn't hot enough the heat won't get through to the glue to re-melt and dry it. As a rough guide, the iron should be hot enough to make a drop of water, splashed on, just begin to sizzle slowly. I'm afraid this doesn't convey a very accurate temperature, so you'll have to experiment a little!

Slightly dampen the blistered and cracked veneer with a wet rag or sponge and leave for a while to soften. Then, as with the caul method, inject and spread hot glue under the loose veneer, working very quickly. Place a sheet of waxed paper over and roll gently with the wide roller to spread the glue underneath. Wipe away surplus glue and damp the veneer again.

Put another piece of waxed paper in place and run your iron over the area. Remove the paper quickly before it sticks, then, with your veneer hammer, apply pressure in zig-zag strokes from the outside of the area to the centre – or work towards the largest join or crack so that surplus glue is squeezed out. With luck, the right temperature iron and if the glue is at the right consistency, the veneer will adhere after the first hammering. If it doesn't, repeat the process until it does.

To test a surface for air spaces under the

veneer, brush the backs of your fingers over the surface and listen for hollow sounds. Alternatively, bounce a pencil on its blunt end and listen for variations in sound. If you find an air space, slit the veneer about it in the direction of the grain, using a craft knife. Apply the hot iron and pat the veneer down with the veneer hammer.

Be very thorough about getting the veneer quite flat. It may look reasonable in its messed-up state, but when it gets a really shiny surface it will show up every bump and undulation. But what about all the mess on the top? You can run your cabinet scraper over it lightly if you like, but there's really no hurry; better to leave it for a while. I will be dealing with methods of restoring the surfaces in the next chapter.

REPAIRING OTHER TYPES OF FURNITURE

I would now like to deal with the odd repairs you might have to do to other pieces of furniture, such as making up missing decorative embellishments. Any piece of furniture classed as antique, which generally means it was made over a hundred years ago, or a piece that is just old is sure to have signs of use or abuse. For instance, a carver arm dining chair may have the edges of the arms worn away by constant handling. The stretcher rails of old oak chairs, dining tables or stools become 'serpentine' on their top edges through wear from heel and toe. Then there are chips and dents in table tops and edges which have been rubbed and polished over the years, until dents become mere undulations.

And you will find unmistakable signs of loving care over the years: the smooth, deep, translucent surface which we vaguely call patina. If only these tables and chairs could speak – what tales they might tell! But let's set aside any thoughts of improving these marks of fair wear and tear and concentrate on actual damage.

As I mentioned earlier, you will often find 'foreign bodies' in furniture surfaces such as nails, screws and holes that have been filled with various materials. Try to avoid using fillers of any kind, as they tend to shrink, work loose, then fall out after a year or two. A piece of matching wood glued in gives a far more permanent job.

Upholstered, stuffed-over dining chairs, couches and easy chairs of the Victorian and Edwardian periods often suffer damage to the surfaces of facings and wood surrounding the seats, backs and arms. These are places where cover upon cover may have been tacked on, advancing further and further over the facings until, when all the coverings are removed, you find tack holes extending far further than the rebate intended for fixing.

What can we do to make these good? 'Surely we will have to use stopping or filler here.' You may have to in this case, but there are alternatives. In the case of a stuffed-over dining chair, the damaged show-wood is just a hardwood facing sometimes only 3mm (⅛in) thick. If it is badly holed or split, it can be removed and replaced with new. A Victorian chair with similar moulded show-wood around the seat can also have the facing renewed if badly split. However, even if it is no more than a case of a row of unsightly holes and no other damage, I think you should take a little more trouble than just pressing in some wood stopping.

Find some similar coloured wood, perhaps a shade or two lighter, and split it into thin sticks. Sharpen each stick at one end and dip into glue. Tap a stick into each hole and cut off. The end grain will show as it's a slightly lighter shade, but remember end grain will show darker when stained and polished. It will be far less noticeable eventually than filler or stopping.

LAYING VENEER

I would like to go a little further on the subject of laying veneer, for it may be that at some time you will need to re-veneer the surface of a piece of furniture.

New veneer can easily be obtained, and your nearest timber merchant who stocks hardwoods will probably advise you where to go for it. Just as you collect ancient wood, so also you can use old veneer. But first you need to know how to remove it from whatever it's on. Here is what I do. First make sure all traces of polish are removed from the surface of the veneer, otherwise moisture will not be able to penetrate. Then lay the veneered piece face down in long grass: after a week or two the veneer usually just falls off.

If you have nowhere available to do this, place damp cloth or newspaper over the veneer and add a sprinkling of water daily to keep it moist.

Let us imagine you have a small rectangular table, with the original veneer on the top – or what's left of it – beyond redemption. Put your glue pot over heat to melt the slab or pearl glue. It will take some time and plenty of stirring before it's ready. Alternatively, you can get Scotch glues that are already in jelly form, and these only need to be stood in hot water until the glue flows. Obviously this is less trouble, and you may prefer to use them.

Meanwhile, clean off the old pieces of veneer, scraping the surface underneath until it is clean and free from old glue. It is advisable to key this surface, and to do this a toothing plane can be used. This is a small plane similar to a wooden smoothing plane, but the iron is fitted in an upright position and the cutting edge is serrated so that it scratches a key into the wood when pushed to and fro. If you have no toothing plane, a short piece of saw blade will do a reasonable job. Make sure that both the surface and the underside of the new veneer are absolutely dust-free.

With the glue hot, put your old electric iron on, and, if it's thermostatically controlled, set it to silk. Have a bowl of warm water, an old sponge and a few clean rags handy, together with a small seam roller (paperhanger's variety) and a veneer hammer. Brush glue evenly over the surface of the table top and the back of the veneer and leave both until the glue gels. Some people like to leave the glue until you can safely brush your hand over the surface without sticking to it.

Place the new veneer in position, dampen the top surface slightly, then run your iron over, slowly, to re-melt the glue. Using your veneer hammer, squeegee-fashion, start from the middle and with zig-zag strokes press down, working to the outside edges where surplus glue and air can escape. This procedure should be repeated two or three times. Damp, iron and press until the veneer is firmly laid.

As with the blistered top of your bureau, test when finished for air trapped under the veneer by tapping or brushing with the fingertips or a pencil. Trim back the veneer to within 3mm (⅛in) all round the top, and leave until thoroughly set before trimming with craft knife and sandpaper right back to the edges.

If you are lucky, one piece of veneer will cover the top. But if you have to use two pieces and make a join, don't worry, it's very easy with the iron-on method. After ensuring that the grain runs parallel in the two pieces, lay down in the manner described for one piece, but this time overlap the edges 12mm (½in) or so. After the first sequence of damp, iron and hammer, place a straight edge down the centre of the overlapping veneers and cut gently with your craft knife, using light strokes, until you have cut through both thicknesses of veneer.

Turn back the top overlap so that you can peel off the scrap piece lying underneath. If it doesn't pull away, because the glue has set, just warm the surface again with your iron. Now damp, iron and hammer once again – and down goes your join, becoming invisible in a perfect fit!

I've talked about collecting useful materials, so why not go one stage further and make a hobby of collecting as many varieties of wood in veneer form as you can? It can be very interesting, and it is an ideal way of learning to recognise the colour and grain of woods used in furniture making.

Squares can be cut – say 50mm × 50mm (2in × 2in) – and either mounted on boards to be hung on the workshop wall or stuck in a scrapbook and suitably labelled. The friend of mine who has the workshop near mine decorates trays, boxes and tables with parquetry tops of every imaginable veneer in hexagonal shapes. The colours and the grains, although different from each other, are beautifully balanced and positioned. He then writes a legend indicating the varieties and hides it underneath. This is an excellent way of collecting woods and at the same time producing something useful and decorative.

Mouldings and beadings also make an interesting study. Short pieces can be saved, mounted and given their correct names, period and dates. Some of the more common mouldings are illustrated *(see fig.30)*.

REPLACING DECORATION

You will often come across furniture that has carving, frets and decorations of several kinds applied to the surface of woodwork. As they are usually applied only with glue, they are prone to getting knocked off and lost. To make many of these ornaments, such as bosses, finials, split turnings, bluebell drops *(see fig.31)*, you really need a lathe. You can then have fun copying them by turning and carving.

The split balluster or pillar is easily turned on a lathe *(see fig.32)*. Before being mounted in the lathe, the wood is cut down the centre, then glued together again with hide glue. After you have turned the pillar, the two halves can be separated by cutting through the glued joint with a hot knife. This is far easier than trying to saw a finished moulding in half!

If a complete half pillar is not required, then two cuts should be made and glued together, so that eventually only about a third of the pillar is used. Small blocks must be glued to each end of the wood to be turned, so that the lathe centres do not force the joint apart.

Always think out the easiest way to produce ornaments and decorations. You may need to replace a number of similar pieces, so find a piece of wood from which you can produce them all in one operation, if possible. If a number of frets have to be

Fig.30

cornice mouldings

simple gouge carved moulding

nose edge mouldings

reeding   gadrooning

astragal for glazing bars   double half round edging

bubble beading

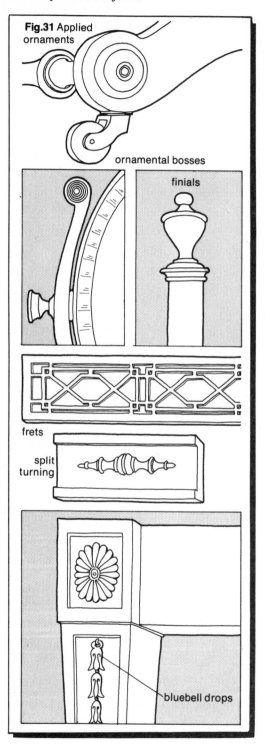

Fig.31 Applied ornaments

ornamental bosses

finials

frets

split turning

bluebell drops

replaced, they can be set out on top of a sandwich of layers, then cut through in one single operation.

To make large bosses, like those on the centres of 'X' chairs, or very small ones, as on dressing mirror stands, choose a long piece of wood of appropriate thickness so you can turn and cut off as many as you require in one operation. The small bosses on dressing mirror stands are very often made of ivory – and that's another useful commodity to have by you. In my workshop I have a drawer in which I store old knife handles, pieces of bone, ivory and riding boot hooks. Round handles are particularly useful for turning knobs and bosses. The old white ivorine, as I think it was called, in items such as piano keys is also worth saving, for much of the ivory-like stringing in chairs and tables produced at the beginning of the century was made of this.

Carving is, as you know, a craft on its own, but in furniture repairing you will have to dabble to a certain extent. Carving is a

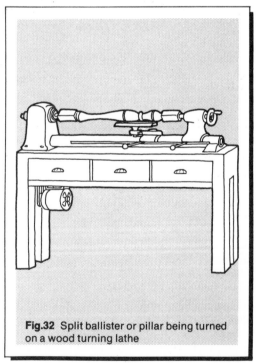

Fig.32 Split ballister or pillar being turned on a wood turning lathe

matter of a lot of common sense, but you do need an extremely good knowledge of wood and the ways in which it can be cut. Also, skill must be acquired in the use of woodcarving tools.

The repairs you are most likely to encounter are to replace missing applied carving. This is wood that has been carved and stuck on to the main body and therefore differs from the carving which has been cut into the actual body wood. On carved chairs you are likely to find missing parts of decorations, from leaves and scrolls to missing chins or noses, broken from figures or heads of animals. To repair these may involve no more than chiselling the broken surfaces flat, then sticking on a matching piece of wood. When it has set, it can be carved back to match the surrounding original wood.

With more elaborate carving – such as an acanthus leaf – it is best to cut out the profile first, using a simple cardboard template copied from another similar leaf. Much of

Fig.33 A chair splat in this condition becomes weakened and if left will break up altogether

front view of chair back

direction of the grain

a 'feathered' bridge across break in splat viewed from the back

the carving, to remove surplus wood, can then be done before the piece is attached. The method of attaching will have to be thought out, and it's usually best to have in mind small dowels or pegs to make a really strong fixing.

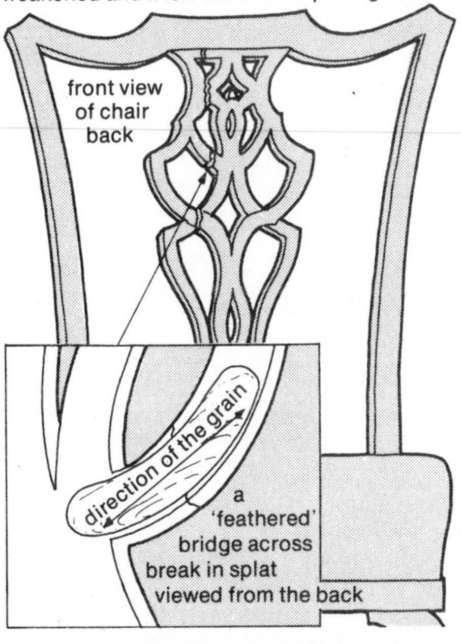

With pieces that are pierced (holes right through) and carved, you very often find that the carving has split from piercing to piercing, along the grain. A chair splat (*see fig.33*) in this condition becomes weakened and if left will break up altogether. The difficulty here is that you most probably will not be able to remove it from the chair; so what can you do in this case? Work glue between the breaks and bring them together with cramps, binding with twine or tape. Make sure you know where the breaks were, for you may be able to strengthen some of them by drilling and pegging through at an angle.

Where this is not possible, bridge across the back with thin strips of hardwood, just glued on. Do not use panel pins or screws, as they will do more harm than good. These strips should be well cramped, then when set they can be carved down and feathered in all directions so that, although thicker over the repaired split, they will resemble an integral part of the back of the carving.

GESSO

While on the subject of carving, I want to mention gesso work. Even if you don't come across furniture decorated with this, you will probably meet the occasional picture or mirror frame with pieces broken off and missing. The old gesso was made of whiting or chalk mixed with parchment size. But a good, strong, modern gesso can be made with plaster of Paris and liquid resin glue. You need to work fast with this mixture, for, although the resin glue retards the plaster setting, it will 'go off' in about fifteen to twenty minutes.

I have made gesso with 'Brummer stopping', which is virtually a very thick distemper, and liquid resin glue. It makes a very hard gesso but can still be carved. This type needs to be applied in thin layers, as it tends to shrink and crack. Plaster of Paris and resin glue, plus a dark pigment, is a mixture suitable for use when replacing a pane of glass in a bookcase door. It is smooth and easy to bevel from glass to glazing bar.

With some types of shallow, flat, repetitive carving in gesso you may find it possible to take an impression with plasticine or paraffin wax and then cast a section for a missing part, using a thin mixture of plaster of Paris. If you use plasticine for your mould, coat the inside with shellac (french polish or patent knotting will do) before pouring in the plaster. Most likely the carving will be too elaborate or undercut to use that method, so you will have to build up the missing parts with gesso made thick enough to stand up. Where possible, reinforce large areas with wire or thin wood. When the new gesso is hard, you can carve it to match the original. After smoothing them with fine glasspaper, touch in the new places with gold paint, shellac and bronze powder or gold leaf, whichever is best.

A modern method of casting is to use a special rubber mould material which can be melted down and used any number of times. As it remains flexible, it is easy to extract intricate castings. Many craft shops stock this material.

Restoring surfaces

Having got our pieces of furniture into a reasonable state of repair, let's see what tools, equipment and products we need for renovating, stripping and re-polishing. First, there's abrasive paper, and you'll find that quite a variety is available, ranging from coarse to fine.

The coarsest I have is some aluminium oxide sanding belt pieces. You can obtain these from tool shops which stock accessories for belt sanders. Then I have garnet papers Nos. 1, ½ and 0, and carborundum paper (wet or dry) Nos. 320, 400 and 600. Also I keep some No.1½ English glasspaper for use on new bare wood.

To go with these I have a number of sanding blocks around which the paper can be wrapped. One or two are made of cork, but I prefer to cut blocks of thick plywood about 125mm × 76mm (5in × 3in) and then stick a layer of 12mm or 6mm (½in or ¼in) foam to one side. This, when covered with abrasive paper, makes an ideal flexible sanding block, as the foam ensures a good all-over contact with the surface to be smoothed. It also prevents the paper clogging so quickly.

Looking along my shelves, I notice fine steel wool, various kinds of liquid and paste abrasives, as supplied to the motor industry, and bottles of cleaner and reviver, the recipes for which I will give later. There is also a goodly supply of white spirit (turps substitute) and methylated spirit, a range of Naphtha wood dyes and oil stains and a few spirit stains in powder and crystal form.

Tins on the 'wax polish' shelf contain three basic colours: light (pale yellow), medium (light brown) and dark. Then we come to the row of cans containing shellac polish – and every polisher has his favourites. There is pale shellac varnish (for brushing on), light french polish (light yellowy brown), french polish extract, which can be thinned as required and is a mid-brown colour, transparent polish, a dark brown garnet polish which the makers call 'table top polish' for the want of a better name. And there is a can of white oil for use as a 'vehicle' for all of these.

All these polishes are shellac and ethanol mixtures with an extra hardener included. Unfortunately many of them cannot be bought in local shops. This is another reason to make friends with your local cabinet-maker or french polisher! Alternatively, hunt out a company which specialises in wood finishing products, such as Rustins of Waterloo Road, London NW2, with years of experience in dealing with timber.

Another material I keep in stock is clear polyurethane, in gloss and flat finish. This, of course, is not for use on antiques. It is easily obtainable in most areas.

Very few tools are required for wood finishing. Good brushes are essential, such as long-bristled varnish brushes 25mm (1in), 38mm (1½in) and 50mm (2in). You also need small scrubbing brushes, such as old tooth and nail brushes or stiff-bristled shoe brushes, and some small squirrel or sable pencil brushes.

You also need a fairly large tin with an airtight lid in which to store your 'rubbers'. I'll tell you what they are and how to make them later on.

Now let's get back to the bureau. Get it into good light and examine it once again, starting with the top. The veneer seems well set down, but there is no doubt about the surface. It will have to be cleaned down to bare wood and re-polished.

The inside with the pigeon holes and small drawers doesn't seem too bad, but what a pity that ink was spilled on the felt writing surface. It has run over the wood surround too. The front of the fall is not in bad condition, though of course there are the new pieces of wood which you inserted as repairs. These are bare wood, but that's nothing to worry about.

The drawer fronts are scratched and dull but not bad enough to warrant drastic measures. And the new wood in the bottom drawer will need some attention. Looking around the sides, we see that one side is a perfect colour but the other side is almost yellow. This has had a lot of strong light – including the sun – shining on it. You can feel that the surface is rough, and I'm afraid this will also have to be taken back almost to the wood. There are new and old parts to the bracket feet, so I think it will be best to strip all the feet, making it easier to get them all the same colour.

Having assessed the extent of the work, begin by taking off all the handles and knobs and putting them safely in a tin or box. Now, as we will not be stripping the whole of the bureau, we must try to determine the nature of the polish that was originally used on it. At the age and period we've described for our bureau, it almost certainly will be shellac – or, in other words, french polish. An expert eye can tell just by observing the ageing symptoms of various surfaces.

However, you can test for shellac easily enough by putting a drop of methylated spirit on an unimportant corner and leaving it for a few minutes to see if the surface blisters and dissolves. If it doesn't, then it's some other finish, such as cellulose.

Before you start french polishing, there are two very important requirements you should bear in mind if you are to achieve a good finish. First, a warm temperature – not less than 18 degrees centigrade (65 Fahrenheit) and, second, low humidity. If you have central heating and your workshop is in the house, then as long as the right temperature is maintained you can polish away all year round. But if you intend working in your shed or in the garage, then late spring to early autumn is the only time you will be able to make any sort of a job of french polishing.

Low temperatures and damp air cause the polish to 'bloom' to a silky whiteness, and the polish will not dry quickly enough to enable you to work continually on one area to 'body in', or build up, the depth of polish required for a first application.

But before applying any new finish, we must prepare the bureau, beginning with the top. With the cabinet scraper, take off all the old surface, plus the mess we left when we re-stuck the veneer. When you get down to bare wood, go gently, for remember it is only a thin veneer. Make strokes with your scraper at a slightly oblique angle (but still following the direction of the grain), going one way for one stroke and the opposite way for the next – and so on. This helps to prevent undulations forming in the surface – always a danger when preparing wood with a scraper.

Make sure you leave no 'stop marks'. These are hard lines across the grain where too heavy scraper strokes started and finished. The scraper should be still moving in the same direction when it comes off at the end of the stroke. In this way, no marks will occur. Couldn't we smooth the marks away afterwards? Yes, if we spent a lot of time rubbing, but very often, when you think the mark has gone, it is only filled with wood dust! Then, as soon as you start to polish, there it is, showing as a fine ridge – much to your annoyance. It is far better to be meticulous over each stage. It saves time in the end.

When the top is scraped clean, examine the surface closely. There may be one or two places on the extreme edges where some old polish is left, for it's very difficult to scrape up to the edges. But if you keep your scraper at an angle, as I have said before, it'll go over the edge safely without taking lumps out.

Never scrape directly across the grain,

for, if you do, look closely and you will see that the grain is torn up. Where this happens accidentally, you must go over the area again, working in the direction of the grain, for, even with a great deal of papering, it could still show when polished. While you have your scraper handy, take down the new wood on the fall and the bottom drawer. Work very carefully until the new wood is flush with the surrounding surface.

Now tackle the sides, first the badly bleached one. The surface will have to be cut back until you have removed all the bleached shellac and you can see the true colour of the wood. For this, use No.320 wet or dry carborundum paper wrapped around a foam-covered rubbing block. You also need white spirit and plenty of rags.

It's best to do this job either out of doors or in a well-ventilated room, because white spirit can make you feel ill if you breathe in too many fumes. I learned my lesson years ago and now wear a small face mask – and advise you to do the same when using liquids which give off unpleasant fumes. Masks and refill pads can be bought very cheaply from many builders' merchants or hardware stores.

Pour some white spirit into a shallow dish or tin, from which a sponge can be charged. Then, with your bureau on its side, thoroughly wet the area to be treated with white spirit and rub down with carborundum paper and block. Sponge the surface all the time to keep it wet. You will have to rub and rub, but persevere until you see the dark colour of the wood coming through the bleached surface.

Wipe away the 'mud' at frequent intervals and sponge on fresh white spirit. Continue until you're satisfied that you have cut below the bleached layers, then give a final wash off with clean rag and spirit to remove any remaining deposit.

As the surface dries, you will probably find you have missed a few places, so repeat the process until all the bleached patches have disappeared. Then, for an extra smooth surface, go over the whole side again with 500 or 600 wet or dry paper.

Wouldn't it be easier just to scrape it off? The stripping part would be that much easier, but the reason for cutting back is to leave the grain filled or, as we say, 'bodied in'. You will find this makes the polishing stage far easier.

While you have spirit, sponge and paper to hand, clean down all the remaining surfaces including the drawer fronts. You will not have to spend so much time on these surfaces, for all you need do here is to take off the top layer to remove the surface scratches and give a good 'key' for the new polish you will be applying.

Next, look at the inside. The green felt writing surface is beyond redemption, so remove it by damping with warm water and stripping off with a scraper – such as a wallpaper stripping knife. Soak and scrape off any glue left on the wood, leaving it smooth and ready for new felt, or leather if you prefer. This will be fitted after polishing is finished.

Now, you'll probably find it difficult to remove that horrible ink stain. Luckily most of it is on the felt, but some ran over the wood surround. What a pity it wasn't mopped up right away!

First, strip the whole of the border, all round the recess made for the felt, with your cabinet scraper. By the way, do keep good edges on this tool, and, as soon as you find you cannot get a good shaving off with any of the four edges, stop to sharpen and turn them up in the way I explained to you on page 19. It saves time in the long run.

You will remove a lot of the ink stain with the shavings, but my guess is that it will have gone down deep into the wood. The only way is to bleach it out using hydrogen-peroxide or any strong household bleach. Mind your eyes! Apply this to the ink stain only, using a fine pointed brush (an old one, for this operation will probably ruin it), and re-apply as necessary until the ink mark disappears.

Neutralise the area with a weak acid such as vinegar, then give it a good wash over with white spirit and leave to dry. You will be left with a light patch, which, after you have smoothed down the surface, will eventually have to be carefully touched in with stain to match the rest of the wood.

The pigeon hole and little drawers inside are not in bad condition; just a few scratches here and there. Clean these out with rag and white spirit. The fronts of the little drawers can be rubbed down with what we in the trade call finishing cream. This is a fine abrasive suspended in liquid. As I suggested earlier, you have probably got something similar in your garage called car paint cleaner – not to be confused with cleaner and polish mixed. If you haven't, try your local friendly cabinet-maker or a car accessory shop.

Leave the bureau for an hour or two to allow the spirit to dry out. You can then come back to it with a dry cloth to rub off all the smears. Now you need some stain – oil or naphtha – and to obtain the right colour a walnut oil stain might be best. Each stain colour is named after a type of wood – mahogany, light oak, teak, walnut and so on – and this misleads many people, who think that, for example, when staining mahogany you must use a mahogany stain. If you do this, however, you end up with a piece of furniture nearly blood red in colour!

Staining wood is something you must experiment with, using each stain as an artist uses the colours on his palette. Don't be frightened to mix the stains until you arrive at the right shade, as long as they have the same base – spirit with spirit, and so on. When you apply a stain, the colour when still wet will give a good indication of the colour it will be after the surface finish has been put over it. This is not always true, however, so you should err on the dark side, for with french polishing a certain amount of pigment will be taken off with the initial application.

Before you stain, use a transparent polish to cover all the light stringing, the motif on the fall front and the drawer edgings – you don't want these to take stain. Now, apply your stain using a pad of cotton wool contained within a soft rag. Use long, even strokes, overlapping each stroke to avoid missing any area. Cover the sides, front, drawer fronts, pigeon holes and small drawers inside, loading your pad frequently.

Leave for a moment the bare wood of the top and the inside of the fall, for it may be that you will need a lighter stain on these unsealed pieces. Try light oak with a drop or two of walnut mixed in, and remember – it's easy to stain a piece of wood darker. But if it goes too dark, it's a much harder job to get rid of the colour and make it lighter. And on bare wood it may be impossible without re-stripping or planing.

When you have finished staining and are satisfied that the colour is uniform, I recommend you to leave it for a couple of days at least, to allow the stain to set, or cure. Cover the bureau with a large sheet of brown paper, loosely laid over, to keep the dust off.

You could use these two or three days to put in some practice at french polishing – perhaps on an old piece of furniture where it doesn't matter too much what happens.

French polish is applied with a pad called a rubber, so the first job is to make up one or two of these *(see fig.34)*. Fine surgical wool forms the inside of your rubber, not the stuff with lumps and bits in it called cotton wadding. About half a compressed handful is enough, but vary the amount according to the size of the job. For a little table a rubber of 38mm (1½in) is all that's required, but for a large dining-table top one twice this size should be used.

Save all your old handkerchiefs, for this type of fine cloth is ideal for the outside covering of the rubber. This is how you make it *(a)*. Take a piece of cloth about 150mm (6in) square and place your ball of cotton wool in its centre. Take up the four corners and draw them through a ring formed by your thumb and forefinger so that you form a mushroom-shaped pad. Twist the stem once or twice, then hold it in your hand and flatten it against the palm of your other hand. Your rubber is now ready for charging. Put this in your airtight tin to keep it clean while you make some more.

While on the subject of rubbers, here's

something I discovered quite by accident one day when I had run out of good cotton wool and I wanted to start a polishing job. I had at this time been working on some soft cushions and had a small quantity of Dacron fibre. This is just like cotton wool to look at, and I thought it would perhaps do instead. So I made a rubber and started the job. It was marvellous. The Dacron wool seemed to hold more polish for longer and, because it was more resilient, by squeezing you could regulate the flow of polish from the rubber more easily. The best thing about it is that it's virtually everlasting, whereas a rubber made with cotton wool will, after half an hour of use, become flat-faced and dead. I must add that I use this 'synthetic' rubber only for the initial stages. Use cotton wool for the final finish when the amount of polish applied is much reduced.

Put your practice piece at a height which allows you to stand comfortably without having to bend down to it. It must also be in a good light. At your side keep your bottle of shellac polish – I'd say transparent would be best – a small bottle of white oil, a small jar containing methylated spirit and, of course, the rubber which you must now charge.

Untwist the stem of the rubber and turn back the cloth from the wadding. Hold the wadding to the neck of the polish bottle and tip up for one second (b). Pour the polish onto three or four places and the wadding should be charged enough. Pull the covering cloth back over and twist up the stem. Hold it in your hand (c), and gently press on to some convenient flat surface, such as an old glazed tile or a piece of glass. This action spreads the polish equally over the face of the rubber.

Before you start, there's one very important point I want you to remember. Your rubber must never come to a standstill while in contact with the surface. Now begin by applying polish in strokes along the complete length of the surface to be covered, working in the direction of the grain (d). Start at the edge furthest from you, and overlap each stroke slightly.

You should already be moving your hand in the direction of the stroke before the rubber comes into contact with the surface. Continue moving in the same direction after contact is lost at the end of the stroke. In this way, at no point will your rubber be stationary on the surface.

If the rubber should stop on one spot it would immediately stick and leave a nasty mark when removed. In this case, the only thing to do is to leave the job for two or three hours, then gently smooth down the mark with a very fine abrasive paper and white or raw linseed oil (not boiled). Continue with the long strokes until you have covered the surface about four times, charging the rubber every other time. The first few strokes you make with neat polish are designed to seal the wood and set the stain, if one has been used.

Leave the surface for a quarter of an hour, remembering to shut your rubber in the airtight tin. If you don't, within that time it will become hard and of no further use.

The next stage is called 'bodying in'. This means that you are going to concentrate on filling in those microscopic crevices which make up the open grain of the wood. Take a new rubber and charge it as before, but this time take the small bottle containing white oil in your free hand. With your index finger covering the open top, tip it up, then dab this fingerful of oil on to the surface of the rubber.

The addition of oil allows you to go over and over a half-dried surface without it sticking. However, the oil is only a vehicle, and it forms no part of the finished polish. The more oil you use, the more you will have to remove at the end of the job – so it is best to go sparingly.

Now use a variety of strokes, starting with small, circular movements of the rubber (e) and gradually moving across the surface. After this make a few straight strokes, following the grain. You can also use a large figure-of-eight, working first with and then across the grain (f).

A good rhythm of movement must be acquired for all these strokes. The wrist must play an important part and pressure is

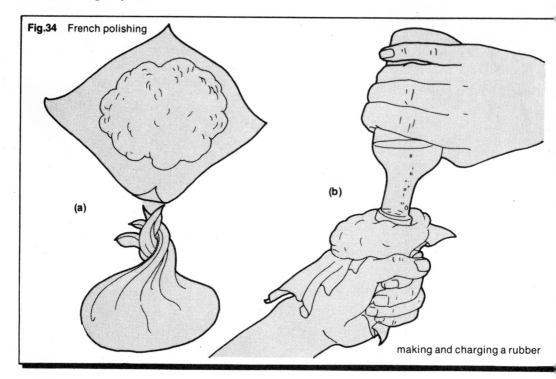

Fig.34 French polishing

(a)

(b)

making and charging a rubber

important too. Use light pressure on the rubber when it's first charged, and increase the pressure as the amount of polish in the rubber diminishes. Above all, take it slowly and easily, and when doing the circular action never go faster than about two circuits a second. Even one stroke is acceptable.

I find that most people, when learning to french polish, go at it like a bull at a gate. They rush away, anxious to see a result, and all they get for their wasted energy is a gummed-up sticky surface – all ridges and surface marks. Remember – slowly does it!

Another important point to bear in mind is that what is important is not the amount of polish you put on but the way in which it is applied. And don't overload the rubber: just the three tip-ups of the bottle, as I mentioned earlier, will be enough, plus one finger of oil. Work away until you feel there is nothing left in the rubber. This may take up to ten minutes.

There is also an art in knowing just when

to stop and leave the work to cure. If you go on too long with a first application, you may find that the polish is building up in ridges, accentuating the microscopic raised grain ridges of the wood. Also, little knops or nibs will appear where specks of dust have fallen unnoticed and the polish has built up over them – or perhaps where a small hair or fibre has become embedded.

If you've gone on too long and put on too much polish, you will suddenly find that parts of the surface start to 'ripple' under the pressure of your rubber. If you can stop before any of the symptoms occur, you'll save yourself a lot of trouble; so spend not more than half an hour on your surface, then leave it until the next day.

By then you will find that the polish has settled into the wood, hardened, and is ready for another half-hour session. Continue daily, until you have a complete, unbroken surface with no open grain pores.

I expect that by this time the surface will be marred by a number of small bumps,

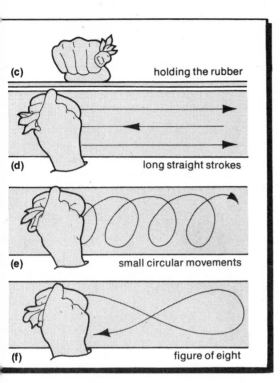

(c) holding the rubber

(d) long straight strokes

(e) small circular movements

(f) figure of eight

So, to spirit off, find the rubber you used at the beginning when sealing the wood with those first long strokes – using no oil. With the jar of methylated spirit by your side, place the palm of your free hand over the open jar and tip up. Put down the jar and with the rubber mop up the spirit that is on your hand. Don't bother to take off the cloth cover.

Now, with fairly quick, long strokes in the direction of the grain, go over the whole of the surface, then leave it for about two minutes. Apply another dab of spirit to the rubber and repeat the operation. You will see that you are picking up oil, because the smear trails following the rubber strokes become fainter. After this you can put the treated surface away for a couple of days. If, after then, oil smears have appeared, 'spirit off' the surface once again.

French polish, although quick drying, does not cure and harden right through for some time. So if you want to use the surface, put it away for at least a month until it is really hard.

After making a success of your practice piece, perhaps you feel confident enough to start polishing your bureau. But first, I'll give you a few tips. Don't do the polishing piecemeal. Each stage should be done to all the surfaces of the bureau – except perhaps the inside. This would involve resting the half-dry surface of the outside of the fall on the fall bearers. So it is best to polish the inside to a finished state first.

Before you start on the outside, apply polish carefully to the mouldings with a soft squirrel or sable brush, concentrating on the areas where it will be difficult to get a rubber. For inside corners, crevices and mouldings, make a special rubber with a pointed end *(see fig.35)*. And, finally, don't forget to work slowly! Don't be anxious to see a quick result, and remember to stop, leave for a while and cut back the surface if it starts to get ridged or lumpy.

I hope I haven't made it all sound too easy. I think you will need to spend time and practice before achieving good results. But don't despair, it will come. If my directions

lumps and undulations, which must now be cut back evenly using a rubbing block covered with a No.400 to 600 wet or dry abrasive paper lubricated with white spirit. Be very careful at the edges. It is so easy to cut through to the wood at an edge, so start in the centre, rubbing in the direction of the grain and going very lightly when you reach the edges.

Make sure you wipe away all the ground-off polish with lint-free rag. Then, when all is thoroughly dry, the final coat can be applied. For this you need very little polish on your rubber – just one tip-up of the bottle and as little oil as possible. Use the basic strokes already mentioned and the surface should now quickly assume a lustrous, even shine and be ready for 'spiriting off'.

This term refers to the final act when you remove all the oil which by now has risen to the surface. Run your finger over the surface and see how it smears. If this oil were left on, it would slowly congeal, forming a dull film which is hard to remove.

seem rather inadequate, it will make better sense when you actually try.

In french polishing, many things can go wrong. And things which can cause problems include imbalance of polish and oil on the rubber; too heavy or too light a pressure on the surface; and the consistency of the polish before use. Most of these things cannot be measured but are learnt by experience. They become instinctive after a time.

With the polishing done, your bureau is finished, apart from adding a new writing surface and re-fitting the handles. Some of these handles may be bent, and all are probably very dirty, so I will deal with these problems in the next chapter. The best way to apply the new felt is to measure and cut it out accurately to size, rather than cutting oversize and trimming into the recess.

Use a white pva glue to stick it down, thinly coating the wood only. If you are fitting what is called a 'loose leather', it is better to trim this when it is in place so that

Fig.35 Rubber with pointed end

edges can be slightly undercut for a good fit. Leathers and skivers with gold-tooled borders are called loose by the manufacturers, but nevertheless they are stuck down in the same way as the felt.

REMOVING SMALL SURFACE MARKS

While many faults on the bureau have been dealt with by stripping or cutting back, there are certain kinds of damage which can be cured without resorting to such drastic action. The most common is the round white water mark caused by the wet base of a flower vase. If caught in time, it can be removed quite easily.

The white mark shows because the surface of the polish which has been in contact with the damp glass becomes microscopically roughened, causing opacity. If you can smooth it down, the mark will disappear. Use the finishing cream or car paint cleaner I mentioned earlier. Some people advise the use of metal polish but, while I admit this does work, I find the liquid in which the abrasive is suspended rather too strong. It sometimes acts like a stripper on shellac polish.

Alcohol marks occur on small tables and dressing tables, the latter being caused perhaps by spilt perfume or hair lacquer. These marks are more difficult to remove, for in most cases the surface is partly dissolved. However, if the damage is not too deep and the colour has not been affected, it is possible to repair it by cutting back and re-building the surface with rubber and french polish. Remember, we are talking only of shellac-type polish. The cellulose-sprayed finishes will not respond in the same way, and damage to this type of surface usually means chemically stripping the whole section and starting afresh.

RESTORING POLYURETHANE SURFACES

On much modern furniture, the finish is polyurethane which is far superior to shellac in durability. But its appearance can be so glass-like and perfect that it gives a plastic look even to the wood underneath. Although polyurethane is very tough, damage can occur in the form of scratches, chips and broken edges.

These can be made good, so long as the damage is confined to the finish and the wood and colour underneath is undisturbed. You must cut back and re-coat several times. Matt the surface surrounding the damaged area with fine carborundum paper used dry, then use a fine brush to paint in the scratch, chip or dent with polyurethane and leave to dry.

Patiently build up, coat upon coat, until the new material is slightly higher than the rest of the surface. Then, when it is thoroughly dry, rub down until the whole is smooth. Finally, ensure that the whole surface is clean and wax-free by washing over with white spirit. Then apply a thin coat of polyurethane to the entire surface.

If you have to strip a polyurethane surface because of deep damage, then you must make sure you neutralise the paint stripper properly – according to the manufacturer's instructions. Building up a new polyurethane surface is quite a simple matter, requiring only a good brush and a dust-free room. Temperature is not so important as when french polishing, but, even so, very low temperatures slow down the drying process and prevent a good gloss from being formed. Here is how you do it.

After carefully preparing the surface so that it is perfectly smooth and clean, apply stain with either a brush or a pad. It helps to add to the stain a small quantity of polyurethane. This acts as a fixative – but do this only with oil stains. Leave the job for at least four days for the stain to cure – after which you can apply the first coat. Thin this to about nine parts varnish to one part white spirit. Then, with a brush, apply it using light strokes. Even though the stain is fixed, there is still the danger that it may streak. When you put on this first coat, brush only with the grain.

If you are varnishing natural, unstained wood, the first coat should be thinned to half and half polyurethane and white spirit.

Apply it with a pad made of cotton wool and covered with cloth, rubbing the varnish well into the grain. Thereafter, use the varnish at full strength, applying at least seven coats in all, cutting back between coats from the third onwards.

To cut back, take a wet sponge (water is used) in one hand and your rubbing block with No.400 wet or dry paper in the other. Wet the surface, then rub in the direction of the grain, keeping the work wet all the time. Clean off with a fresh rag and leave to dry thoroughly before applying the next coat.

Before the last coat is applied, cut back very gently with the finest paper – No.500 or 600 carborundum. After seven coats, you should have a perfect, unbroken glass-like surface, which, when cured in about two weeks, will stand up to knocks, bangs, spilt drinks and water. Polyurethane may be applied over cellulose providing this is well cut back to a matt surface to give a good key. But it will not adhere to shellac polish.

To renovate an old polyurethane or cellulose surface which doesn't need stripping, use the finishing cream or car cleaner previously mentioned, then polish with a good car wax. It'll probably come up looking like new.

REMOVING SCORCH MARKS

Another very common accident which occurs to polished furniture is scorching. You will probably come across chair or table legs which have been too close to the fire – and strong, hot sunlight can also produce similar symptoms. The legs get hot; the polish starts to melt and bubble up; the bubbles burst; and you're left with very nasty marks.

Treatment, if the damage is bad, will mean stripping the whole leg, endeavouring to leave the stained surface underneath unmarked. Sometimes you can treat the affected area by rubbing lightly with dry, fine glasspaper or garnet paper. Be very careful not to rub through the stain.

Finish rubbing down with a very fine wet or dry paper lubricated with white spirit until all traces of the blisters have gone.

You can then re-build the surface with shellac polish.

OTHER FURNITURE

You must give a lot of thought as to the best way to tackle each piece of furniture requiring renovation. For example, a Victorian show-wood chair which has been liberally coated with thick varnish will, most likely, have to be given the full treatment – back to bare wood. You will have to experiment to see how best to get shellac varnish or old polish off.

Sometimes you find that the varnish has deteriorated to such a degree that a light rub with medium garnet paper or fine wire wool brings the lot off in fine flakes or dust. The chances are, however, that the surface will be much tougher, with the varnish well keyed on. In this case, try dry scraping – with scrapers variously shaped to cope with the contours of mouldings and legs. Another method is to rub down with white spirit and wire wool.

If these methods prove too tedious, you will have to resort to 'scrubbing down'. For this you need a shallow tin containing methylated spirit, another of white spirit, and a small nail brush, tooth brush or similar small, stiff-bristled brush. You also need plenty of rags and an old paint brush with which to apply the methylated spirit.

Apply meths liberally to all the surfaces, then leave for five minutes. Give the surface another wash over with methylated spirit, and you should find that the varnish is starting to dissolve. Now get to work with the scrubbing brush. Dip it first into the meths and then into the white spirit. The white spirit keeps the dissolving varnish in a fluid state for a little longer so that it can be mopped away with a rag. Otherwise, it could be setting again before you are able to remove it.

Scrub away, keeping the whole of the piece well soaked all the time. When you are satisfied you have removed all you can from the moulding, carving and turnings on the legs, give the whole lot a thorough wash with meths, using clean rags.

One side effect that methylated spirit has on many woods is to raise the grain, causing a roughening of the surface. So, when all is dry, go over it again, this time with fine glass, garnet or carborundum paper, smoothing it down prior to re-staining and polishing. It is this effect that makes me hesitant to recommend spirit stains. These consist of crystals dissolved in meths. Water stains also have much the same effect, raising the grain fibres into minute ridges that remain prominent even when the wood has dried out.

If you try to smooth down after staining, very often you leave flecks of bare wood where the ridges were. It all depends upon the type of wood you are staining, so I recommend that you try the different types of stain for yourself, on scrap pieces, and learn by experience.

While we are on the subject of wood grain, there are some woods which have a very open grain – among them many of the redwoods (mahogany types), oak and, perhaps the worst of all, ash. Such woods, if french polished with no other preparation other than smoothing and staining, would take weeks to get 'bodied in'. So we use a grain filler to bring the surface forward.

Grain-filling materials usually consist of china clay or fine whiting suspended in a white spirit, linseed oil medium. I say suspended, but the mixture must be constantly stirred to keep it in this condition. The mixture also contains pigment or stainers to colour the otherwise white clay or chalk. You can buy this filler ready prepared, and it will be labelled with a wood name, to give a rough guide to colour.

I find it best to fill the grain after staining the wood, letting it dry for a day or two. Even so, you are bound to remove a lot of the stain when applying the filler, so I like to add stain while I'm filling. This is how you do it – and a fair amount of speed is essential. Have to hand sheets of newspaper rolled into loose balls, with one flat side, rather like your french-polishing rubber, only much larger. If you are working on a very light piece, use a tough tissue paper or any semi-absorbent paper instead of newsprint, because a certain amount of printing ink comes off.

Stir your filler well and paint on thinly over the entire area. Quickly take up a paper pad and rub the filler into the surface. The idea is to get the open grain filled level while leaving no trace of filler on the actual surface. Paper will do this, but if you wipe with a rag you will find that the filler is taken out of the grain by the cloth fibres.

As soon as one ball of paper is clogged, throw it away and continue with another until the surface assumes a sheen. At some time during the process of rubbing off I like to add a wipe or two of stain to make up for the stain that is being rubbed away. So long as it is oil or naphtha stain, it will not affect the filling process.

The job should then be left for a day to cure, after which you can start the french polish as already described.

POLISHES AND REVIVERS

To end this chapter, I would like to give one or two recipes for polishes and revivers. Over the years an old piece of furniture will accumulate an incredible amount of dirt on its surface unless it has been well cared for. And too many people today associate antique furniture with dirt and grime. They think it is an integral part of the finish.

Many times have I gazed through the windows of small antique shops at quite attractive pieces displayed there – my fingers itching to get to work at cleaning them up and getting rid of all the muck in the mouldings and the black dirt in corners of panels, as well as improving their general dingy appearance.

Some folk advocate vinegar and warm water for cleaning, but I would not recommend using water on any furniture. Here is a recipe for a much better reviver. Use 50 parts raw linseed oil, 48 parts malt vinegar and 2 parts methylated spirit. A graduated chemistry tube will help you to measure. Put the linseed oil in a small bottle, filling only a quarter of it. Add the methylated spirit and shake well. Add the vinegar a little at a time

and shake well before adding more. This should form an emulsion with the consistency of cream and the colour of mayonnaise – so label the bottle clearly!

This makes an excellent polish restorer which will clean off old wax and surface dirt, leaving a bit of a shine.

In the early days, furniture made of oak was finished by rubbing in linseed oil, then polishing with beeswax. Later, walnut was also treated in this way, creating over the years the beautiful dark brown colour. This differs greatly from the rather (to my mind) nasty colour of walnut from the late nineteenth century that has been french polished and which will never assume any other colour – even in another hundred years' time.

With the advent of mahogany, a little more sophistication was introduced. A piece of furniture was liberally coated with linseed oil and left to dry for a day or so, then finely-ground brick dust was rubbed into the surface with the aid of a piece of cork. The brick dust made an excellent grain filler. Then, coat upon coat of linseed oil was applied over long periods, resulting in a surface which was more permanent than many finishes known today.

A more modern method of oil polishing is to substitute brick dust for the modern type of grain filler I mentioned earlier. This is applied first, then when thoroughly dry a mixture of half raw linseed oil to half turpentine or white spirit is brushed on and lightly rubbed in with pads of semi-absorbent paper such as newsprint.

This will then have to be left for perhaps a month, as linseed oil takes a long time to oxidise and dry. Coats of a slightly stronger mixture (more linseed oil) can be rubbed on at intervals of several weeks until a good depth of polish has been achieved. This is a very slow process but immensely rewarding in the end.

There are a number of recipes for wax polish. An early one is recorded by Thomas Sheraton in the *Cabinet Dictionary* of 1803. It reads as follows: '...take bees wax and a small quantity of turpentine in a clean earthen pan, and set it over a fire till the wax unites with the turpentine, which it will do by constant stirring about; add to this a little red lead finely ground upon a stone, together with a small portion of fine Oxford ochre, to bring the whole to the colour of brisk mahogany. Lastly, when you take it off the fire, add a little copal varnish to it, and mix it well together, then turn the whole into a bason of water, and while it is yet warm, work into a ball, with which the brush is to be rubbed as before observed. And observe, with a ball of wax and brush kept for this purpose entirely, furniture in general may be kept in good order.'

If you try making up this recipe you must substitute burnt sienna for red lead for a mahogany colour or burnt umber to give a dark oak colour. The inclusion of red lead would make this polish a very dangerous substance to use.

A simple wax polish can be made by shredding or grating beeswax into turpentine or turps substitute and leaving to dissolve, stirring daily and adding more flakes of wax until a thick cream is produced.

The best wax polish for building up a really hard surface that will not finger mark or remain sticky can be made with approximately 40 per cent beeswax, 15 per cent carnauba wax (a very hard wax obtainable from varnish manufacturers and merchants) and 45 per cent white spirit. Melt the two waxes in a container and take away from the heat. Then add the spirit and a colouring pigment if required. Stir well and then leave it to cool.

Creamed Beeswax Polish A Cornish recipe by courtesy of M. Putwain Esq, Marazion.

This makes an excellent polish for smooth sealed surfaces. I would not recommend it to be used on open grained wood or woodwork with many crevices, carvings or mouldings unless used with brushes to ensure that no cream is left behind.

It is an expensive polish to make so I halved the quantities of the ingredients and found that it made about 570g (1¼lb) of cream. The ingredients are:

6dl (1 pint) turpentine (genuine)
6dl (1 pint) water (warm)
127g (4½oz) beeswax
1 tablespoon ammonia.

Melt the beeswax in a container standing in warm water (I used an old double saucepan). Don't place a container with the wax in it directly over a naked flame!

When the wax has melted, pour in the turps and stir well. Add the ammonia to the warm water and then pour it into the wax and turpentine mixture, stirring vigorously. Fill previously warmed shallow jars or tins with the polish while it is still liquid.

When polishing with wax, don't assume that the more polish you put on the better will be the shine. If you put a lot on, you will spend much time rubbing, until most of it has come off on your polishing rag and is wasted. Remember, a small amount of polish and a large amount of 'elbow grease', and rub like mad!

With the hard wax polish I have mentioned, made with carnauba wax, it is best to apply polish to a small area, then polish off before going on to another similar area. With furniture cream, you can cover a whole area and leave for some minutes before polishing off. Avoid using the cream on furniture with open wood grain or pieces with many crevices, corners or carvings, as the cream will tend to dry white in these places and look unsightly. Use a more full-bodied material.

Some people overdo polishing, treating it, perhaps, every week. The result is a build-up of wax on surfaces into a sticky film, for which the only cure is a good clean-off with the vinegar and linseed oil reviver, and start again.

One polish every two months is quite enough, and, with a hard wax, every six months is sufficient. In the meantime, a rub with a soft duster every other day will keep everything shining.

Repairs and treatment of metals on furniture

Don't be alarmed at the thought of tackling metalwork. I am no metal worker myself, so all I intend to do in this chapter is to discuss very easy and minor repairs, plus general care of the metal parts found on furniture. Major repairs, or repairs to metalwork on valuable pieces of furniture, should always be taken to an expert.

EXTRA TOOLS

First, a list of a few more tools you'll need (*see fig.36*). A small engineer's vice with 50-76mm (2-3in) jaws which should be mounted on the end of your bench. Pliers of various sizes; a small pein hammer – that's one with a knob on the end; a good hacksaw and blades; saw files, which you already have – but square, flat and rat tail files will be a useful addition. A soldering iron, electric or the simple 'heat in a flame' type; flux and a bar of fine solder; also tin snips for cutting thin sheet metal. You already have carbon drills, but now you can add to these some much smaller sizes.

HANDLES AND KNOBS

Metal handles are probably the most common items on furniture. So let us look at

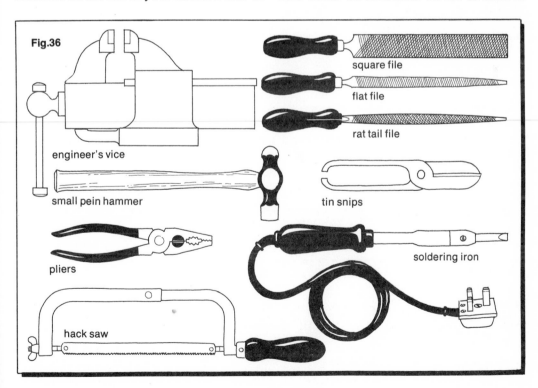

Fig.36

engineer's vice

square file

flat file

rat tail file

small pein hammer

tin snips

pliers

soldering iron

hack saw

your bureau and see what needs to be done to re-fix the handles and knobs. The small knobs for the inside drawers screw in, so they are easy to put back – except for one, which we'll assume is a very loose fit. The hole in the drawer has become enlarged.

Don't be lazy and simply stick a matchstick into the hole as is often done. Do the job properly and glue in a peg of some more substantial wood. Then drill a hole a fraction smaller than the screw shank on the knob, and screw the knob in. It will now stay put!

There is not much wrong with the large drawer handles, which, by the way, are called 'swan necks'. I see one or two are bent inwards, and this means that if they are pulled hard they would probably come out of their sockets. Try to open these out very gently with pliers, being careful not to scratch the brass. If they feel stiff and won't bend easily, don't force them or else they may break.

ANNEALING OLD BRASS

Brass becomes hard and brittle with age and must be annealed (made more pliable) before it can be bent. To do this, heat must be applied to the handle. Hold it over a gas flame until it is red hot, then drop it immediately into a container of cold water. You will then find that you can bend your handle quite easily without fear of breaking it. However, you will have a problem after the heat treatment, because the flame will have left the metal very dull. Hard work will be needed to restore the brass.

CLEANING HANDLES AND METAL-WORK ON FURNITURE

This brings me to the controversial subject of whether to clean or not to clean handles and other metal on furniture. I admit that nothing looks nicer than a chest of drawers with handles gleaming, but there again, nothing annoys me more than seeing gleaming handles surrounded by a white encrustation of metal polish dust. I suppose polishing smooth, simple, swan neck handles such as the ones on your bureau is no great sin; after all, I expect they started life that way. But with older, more ornate, finely modelled or

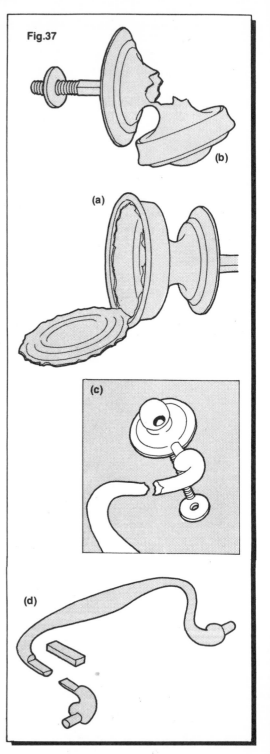

Fig.37

(a)

(b)

(c)

(d)

chiselled handles, cleaning is frowned upon by experts.

Over a period of time, handles and knobs of brass, bronze and other similar metals gain a coating of oxide, which, with use, gets rubbed and smoothed to become a good protective deposit. As with the old polished wood, a patina is formed, the colour of which cannot be imitated. So I think it's best not to polish. After all, you are not only taking off dirt and oxide but also a quantity of metal as well.

I have seen knobs on Regency chests of drawers – the type that are made of pressed brass and are hollow inside – that have been cleaned and cleaned until the metal has become so thin and brittle that they have eventually cracked and broken.

REPAIRING HOLLOW BRASS KNOBS

A good way to repair hollow knobs is to fill, or fill partly, the hollow metal knob with one of the resin-hardener repair materials that are used for repairing car bodies. You can buy small kits in garages and hardware stores in two tube packs.

The usual place in which a knob breaks is around the waist between the front part and back but I have come across knobs with the whole front face hanging only by a thread *(see fig.37)*. These are the easiest to repair, for you can pack the knob from the front with filler, then push the front face on to it – like closing a lid *(a)*. With the break at the waist *(b)*, it is best to coat the interior of both halves with liquid quick-setting epoxy resin adhesive with hardener mixed in, then put both halves together, sealing the join with tape or plasticine. Slowly revolve the knob in your hands, over and over until you are sure that the resin has hardened. A quick-setting adhesive doesn't take long to go off. If you leave a dab on something nearby, you can keep a watchful eye on it as you're turning the knob, and you will then know when it is safe to stop.

When a knob has a very slender waist, fill both halves with resin. Then give some added reinforcement by pushing in pieces of wire before bringing the two halves together.

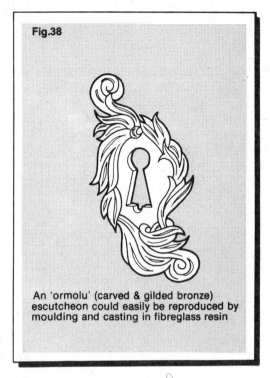

Fig.38

An 'ormolu' (carved & gilded bronze) escutcheon could easily be reproduced by moulding and casting in fibreglass resin

RESIN-HARDENER (OTHER USES)

The resin-type repair material can be used in several other ways. For instance, if a piece of decorative brass is missing it can be reproduced by making a mould from part of the original in the same manner as I described on page 52 for making gesso moulding and carving. When the piece has been cast, it can be fitted and stuck in place with more resin. Strands of glass fibre can be laid across the joints to add strength. Pieces of missing ormolu can be cast *(see fig.38)*, and bronze dust added to the liquid will give a metallic bronze effect. Metallic resin-hardeners in a number of colours are available from handicraft shops.

SOLDERING

To return to the subject of handles *(see fig.37)*, a solid cast brass handle like the swan necks referred to on our bureau may break in two *(c)*. This is a problem, but it may be possible to let in a bridging piece at the back, making a similar repair to the scarf joint I mentioned on page 34 for repairing a broken chair stretcher rail. This time, however, you cannot glue the piece in; it will have to be soldered.

Take your broken handle and place the pieces together, holding them in position against a board with small clamps – the back of the handle uppermost. Leave room between your clamps to enable you to file out for the bridging piece. With a square file cut a recess down to half the thickness of the handle, across the area where the break has occurred. With a hacksaw, cut out and file up a piece of brass to fit in the recess *(d)*.

Now, get out your soldering iron, bar of fine solder, flux, a flat-bladed knife (an old table knife with a sharp, straight edge will do) and a pair of pliers. You also need a small piece of stick to dispense the flux and a small square of fine emery cloth. If you are using an ordinary soldering iron then you will need a heat source, such as a gas ring, blowlamp or camping stove.

The watchword when soldering is cleanli-ness, for the enemies that will thwart you are oxide, grease and dirt. You must make sure that all the faces to be joined are absolutely clean. Even an hour after you have filed the brass to shape, oxidisation will have started on the exposed surfaces. You won't be able to see it, but there will be enough to prevent solder taking hold.

Also, how many times have you handled the pieces? Every time you touch metal, oil from your skin is left on the surface, and this also will prevent solder from holding. So here's what you have to do to get the surfaces really clean.

Clean off the tip of the soldering iron by rubbing it on a piece of fine emery cloth. Go easy with the cleaning if you have an electric iron. Heat the iron, and when it is hot scrape the tip with your flat-bladed knife, not hard, but just enough to get rid of any dirt, oxide or grease that may be stuck to it. Then dip it into the flux immediately. Apply the tip of the iron to the bar of solder; providing it is hot enough, the solder will melt and stick to

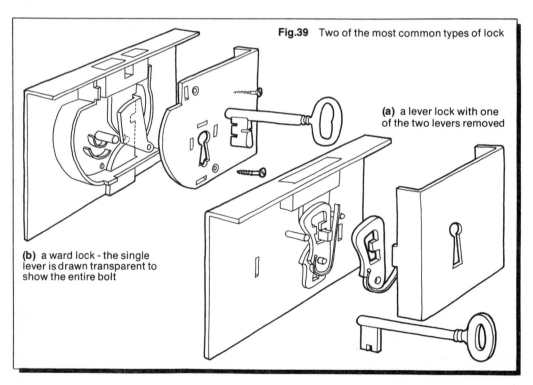

Fig.39   Two of the most common types of lock

(a) a lever lock with one of the two levers removed

(b) a ward lock - the single lever is drawn transparent to show the entire bolt the cleaned tip. This is called tinning. Flux, by the way, is a substance which keeps metal free from oxide, thus helping the soldering process.

Now, scrape the parts of the handle to be joined, using the knife as you would a cabinet scraper. As you scrape, although you cannot see it, you are paring off all the microscopic blotches of oxide and finger-print grease.

With the small stick, quickly coat the newly-scraped bright metal with flux. When all the appropriate surfaces have been treated, the next step is to tin them. Pick up a drop of solder on the tip of your iron, place the bridging piece flat on the bench, and touch the iron on the metal. There is no need to try to spread the solder along – just leave the tip of the iron resting on the metal and, providing it is at the right temperature, the solder will melt and run over the whole surface just like quicksilver.

Now tin the recess you have made in the back of the handle in the same manner. Pick up the bridge piece with your pliers and place it in position. It won't go down into the recess yet because of the layer solder. Just put the tip of the hot soldering iron on the centre of the bridge and wait.

In a moment or two, when the metal reaches the right temperature, it will suddenly drop into place. Keep the iron on the metal while you make sure that the piece is exactly in position, then remove the iron and leave to cool. Remove the handle from the bench and file the new metal back to match the contours of the original parts of the handle.

This handle, although well repaired, is bound to be a little weaker than the others, so, when putting it back, exchange it for a handle on one of the least used drawers.

HOW TO DETECT ORIGINAL HANDLES

Often, when we see a nice old piece of furniture – maybe a chest of drawers, bureau or tallboy – we may ask, could the handles be original? Look inside a drawer and very often you will see another two or perhaps four holes made for previous handles. And

perhaps between them you will see a larger hole which has been pegged or filled up where, in Victorian times, a fashionable knob had been fitted. You can also spend time in detective work, looking up books to see if the period of the handle really matches the period of the piece of furniture.

LOCKS

Locks are perhaps the most fascinating metal-made objects on furniture, as they show the ingenuity of the metal craftsman. You will be able to do only the simplest of repairs to locks – perhaps renewing a spring, fitting a key or straightening the mechanism – but even these jobs are worth a word or two of advice.

There are two main types of cupboard and drawer locks (*see fig.39*): those which rely on levers for their security (*a*), and those which have fixed wards (*b*). The earlier ward lock has usually only one lever, while the wards, those little semi-circular fences of metal around the key pin, prevent any other key from fitting.

Examine the key that fits this lock, and you will see that castellations or slots are filed into the leading edge of the key flange to match the pattern and position of the wards exactly. In contrast, the key to the more secure lever lock has castellations along the side of the flange, enabling a number of levers to be raised to different levels, thus aligning a gap in their centres to allow the free passage of the lock bolt.

Most of the better-made locks have a cover plate secured by small machine screws. In some early locks and modern cheap locks this cover plate is fixed by flanges which go through slots and are burred over on the outside.

Minor ailments common to locks are: lever springs breaking; key pins working loose or coming out completely; and, with old locks, wear occurring in the key gap in the bolt, causing the bolt to be thrown only part of the way out and thus not to be locked in position by the levers. Let us look at these faults and see what is the best way of putting things right.

Take the lock from the door or drawer and remove the cover plate. This is easy enough with the better locks secured with screws, but with the flange and slot type it is a trifle more difficult. Where the flanges are protruding and burred over, file off the burr and lever off. You may come across a lock where these flanges have been filed flat to the surface of the plate. In this case the only thing to do is lever off by inserting old knife blades under the cover plate each side of the flange. By inserting several blades one on top of the other, you will gradually force the plate off without buckling it.

Examine the lock carefully, noting the action and purpose of every moving part. This is yet another outlet for your 'magpie instinct', for the parts from any old cupboard and drawer locks you can collect and save will very likely come in useful. For instance, where a lever spring is broken, you will see the pieces in the lock you have opened. It is a small, thin spring that curls over and is slotted into the lever. Its purpose is to keep the lever down on to its rest.

Most locks for drawers or doors have a pin in the centre of the keyhole; the key itself has a hole in its end so that it fits over the pin. Very often this pin becomes loose, falls out or even falls down inside the lock, jamming the works. This pin is made with a shoulder *(see fig.40)*, and it fits into a hole in the back of the lock. The shoulder on the pin ensures that it is fixed at right angles when riveted over from the outside of the back plate. Should this pin become loose, you can tighten it by tapping and burring up the end behind the lock while holding the front part of the pin firmly in your vice.

If the pin is missing, you will have to make a new one. Find a nail, or something similar made of mild steel, which will fit into the barrel of the key and is also big enough to enable you to reduce one end to fit the hole in the back plate.

Cut off the point of the nail and round off any sharp edges. Measure the length required by inserting it into the key barrel, then adding the length required for it to pass through the back plate and protrude 1mm

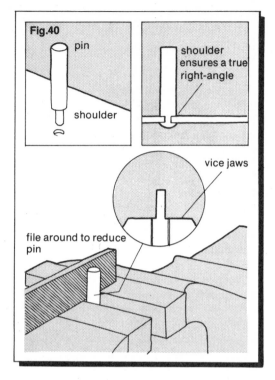

Fig.40

pin

shoulder

shoulder ensures a true right-angle

vice jaws

file around to reduce pin

($^1/_{32}$in) at the back. To make the shoulder near the end of the pin, mark how deep it goes into the key barrel with a file, then fix it firmly in the vice, keeping the mark you have made level with the top of the jaws.

Make sure the pin is at right angles to the jaws, then with a square file carefully file round the pin, using the vice jaws as a guide. Try the hole in the back plate over the pin frequently, until you have a good tight fit. Raise the pin a little higher in the vice and put the plate in place on the pin. Then, with your small hammer, burr over the protruding part of the pin until secure. Check as you do that the pin is still at 90 degrees. Try the key, and if all is correct start to re-assemble the lock.

With an old lock in which the key and the part of the bolt where the key makes contact are badly worn, the bolt may be thrown only partially out or in. This is very awkward on a close-fitting door, because the bolt will remain partly out when unlocked and the door will not open. If you are faced with this problem, a very thin-bladed knife inserted over the bolt may work the bolt back, providing there is enough gap between door and stile.

What can you do with a lock like this? The thing to do is to provide another key which has a longer flange to cope with the worn bolt. Maybe you have a collection of old keys around the house somewhere: if you're lucky, one of these could be adapted. If not, blank keys can still be purchased at a good old-fashioned ironmonger.

CUTTING KEYS

Key cutting is quite an exacting task, but you can do it if you have some good files – especially the thin varieties used for cutting slots in wards or levers.

For a ward lock, the type with the semi-circular fences, first remove the cover plate and by trial and error file the key flange to the correct length so that it will throw the bolt to its full extent. Then mark the position of the wards on the leading edge of the key flange with a scriber and file or cut them out with a hacksaw. I have seen many a lock ruined by lazy people who, instead of fitting the key to the lock, fit the lock to the key by pulling out all the wards!

When fitting a key to a lever lock, first remove all the levers, but keep them in their correct order. As with the ward lock, file the flange to the length to throw the bolt. Then replace the first lever; mark its position on the key, and file out a slot in the edge of the flange as wide as the thickness of the lever. This should be deep enough for the lever to be raised sufficiently so that the lug on the lock bolt clears the gap in the lever slot. Repeat the process for each of the levers in turn, making sure that the flange of the key is the correct width for the thickness of the lock. Put on the cover plate, and the job is finished.

HINGES

Hinges are found in many shapes, forms and sizes and they often bend, break or come apart. Ordinary hinges are not usually worth repairing as they can be replaced, quite

simply, with new ones of the exact size. Many hinges, however, meet an untimely end, through no fault of their own, by being strained by ill-fitting doors, bureau falls or lids. So, before fitting new hinges, look for the cause of the trouble.

A cupboard door may rub or stick at top or bottom and have to be pushed hard to close it – thus putting strain on the hinges. A bureau fall may be resting on slides that don't stand out at right-angles but sag because of wear or loss of a kicker (the top runner). This means that the flap hinges are subject to considerable leverage and are consequently pulled apart.

The hinges on box lids may break when a lid stay or strap has come away and the lid is allowed to drop back – sometimes splitting the back of the box as well.

One simple repair you can do to hinges is if the pin slips or falls out. This often happens on cupboard doors. It is a simple matter to remove the two parts of the hinge and either to replace the pin or to make and fit a new one from, say, a long nail of the right thickness. The ends of the pin should be burred slightly to prevent it coming out again.

There are many kinds of hinge dating from Victorian times and before that cannot easily be replaced by new ones. Two that readily come to mind are the pin hinges found on Victorian wardrobes – forming pivots at the top and bottom of the door – and the 'flail' type that hinge the tops of card tables with swing legs and are let into the side edges of the top *(see fig.41)*.

The wardrobe pin hinge is easily repaired, and it's probably within your scope to make a new part, for it is the plate with the hole that wears out. The hole plates are slotted flush into the cornice and plinth, so to remove the door the cornice has first to be unscrewed. The door can then be lifted out and the hinge plates removed *(a)*.

When re-assembling, do make sure that both plinth and cornice are securely screwed down. I've had to deal with several nasty accidents involving this sort of wardrobe. One, I remember, had a plate-glass

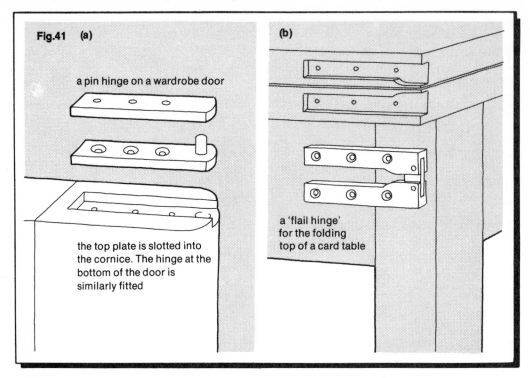

Fig.41   (a)

a pin hinge on a wardrobe door

the top plate is slotted into the cornice. The hinge at the bottom of the door is similarly fitted

(b)

a 'flail hinge' for the folding top of a card table

mirror in the door. It was 9mm (⅜in) plate glass, weighing a ton, and when the owner tried to move the wardrobe to clean behind, it came off its plinth. The door dropped out of the top hinge and came crashing down on top of this unfortunate lady. Luckily she was not badly hurt, but it could have been serious had the mirror broken.

The 'flail' hinges on card tables, of the type where you pull out a leg, or legs, at the back and the top lifts up and over, disclosing a felt-covered playing top, are double-jointed, with a link to give distance when folded *(b)*. If it's just a question of putting in a new pin or two, this you can do, but very often the pin holes through the brass are worn right through. In this case I would strongly advise taking it to an expert metal worker or engineer.

CASTORS

Castors are objects that take a lot of punishment and suffer neglect until something happens to them and they break, fall off or just cease to work properly. Many times I've seen the beautifully-made castors on Victorian chairs looking very down-at-heel. The centre pins only just clear a carpet, and the swivelling parts don't turn much because they are right down on the base plate.

If such castors had had attention, say just once a year with a drop of oil, they might still be almost as good as new. These and earlier castors are the only ones worth repairing, so let us see what can be done to them.

The minor repairs that you can do yourself are to the bowl, wheel or roller spindle. The spindle very often comes loose, gets rusted inside the bowl or falls right out. It is a fairly easy job to find a piece of rod and make a replacement. Care must be taken, however, when dealing with castors that have porcelain bowls, for when burring over the ends of a new spindle you can easily damage porcelain if your hammer misses its mark.

Occasionally you'll find a castor has

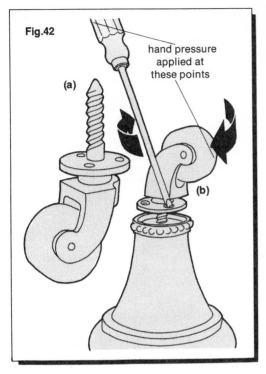

Fig.42

hand pressure applied at these points

(a)

(b)

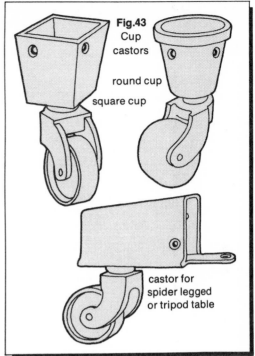

Fig.43
Cup castors

round cup

square cup

castor for spider legged or tripod table

completely seized up, because it has stood in a damp place over a long period and rust has set in. Take the castor off and immerse it in penetrating oil or, better still, in a rust-dissolving fluid.

Most wear occurs around the steel swivel pin of the castor. This pin fits into a hole in the bowl assembly, which is usually made of brass. As brass is a much softer metal, it wears away if not regularly lubricated. The hole eventually becomes so large that the castor ceases to work. There is nothing you can do about this unless you are an engineer, so try your local garage man or a small engineering firm. They can probably fill up the enlarged hole with bronze, then re-bore it for you.

It is important that the castor should be fixed firmly to its leg *(see fig.42)*. Many become loose and not only look unsightly but also rattle about whenever the piece of furniture is moved. This may cause damage to floor covering and may also put undue strain on the leg.

The most common fixing for old castors is a centre woodscrew pin and a brass screw plate with three holes for small screws *(a)*.

Where a castor is loose, the hole must be filled with a peg of wood glued in, then a hole made in the peg a size smaller than the screw pin. The castor can then be screwed in securely. 'How does one screw it in when there's nothing to hold?' You will see at *(b)* that, by inserting a smallish screwdriver on the slant with a corner of the blade firmly in one of the small screw holes, you can turn the castor bowl assembly against the screwdriver shaft with enough purchase to screw it in. To aid your efforts, put a small knob of paraffin wax into the hole before you insert the castor. This will act as a lubricant. And don't forget to put in the three small screws – not that they count for much in the fixing, but at least they prevent the castor plate turning and unscrewing itself.

Not every castor of this type has a threaded pin, so don't be surprised if you encounter one which just goes round and round and won't come out. The chances are that it has a plain, straight, unthreaded pin and just pulls out. Some continental castors of the same period are like this.

The cup castor is another type found on Victorian and earlier furniture *(see fig.43)*. There are three main kinds: the round cup, the square cup and the kind that fits sideways on to a leg, usually of a spider or curved leg pedestal table, often in the form of a lion's paw. One fault common to all these castors is a loosening of the swivel pin which is riveted into the cup.

If the swivel pin is not worn too much, it can be tightened by burring the end of the pin inside the cup. This pattern of castor is still made today and fitted to reproduction furniture. Some are made of solid brass, but the majority are cast from some inferior metal and gilded to look like brass; if these break, they are almost impossible to repair as they cannot be soldered or brazed.

INLAID METAL

Metal inlaid in furniture may vary from just a simple string made of pewter let in around the top of a small Edwardian box to the intricate designs in brass set into the top of a Regency table. I would suggest that with repairs to this kind of work you should confine your efforts to only the simplest jobs – such as sticking back loose but undamaged portions of metal. If metal needs considerable re-dressing, flattening or joining, take it to an expert.

Where damage has been caused by a duster catching and pulling up a corner of brass stringing, repair it by working glue into the groove under the metal without lifting it too much, which would cause it to bend or kink. Then press back the string, place a waxed block of wood over it and cramp down firmly. The wax prevents glue sticking to the wood.

The best adhesive to use for this job is a two-part rapid epoxy resin type. It will stick firmly to both wood and metal.

Part 2: Upholstering and Re-covering Furniture

Introduction

To my mind, upholstery is the poor relation of the furnishing trades' family. Upholstery work has to put up with being sat on, ill-used and often ignored completely.

Yet a good furniture upholsterer has to be an amalgam of trades, skills and arts.

He must be an engineer when judging and setting the tension and resilience in the seat or back of a chair, an artist with a good eye for balance and good judgement of comparative sizes, when, for instance, he is making both arms of an easy chair the same size and shape. And, most of all, he has to be a sculptor, for his job has to do with the creation of shapes – shapes which are pleasing to the eye and, more important, bring comfort to the sitting or reclining body, offering support in the correct places and firmness and softness where it is needed most of all.

Traditionally, the upholsterer had also to be skilled in the arts of all soft furnishing – curtains, blinds, bedding, floor coverings and general house fitting. Furniture upholstery has evolved slowly over the years, and skills reached a peak at the end of the last century, since when I believe they have declined. Now many of today's so-called upholsterers are no more than assemblers of ready-made components and shapes for which very little skill is required.

However, we must be realistic and not stand in the way of progress. After all, upholstery is for the comfort of mankind and not just for glorification of the upholsterer, and many modern pieces have been scientifically designed to give maximum comfort.

I would also defend the traditional upholsterer and say that nothing can be more comfortable or beneficial than, say, a well-made, well-upholstered Victorian spoonback chair or an earlier high-seated, straight-backed wing easy chair. Of course, every individual has a slightly different shape, and many of us have our favourite chair, a chair which over a period has shaped itself to us – or is it we that have altered to the shape of the chair? A bit of both, I'd say.

I remember a gentleman coming to me requesting the refurbishing of his favourite wing easy chair. He explained that it was so comfortable that he wanted no alteration made to the seat. I went to see the chair, and it was obvious that it had been of good quality and nicely upholstered many moons ago. But I looked aghast at the seat, if what remained could be so called.

It has a great dip in the centre, and the front had been pushed well back. I looked underneath. The webbing had given way, and the springs were resting on the floor!

'You see how comfortable this seat is, and how it suits me,' said the gentleman, flopping down and almost disappearing into the chair, legs straight out and arms crooked over the arms of the chair so that his shoulders were on the same level as his elbows.

I gently explained that I would never agree to cover a seat and leave it in that shape. But not until I downright refused to do anything did he relent on condition that the seat was made super-soft so that he could sink well into it.

How far we have moved from the times when people sat on hard wooden chairs such as the old high-backed Windsors, the type with the beautifully-shaped seat board. They are comfortable, but I think people today would find it irksome to sit for more than an hour in one, after being used to soft squashy modern upholstery.

An expert, dealing with all sorts of upholstered furniture, gets a pretty good picture after a time of the evolution of upholstery. For instance, I once came across a very old stool which I guess was made in about the early seventeenth century. I set to work to remove layer upon layer of covering materials from the seat – seven different cloths in all, the last of which was in shreds. Under all this, I found a pad of hay, seeds and all.

But the most interesting thing was that when I removed the hay, there, underneath, stretched across the frame and fixed with large-headed hand-made nails, was a piece of goatskin, hair-side uppermost. This skin had become dry and mummified but had been strong enough to support that seat for hundreds of years. I had been puzzled when I first looked underneath the stool, and at the time I thought that someone had put a wooden board under the seat. But I couldn't make out why this 'board' had bellied downwards. Of course, I left the skin intact and put new webbing and upholstery on top.

Then, one comes across William and Mary and Queen Anne period chairs where you can see that the upholsterers have refined their skills a little by softening the edges of seats with rolls of straw covered with hessian and bound together with twine, then adding a top stuffing of sheep's wool. You find little if any of the original webbing and hessian used for the basic support on these early chairs. These have usually been replaced with new several times over the years, the pad made with straw and with bound edges having been taken off and put back each time.

In early Georgian times we find a little more sophistication, with horsehair used for the first stuffing. And we find the first signs of blind stitching (which will be explained later) holding the horsehair up to the edges.

The trade gradually improved from that time on to the end of the nineteenth century, when very fine upholstery was done. Much time and thought was spent on achieving a good, firm, lasting foundation to support a variety of shapes of seat, arm and back.

Springs in seats were introduced in the nineteenth century, and if you take the upholstery off an untouched Victorian chair you will find some wonderful hand-made springs. Many of these are so well made, having twice as many coils as their modern counterparts, that they might well be retained in service in a new seat.

You will find earlier chairs, never designed for springs, which have had springs added at some later date – and, likewise, chairs that should be endowed with springs which no longer have them! There is a clue or two in the construction of a seat frame which determines whether or not springs should be present.

For example, in a dining chair seat of the stuffed-over type where no springs were intended, you will notice the peculiar corner bridges slotted into the tops of each rail. Their purpose is obvious. When webbing is fixed tightly over the top of the frame, the strain is taken and transferred from rail to rail preventing the twisting of the rails at the mortise and tenon or dowelled joints at the corners.

Now, when springs are employed, the webbing is fixed underneath seat rails, so corner glue blocks are used, glued and screwed securely in place.

In late Victorian times and into the twentieth century, good upholstery continued to be produced, but at the same time much cheap furniture was made. It wasn't only that frames were poorly assembled and made of inferior wood, but the upholstery was also botched, and many short cuts were made to achieve the shapes that previously had taken so much time to build up.

You may be unfortunate enough to discover this for yourself if you make the mistake of buying from a junk shop a couch or chair marked late Victorian – as did a young couple I know. They asked me to examine the couch they had purchased, with a view to re-upholstering and covering it. I took one look at it and felt very sorry for them, for they had paid a goodly sum. Turning it upside down, I pulled off part of the bottom canvas and showed them the inside: seat rails so thin that extra battens had been nailed on the insides to give enough width to attach webbing; legs halved then glued and nailed to the inside of the frame. Then I pointed out the numerous short lengths of wood which had been roughly nailed, one on top of the other, to build up the seat edges all round to the required depth. I explained as tactfully as possible that I could never make this into a good piece of furniture. They were very disappointed and realised they had paid dearly for the experience.

In the 1920s and 1930s, many club type chairs and smaller easy chairs with scroll arms came into vogue. And as this style is still being revived, chairs like this are well worth spending time and money on.

There are several things to look for when buying upholstered furniture for refurbishing. For example, with the chairs with the scroll arms I have just mentioned, look at the castors. The makers of a good class of chair would always fit good quality brass castors. Note the line of the back legs, and shun chairs where the legs follow in a straight line the slope of the back; they should curve backwards or even form an ogee curve in the best chairs.

Feel through the covering to gauge the thickness and width of the bottom rails of the chair frame. They should be at least 50mm × 50mm (2in × 2in), the bigger the better. These are the parts that have to be really strong.

I described earlier the method of testing the strength of a chair frame by lifting diagonal corners and finding out if the joints are sound. But there is one fault you cannot look for thoroughly until the covering is removed – and that is woodworm. However, as an attack usually starts in the bottom rails, one or two holes may be apparent in the legs. Or it may be possible to pull up a corner of the bottom canvas and take a peep inside, looking for signs of woodworm dust.

On earlier chairs, couches and settees, apart from watching for the points already mentioned, examine the show-wood wherever present. Is it good quality timber with no shakes or cracks that have been filled up? On spoonback chairs, look at the sweep of the moulded show-wood round the back. Does the curve on the left side correspond with that on the right? Look at the back legs of easy chairs. They should be of the same wood as the front legs. On cheaper chairs they will be of beech or birch; this is because they are a continuation of the back upright of the frame.

The legs of good couches and Chesterfield settees will have plenty of wood in them and will be well turned and finished, being made of mahogany, walnut or oak. The legs of cheaper articles will be thin and skimped, perhaps made only of beech, doctored up to look like a better wood. Also, examine any carving to see if it is well executed and finished and uniform in design.

I would like to point out, especially to the ladies, that upholstery and dust go hand in hand. So be prepared when you are ripping off and unpicking that old chair, couch or settee. It's a job you cannot do in the drawing room. And, as I mentioned in the first section, wear a small mask to avoid inhaling dust.

I well remember my training as an upholsterer. That was in the days when stuffed mattresses were still in fashion – not many spring interiors about then! With a good, hard, horsehair mattress, you could always reckon on a fog of dust so thick that you couldn't see across the carding room even with an extractor fan going. My doctor assures me this dust is not harmful to health; nevertheless, do wear a mask.

Things are better today, with more synthetics such as plastic and rubber foam, ready-made cotton felts and acrylic fibre 'wool' being used.

Tools and basic materials

An upholsterer does not use nearly as many tools as the cabinet-maker. Nevertheless, there are items that you won't have met so far. So let's get an idea of what we need in the way of equipment, tools and materials. So, come up to my workshop.

Carding machine Through that door there is the carding room, so come in and meet the 'old devil' – which is what we call the carding machine. It is 1927 vintage, and it's for 'teasing' the fillings and stuffings. You put in lumps of matted horsehair, wool or fibre that have been in chair upholstery, sat on for years until compressed, dusty and horrible. They go in the hopper at the top; travel between and over spiked rollers which separate and comb the fibres while all the dust is sucked out by an extractor fan at the back. Then the filling comes out at the bottom, all clean, soft and springy, ready to be re-used.

The carding machine is the upholsterer's most expensive piece of equipment, but it is not so necessary for an amateur since, these days, you can buy ready-carded stuffings and fillings – but at a price, mind you. So if you intend to do a fair bit of upholstery and you spot an old carding machine in a sale or junk yard, buy it – that is if you have room to set it up, for it needs a shed of its own. Then it will pay for itself, all ends up.

Another idea is to gather together a group of people as keen on upholstery as yourself, club together and set up a carding and machining centre in someone's garden shed. You can all take your stuffings there and rejuvenate them. The other alternative is to get to know your friendly neighbourhood upholsterer, who, for a fee, may do your carding for you!

Sewing machine This is the next largest piece of equipment. You can probably get by with an ordinary domestic model, but this will not deal with very heavy fabrics such as tapestry and thick, modern leathercloths. These may have to be fed through in four or more thicknesses, as in making piped cushion covers. My machine is under the window. It's an old one, but still a good heavy industrial model. If you have to manage with a domestic machine for a start, fit it with a thicker gauge needle.

Trestles It is always important, for both comfort and efficiency, to have the work at the right height, so adjustable trestles, or trestles of differing heights, are necessary. I have three sizes: a pair of high trestles for working on seats; medium, for doing arms; and then a pair of low ones for working on backs and wings.

Each trestle has a groove, or trough, in the top. This takes the castors and legs, so preventing the chair or settee from moving while you are working on it. I intend, some time, to make an adjustable stand which will take any size of chair and which can be moved up and down and swivelled and fixed in any position. The idea is in my mind, and one day I may find time to make it!

HAND TOOLS

Now let's work through the tools needed (*see figs.44 and 45*).

Ripping chisels In my rack I have several ripping chisels. These have specially hardened tips and are sharpened with thick bevels on each side. These are used for knocking out old tacks, and the hard steel with the short, thick bevels does not gap or break when metal meets metal.

Mallet A small mallet is used with the ripping chisel; if you already have one in your woodworking tool kit, use it.

Knives I have some long-bladed knives which I use for cutting plastic foam and some with shorter blades for slicing through string and webbing and also for general unpicking jobs.

Tack-lifters A tack-lifter resembles a screwdriver but has a claw at the end. It is very useful and essential for getting out dome-headed ornamental chair nails.

Scissors I have many kinds and sizes of scissors, but you really need only two. A small pair with about 76mm (3in) blades and larger cutting-out shears about 175mm (7in). Those are the destructive tools you need – for ripping things apart. Now the tools for construction!

Webbing-stretchers I have illustrated two varieties of webbing stretcher *(see fig.45)*, one with a hinged metal strap, the other with peg and chain. I also have some steel plier-type stretchers, sometimes called hide strainers, though they can also be used for webbing.

Hammers The upholsterer's hammer is unlike any other, and looks more like a small ice axe. I have three in my collection which I regularly use. The first is an old hammer I have had since my youth, while the next is a modern magnetic type. The magnet is in the head, and it is a great help when working in rather inaccessible places. Also, if you drop a tack, you can reach down, pick it up on the hammer head, and it's ready and in position to be banged in.

The third hammer, although similar in design, is called a pin or cabriol hammer, and if you look closely you will see that the leading part of the head tapers to a very small area which forms the tacking face. This hammer is used when fixing material up to or into rabbets or facings, where a larger-faced hammer would be likely to damage the woodwork.

Needles I have a long narrow box full of needles, some of which are illustrated *(see fig.45)*. The double-ended ones, pointed at each end, are called mattress needles,

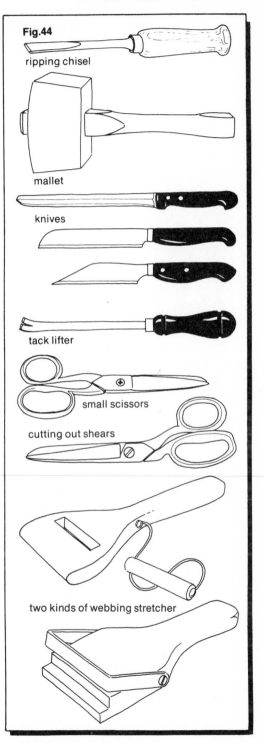

Fig.44

ripping chisel

mallet

knives

tack lifter

small scissors

cutting out shears

two kinds of webbing stretcher

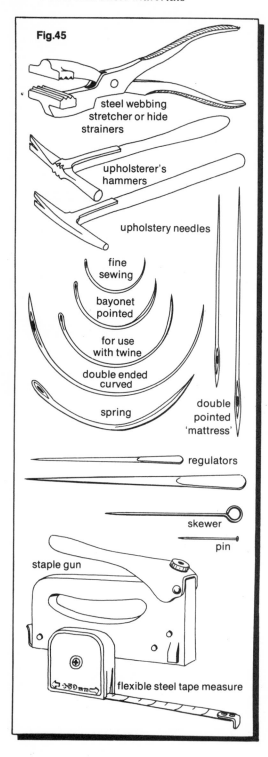

Fig.45

steel webbing stretcher or hide strainers

upholsterer's hammers

upholstery needles

fine sewing

bayonet pointed

for use with twine

double ended curved

spring

double pointed 'mattress'

regulators

skewer

pin

staple gun

flexible steel tape measure

though they are seldom used on mattresses these days. Of these you need three sizes: a very long one, 350mm (14in), 12 gauge (thick); one of medium length, 250mm (10in), 13 gauge; and a short one, 175mm (7in), 14 gauge.

The slightly curved needle is called a spring needle and is used for sewing in springs. It has what we call a bayonet or square point. You will need one that measures 150mm (6in).

Now we come to the sewing needles in a smaller box. They are all curved to form a semi-circle, and the size is determined by the length of the needle measured around the curve. The largest you will need is a 150mm (6in) one, and if you can also buy one with a point at each end so much the better. If not, you can modify the one-pointed curved needle for a certain type of work, as I will tell you later on. These are used for sewing with twine.

Of the much smaller curved needles, for use with thread or cotton, you need a 76mm (3in), 17 gauge, bayonet point (for use on tough materials such as leather), a 76mm (3in), 19 gauge, round point, and a 65mm (2½in), 20 gauge, round point. Buy a number of the last two listed, for they break easily and are not expensive.

Regulators There are two things in the large box that are not needles. They are called regulators and have many uses – for packing and distributing stuffing; for marking; and also in button work. And, if you're like me and have rather large fingers, they are very useful as extra fingers for holding material while fixing.

Odd tools There are many tools that you may already have in your woodworking kit that can also be used for upholstery, side-cutting pliers adapted for taking out brads, for instance. These can be very handy for pulling out tacks and gimp pins. You may be surprised at some of the carpentry tools that can be used in upholstery. A fine-tooth panel saw, for instance, is ideal for cutting rubber block foam. A try square is very useful for setting out and getting stripes and threads at right angles to the fronts and sides of seats.

Pins and skewers Upholsterers' pins and skewers are items unique to the trade. The pins look like dressmakers' pins but are at least 38mm (1½in) long. The skewers, as illustrated, are 76mm (3in) or 100mm (4in) long. Both pins and skewers are essential and are used for temporarily holding and fixing coverings, hessians and cushion work.

Rules and measures Rules, rulers and straight-edges will be used in your upholstery work, but the most important of the measuring tools is the flexible steel tape *(see fig.45)*. Nearly all measurements made in upholstery involve distances around and over curved surfaces, so the tape must bend.

Staple guns A tool which has proved popular with upholsterers during the last few years is the staple gun, which is used a great deal in modern upholstery. But I hesitate to use staples on antique work – except in certain circumstances which I will detail at the appropriate moment.

A staple gun is a great time-saver. It can be bought at most hardware stores and, when purchasing one, do take a piece of hardwood in your pocket to try the stapler on. Some have very light springs, and these are of no use except on softwood – and, of course, softwood is what the shop assistant will offer you to try this weapon on!

Fire a staple into your piece of hardwood and, if the gun is a good one, the staple will be driven well and truly home. The gun should take the thin 6mm (¼in) and 9mm (⅜in) staples. The 6mm (¼in) staples will serve most purposes.

BASIC UPHOLSTERY MATERIALS

In my workshop, to one side, are sets of drawers and shelves containing all manner of upholstery materials and sundries. Let us look at some of the basic materials used – materials which, if you are tackling a number of jobs, might be bought to advantage in quantity.

Webbing I find the best and longest-lasting webbing is English 50mm (2in) black and white, though for frame webbing other than seats the Indian jute 4.99kg (11lb) webbing is

sufficiently strong.

Hessians You will be using hessians in three weights. The heaviest, called tarpaulin or 456g (16oz) hessian, is for covering over springs or webbing and for basic first hessian on frames where the greatest strength is required. For parts that require a more pliable material 283g (10oz) hessian is used. And 202g (7½oz) hessian is used for base coverings and parts that do not require much strength.

You will also need some lightweight unbleached calico which will be useful for undercovering.

Twines and cords *(see fig.46)* Laid cord is a misleading name to describe a cord usually made from hemp or jute used for lacing springs together. I have illustrated the cord and twine sizes, as manufacturers seem to have different numbers for the sizes. Next down in size to laid cord is the stoutest twine, usually called number one. This is used for tying springs to webbing or hessian.

A much finer twine, a number three, is

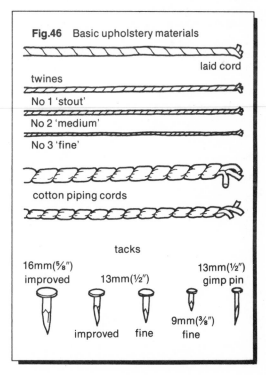

Fig.46　Basic upholstery materials

laid cord

twines

No 1 'stout'

No 2 'medium'

No 3 'fine'

cotton piping cords

tacks

16mm(⅝") improved

13mm(½") improved

13mm(½") fine

9mm(⅜") fine

13mm(½") gimp pin

used for stitched edges and for sewing hessian. Keep a lump of beeswax with your twines and use it to dress the twine. This will preserve and strengthen it. I always keep a 'cop' or two of nylon tufting twine. It is very expensive but immensely strong and is the best for use in button work.

I use cotton piping cord in two sizes, numbers one and two and, for the finer stuff, threads and cottons. I stock a very good Irish linen thread in several colours and in two sizes. No.18 is the stoutest and No.25 a thinner one. I find a No.24 is the best general-purpose cotton for the sewing-machine.

Tacks *(see fig.46)* I also have a nest of drawers where I keep all the tacks needed. You won't need such a variety, so just buy the ones I list, which are obtainable in 456g (1lb) packets. In all sizes there are two varieties: the stouter tack with a large head, called 'improved', and those with smaller heads, called 'fine'.

Starting with the largest, you need 16mm (⅝in) improved; 13mm (½in) fine and improved, and 9mm (⅜in).

All these are termed 'cut tacks'. There is another kind, called 'bayonet', but these are little used by upholsterers as they are more akin to nails, having square, parallel shanks.

Gimp pins are like very fine tacks. They are not merely for fixing gimp or braid and are very useful for general tacking purposes where larger tacks may split the wood. So it is as well to have some of these. They are made in japanned black, white and colours. Black are the most useful; buy ones measuring 13mm (½in).

Adhesives You will need two kinds of adhesive: first, an impact adhesive for joining and building up rubber and plastic foam. This is not quite the same as that used for fixing plastic laminate but is modified to give a 'soft bond'. If you use this when joining pieces of foam, say to make up a cushion, hard ridges of dried adhesive will not form along the joins.

The other glue is a white latex type which is used for putting on braids and trimmings.

Upholstery foam Keep an eye open for bargains in polyether and rubber foam in various thicknesses. The thickness I most use in polyether foam is 6mm (¼in), which is sometimes labelled carpet underlay. The other thicknesses I use are 12mm (½in), 25mm (1in) and 50mm (2in). In sizes above 50mm (2in) I use rubber block foam, which has more resilience and, in my opinion, lasts for a longer time.

You will need other commodities, but these are the basic necessities.

Fixing and fastening

I am writing this chapter realising that the information given will be difficult to relate to any specific job. But I think it best to give these basic instructions now, so that you will be able to refer back to them as we progress to more difficult work.

Upholstery is all fixing and fastening, whether by tying, tacking, sewing or sticking, so, before thinking about tackling any upholstery job, let us go over the various ways and methods of fixing. I will illustrate the knots used and describe their purpose as we go along.

Reef knot *(see fig.47)* This is for joining cords of equal thickness, and the rule is left over right and right over left. This knot isn't used very often, but it is useful if you misjudge the length of cord required – say for lacing springs – and you need to join on an extra piece. It can also be used for tying off cottons and twines at the end of a row of stitches.

Sheet bend *(see fig.47)* This is a knot for joining cords of unequal thicknesses, so it will be as well to learn this one too.

Half hitch *(see fig.47)* This forms part of several knots and can be used for instance when joining on extra twine for blind and

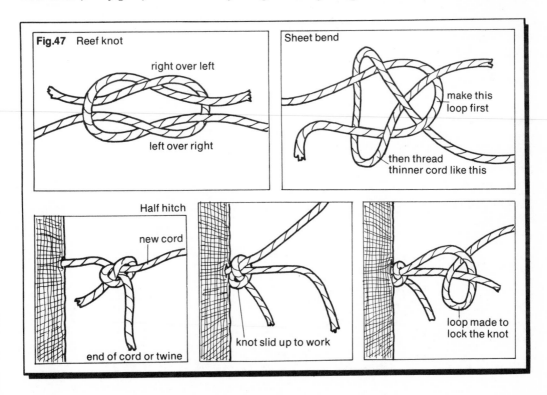

Fig.47 Reef knot
right over left
left over right

Sheet bend
make this loop first
then thread thinner cord like this

Half hitch
new cord
end of cord or twine
knot slid up to work
loop made to lock the knot

roll-edge stitching or joining on another length of thread when ladder stitching (don't worry about these names as all will be made clear later). You need to join the new cord up close to the last stitch.

So, make a half hitch with your new cord around the old short length and slide up to the last stitch that you made. Then tie another half hitch by looping the new length over the old short end and pull tight. Do this twice for security, and don't cut off the old end too close to the knot. Leave at least 25mm (1in).

The half hitch is also used for lacing springs and forms a simple yet fast knot. Also used in spring lacing is the locked loop, which isn't really a knot at all.

Clove hitch *(see fig.48)* To make a clove hitch, which is used on the front part of the coil of a spring, bring the cord over the spring from the back and under, coming up again on the right side of the cord *(a)*. Place your left index finger on top of the spring and wind the cord over your finger so that it comes up to the left of the cord *(b)*. Remove the finger and then thread the cord through the loop where your finger has been and pull tight *(c)*.

Upholsterer's slip knot *(see fig.49)*. This is the most used knot, so you must learn to do it quickly. It is used for fastening twine, thread and cotton to begin a line of stitches or ties and also for tying in stuffings, putting in buttons and for many other jobs. Let us say, for instance, that you are tying in a button and the two ends of the twine are sticking out of the hessian.

(a) Hold both ends together between thumb and forefinger of left hand. The cord end on the right should be at least 100mm (4in) behind the finger and thumb.

(b) Take the end on the right forward and bend across the cords in front of your thumb.

(c) Make two turns around both cords through the loop you have made.

(d) Pull this same cord to moderate tightness.

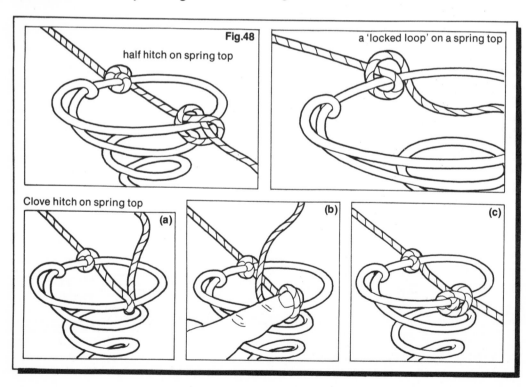

Fig.48
half hitch on spring top
a 'locked loop' on a spring top
Clove hitch on spring top
(a) (b) (c)

Fig.49 The upholsterers slip knot

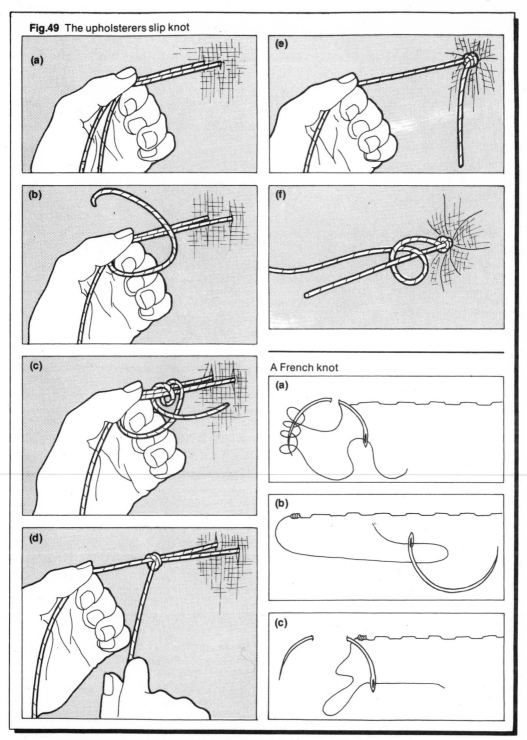

A French knot

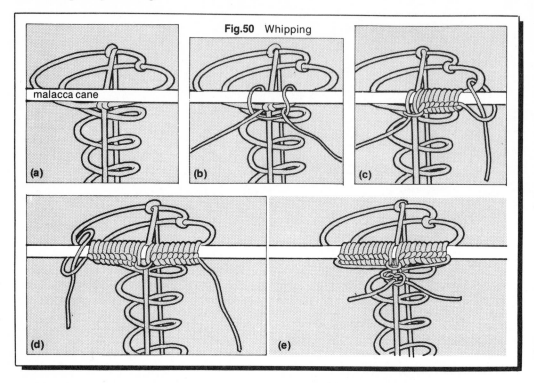

Fig.50 Whipping

malacca cane

(a) (b) (c) (d) (e)

(e) Pull the other cord to slip the knot up to the required tension, then give the shorter cord a tug to tighten the knot.

(f) Lock the knot with two half hitches by looping the longer cord over the shorter one.

French knot *(see fig.49)* We use a kind of French knot for securely finishing a row of stitches.

(a) As the needle emerges from making the last stitch (which should be a very small one), take the trailing thread and wind it around the needle four or five times.

(b) Pull the needle out and tighten the knot up close to the fabric.

(c) Make a further two stitches to give length to the end before cutting off.

Whipping *(see fig.50)* This is a way of binding springs to the front edge wire or cane.

(a) The cane and spring are shown in position.

(b) Start with a barrel hitch in the centre. The illustration shows you how to make this knot.

(c) Moving to the right, make a row of locked loops along about 25mm (1in) from the barrel hitch.

(d) Do likewise on the left side.

(e) Finish by tying both ends together in the centre with a reef knot.

If scissors are out of reach, an upholsterer will often cut off twine and even thickish cord by deftly twisting the cord around the index and middle fingers of the left hand, following it with a quick flick of the right hand. There is nothing magical about this – it is just a manoeuvre to make the cord cut through itself by friction. I'm not going to attempt to describe the mechanics of this, for unless I were to show you personally you might well end up cutting half your finger off!

FIXING WEBBING

While I deal with webbing, I will assume we are using 50mm (2in) width *(see fig.51)*.

(a) Make a 25mm (1in) fold at the end of the webbing and place it on the frame with

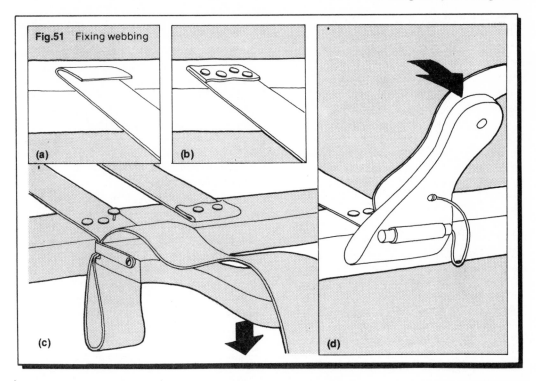

Fig.51 Fixing webbing

(a)

(b)

(c)

(d)

the fold uppermost.

(b) Fix with four 16mm (⅝in) improved tacks in a staggered row. You will have to use your discretion as to the size of tacks. A very hard wood may need only 13mm (½in) improved tacks, but if the wood splits easily, fine tacks will have to be used. And since the fine ones have smaller heads, more tacks will be required in the row.

Be careful how you drive in your tacks. Each should be driven well home with the head perfectly flat and level with the surface of the frame. If a tack is driven in crooked, part of the head will cut into the webbing, weakening the fixing. The whole idea of a large headed tack is to give the maximum frictional surface between wood, webbing and tack head.

(c) and (d) A webbing stretcher is shown in use. You can see how webbing is held and pulled tight on the two different models. Three tacks are used to secure the end being stretched, which is then cut off 25mm (1in) from the row of tacks and folded back on

itself, a further two tacks being used to hold the fold down. These should be placed between the three tacks underneath.

The black and white webbing has little elasticity and should not be overstrained. Jute webbing requires much more stretching and should be quite dry when put on. If applied damp it will be slightly shrunken and will slack when the moisture dries out.

FIXING HESSIANS AND COVERINGS

When fixing hessians and coverings, you have to be certain as to the size and length of tacks required to fix the different hessians to woods of various hardnesses. It's really a matter of common sense. The tarpaulin hessian used to cover springs must be secured with the larger, longer tacks – then the lighter the fabric, the smaller the tacks you will require.

Always make wide turnings when tacking, so that there are always two thicknesses of material held by the tacks. When securing open weave material, use the large-headed improved tacks for maximum holding. Tacks should not be spaced more than 38mm (1½in) apart when fixing hessians and undercoverings – and with top covering fabric they should be much closer together, as close as 9mm (⅜in) if you are using velvet or leather.

Concentrate on achieving straight, evenly-spaced rows of tacks.This not only looks neat and tidy but also makes for maximum fastening.

When using staples instead of tacks, I like to put many more in a row, especially with leathercloth and loosely-woven fabrics, spacing them closely so they almost touch. The manufacturers of some makes of staple gun also supply a metal guide, and by adjusting the guide you can make a very neat row of staples at an exact distance from the edge of a frame.

Sewing A good upholsterer of modern furniture will keep the number of tacks put in to fix the covering material to a minimum. If you look at the outside back coverings of cheaper chairs and settees, most likely you will find they have been secured with gimp pins of a similar colour to the fabric. This, of course, is a quick way to finish the job.

The correct way, however, is to sew the seams. To do this you must learn the slip or ladder stitch, using a circular needle. This stitch is used for all outside cover seams when the material cannot be machined together before fitting.

The method of doing the slip stitch is illustrated *(see fig.52)*.

(a) To begin, take a small stitch just beneath the over-lapping fabric 10mm (⅜in) from the beginning of the seam. Secure with the upholsterer's slip knot.

(b) Make a stitch through the line of fold of the overlapping fabric back to the beginning of the seam. This makes a secure start to the sewing and also obscures the knot and thread, which can now be tucked away beneath the fold.

I sew from right to left, but, should you be left-handed, you will find it easier to sew

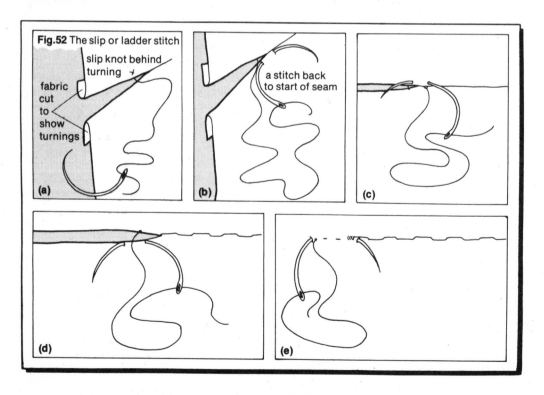

Fig.52 The slip or ladder stitch

slip knot behind turning

fabric cut to show turnings

(a)

a stitch back to start of seam

(b)

(c)

(d)

(e)

from left to right.

(c) Take the first stitch in the direction of sewing by making the point of your needle enter the opposite fabric a thread or two back from the place where the thread emerges from the last stitch.

You will now see the reason for the curved needle, for both pieces of fabric to be sewn together are stretched taut, and nearly always there is part of the wooden frame beneath. To try to sew with a straight needle would prove extremely difficult.

(d) The rule that the next stitch should be started a thread or two back from where the needle last emerged applies all the way, so that as you pull the thread tight after each stitch it disappears completely.

The length of stitch can be varied. For very heavy fabrics such as tweed or uncut moquette, a stitch of up to 16mm (⅝in) would be acceptable. But for finer fabrics, 5-10mm (³/₁₆-³/₈in) will be much neater.

(e) When you come to the end of the seam, the thread must be well finished off, so use the French knot described earlier. Don't cut off the thread at the knot, or it will soon come undone. With the needle still threaded, take two or three stitches back along the seam, then cut off close to the fabric. Alternatively, if your seam ends at the bottom of the chair, a tack can be put in underneath around which the thread can be wound, then the tack driven home to hold it.

FASTENING WITH ADHESIVES

Impact adhesive There is not much sticking to be done in good upholstery, but with modern foam cushions, a standard size foam interior is often too small and must have extra pieces added to back or sides. The impact adhesive I mentioned earlier is used for this, and as with all glues of this type you coat both surfaces to be joined, leave them until touch-dry, then press the surfaces together for an immediate bond. This adhesive is also used for taping cushion edges, which I deal with between pages 130 and 133.

Latex adhesive This is used for fixing braids and trimmings, and again it should be

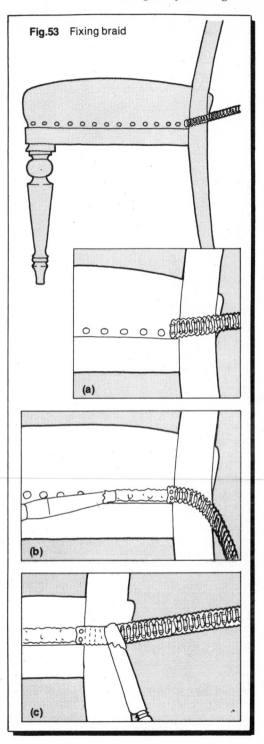

Fig.53 Fixing braid

(a)

(b)

(c)

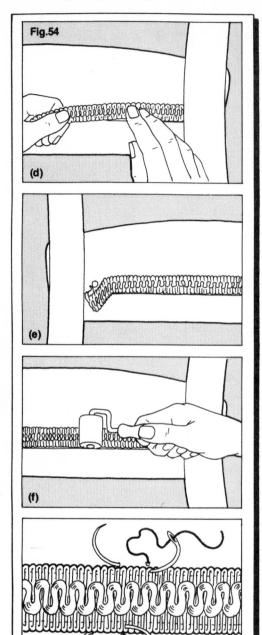

Fig.54

(d)

(e)

(f)

(g)

applied to both surfaces. Care must be taken when applying it, for if you put on too much it may squeeze through and spoil the look of the braid. I use two knives for spreading: a palette knife for putting a line of adhesive along the material (the width of this knife is just under the size of the braid) and an ordinary stainless steel table knife for the braid itself. The best method I find for putting on braid is illustrated *(see fig.53)*.

(a) Secure the end of the braid by 'back tacking' with two gimp pins.

(b) Apply line of adhesive to the material.

(c) Spread the adhesive along the braid, holding it taut and scraping the glue along to ensure a thin, even application. Don't lay the braid down to spread the adhesive, for this way, especially on thin braids, adhesive will go right through to the face. Coat no more than half a metre at a time.

Fig.54 shows the rest of the process.

(d) Stretch the braid along and gently press down with the fingers.

(e) To finish off, cut the braid 5mm ($^3/_{16}$in) too long and fold it under. Put another dab of adhesive on the folded piece and press back into position.

(f) Leave for a few minutes and then roll the braid with a small seam roller.

(g) I never rely on adhesive alone for fixing braid and trimming and like to add a row or two of stitches. I find the latex adhesive lasts up to two years but it is affected by sunlight and by the presence of a gas fire in the same room. Both cause the glue to deteriorate, reducing its tenacity.

For sewing braids, use the stitch illustrated at *(g)*; a row that catches the top loops of the braid and, if possible, another row near the other edge. Make the stitches very small so they cannot be seen.

Finally, it is important to do your fixing and fastening really well, especially on basic support materials. Then you can be sure that all the good work you do on top of this will have a firm foundation.

Measuring up

Having talked about upholstery, let's get down to the practical side of things and start doing something. You may have a nice gentleman's spoonback chair, but this is far too ambitious to start with. So we will take an easy chair with scroll arms and well-shaped wings, and using this as an example, let's see what we can learn from it with regard to measuring up.

HOW MUCH MATERIAL?

Before we start any upholstery work we must measure up and determine how much covering material we need. So have a pad or book especially for measurements, and set out a page as outlined (*see fig. 55a*).

You will need your flexible steel tape, which should be metric, because nearly all furnishing materials are measured by the metre now. The width of the material is important. At present it is generally made 127-132cm (50-52in). Some tapestries and leathercloths run to 137cm (54in) wide.

MATERIAL DIRECTION

Before you start measuring, determine which way the material must go on the chair. With most jobs, the covering material will be put on in the usual manner, with the length from top to bottom on backs, arms and borders, and running from back to front on seats and seat cushions. Fabric patterns will dictate this, and in velvet, or in fact any material with a pile, the pile must run down – or from back to front on seats.

Many materials can be placed either way, and, indeed, some modern suites are designed so that the cloth goes lengthwise across. The long, multi-seat settees with extremely wide backs, for example, are covered in one piece with no joins. But we will assume that our material is going on in the usual manner with the length up and down (*see fig.55b*).

MEASURING

First measure the width of the back and the outside back. If this is 63.5cm (25in) or less, the inside and outside backs can be cut from one width. Measure the length of the inside back, tucking in the end of the tape measure about 100mm (4in) at the bottom, between the seat and back. Allow a good turn at the top of about 25mm (1in). Then measure the outside back allowing a 25mm (1in) turn top and bottom.

Enter whichever is the greater of the two measurements against the two headings bracketed together. If the width of the inside back is greater than the half width of your material, allow the full width, and in the column on the extreme right jot down the size of the piece you will cut off. Do the same with the outside back if this is also too wide.

Luckily, the inside and outside back of the chair we are measuring can be cut from the one width. The inside arms, however, measure well over half the width of the material, so allow for the full width for both arms. Again, tuck the end of the tape well down beside the seat so that about 100mm (4in) disappears. Then measure right over the arm to where the outside arm covering is joined, and allow 38mm (1½in) more.

If I were re-upholstering that arm, I would want to make it a bit fatter, so raise the tape from the arm surface to roughly the contour you think the arm should be. Now read off the measurement – which could

Fig.55

Cut	Length	Off cuts	
		length	width
inside back			
outside back			
inside arms			
outside arms			
seat			
front border			
inside wings			
outside wings			
cushion			
scroll fronts			
piping			
Total			

(a)

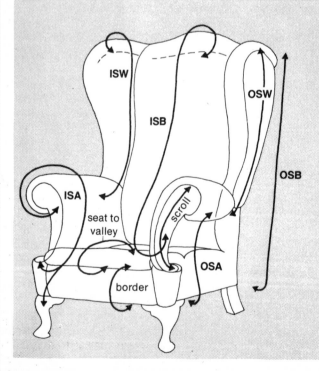

(b)

Measuring a wing easy chair for covering material

abbreviations

ISW : inside wing
OSW : outside wing
ISB : inside back
OSB : outside back
ISA : inside arm
OSA : outside arm

make a difference of up to 50mm (2in). Remember this when measuring over old upholstery, for arms get flattened or sag out of shape. And so do backs, where the stuffing may have slipped down from the top. When re-built, they will be quite a bit higher. Similarly, where seats are low at the front, or where edges have been pushed back, you must judge roughly to where the new seat will be built out and allow for this.

Don't forget to make a note of the surplus material to be cut from the inside arms in the right-hand column. Later you will see how these oddments will serve for smaller cuts.

Now measure the outside arms of your chair. Here again they are too long from back to front to enable you to cut both from one width, so allow the full width and note the surplus. For the length, from top to bottom, measure near the front of the arm. You will see that the distance is greater here, because of the slope of the arm. Allow 25mm (1in) beyond where the material joins at the top and 38mm (1½in) to turn under at the bottom.

Some upholsterers will use half widths on outside arms and join on matching pieces towards the back to make up the width. And some even do this with the inside arm coverings to try to save on material. I try to avoid all such seams, which nearly always show up. And I find that very little extra material is needed to do this if cutting is carefully planned.

We will measure the seat next, so take out the cushion. You will see that the covering only extends back about 150mm (6in) from the front edge. Beyond this is a tough, matching linen union. Note that where the union joins the covering material the line of the seam dips in to form a shallow vee channel. In the trade, we call this a valley. Measure the width of the seat. We find that half widths will do both front and seat border, so write down whichever measurement is the greater against Seat and Border, bracketed together.

Now we come to the wings. Measure the inside wing from top to bottom, allowing plenty for turnings, for the material extends quite a way beyond where it meets the arm. Look in the right-hand column on the list. I think you will find that the two pieces cut from the inside arms will be plenty large enough for the inside wings. Unfortunately, the pieces from the outside arms will not do for the outsides of the wings. They will be just too short, so you will have to have extra for these. Measure the outside wing from top to bottom and record. There will be spare material from this cut also.

Look at the cushion next. Since it's of average size, I guess it will take nearly 1m (just over 1yd). But perhaps you should work it out for yourself. Measure from back to front and add 25mm (1in) for turning. One width will do both sides. Then measure the border depth and add 25mm (1in). Double the last measurement, as two widths will be needed to go around the entire cushion.

Now we come to the front facings to the arms – what we call scrolls. There should be enough length in the pieces from the outside wings, but if not put down the extra needed, which will be the difference between the lengths of the outside wing and scroll.

We seem to have some rather large pieces left in our right-hand column, but these will be needed for making up piping. And they need to be fairly big, because they have to be cut on the bias or crosswise to the weave.

With all the measurements taken, all that remains is to total up and see how many metres are needed. I estimate our wing easy chair will take about 4.6m (5yd).

MATCHING AND BALANCING

Before we order the material, we must study the sample well, for if it is anything but a plain cloth we may have to allow extra for various things. For example, it may have a very large pattern repeat – in which case we must allow half a metre to make sure of the continuity of design, following down from the inside back over the cushion and down the front borders.

Your material may also have a centred design, which means you must allow more material so that these centres can be placed in balanced positions on the back, cushion and arms. An extra 0.75m (just over ¾yd) should enable you to do this – remembering that you have always got two ends of the cloth from which to cut.

MEASURING A DEEP BUTTONED CHAIR

Now let's take a look at your gentleman's spoonback chair. Measure this in the same way and record the findings on the list. You won't need all the cuts listed.

The inside back is buttoned, so here's how to work out the amount of extra material needed for this effect. First study the layout of the old buttonwork to see if we can improve on it. Perhaps there could be another row of buttons and more in the row so that they are closer together.

Take a measurement from top to bottom, allowing a 20mm (¾in) turn at the top, pushing the end of the tape down in between the seat and the back until you feel it touching the tacking rail. Read off the measurement and add to this 50mm (2in) for every button in a straight line from top to bottom. Enter this measurement against 'Inside Back'.

Measure across the widest part of the inside back, allowing an extra 20mm (¾in) for turning on both sides. Count the buttons in a straight line across this widest part and add the same 50mm (2in) for each button. I think that the piece left over from the inside back cut will cover the outside back. Some larger chairs of this type are not very economical to cover and require full widths for all cuts, so that large pieces are left over from which only pieces for the arm pads can be used.

Make allowances when you measure the seat, for the new seat is going to be higher and the front edge will extend further than it does now. Measure the width of the arms. As these are just pads, you will probably find there will be enough left from the seat piece to cover these.

While you still have the tape measure handy, check how much braid is needed, so that when you are purchasing material a good matching braid can be bought at the same time.

Finally, a word or two about measuring other pieces of upholstered furniture.

COUCH

The material to cover a couch should run the length of the seat and over the head in the same direction. If it has a back, it should run from top to bottom and in the same direction on the outside back, seat border and the scroll front of the head.

STUFFED-OVER SINGLE CHAIRS

Single chairs with stuffed-over seats, such as dining chairs, can be very deceptive, for those with wide seats take well over the half-width of cloth. If the material you choose has a pattern which permits a join that will not show up, you can measure for covering each chair in half a width, then allowing extra to join pieces on each side of the seat. I don't like doing this except with striped cloth, and I much prefer to get enough material to cut the correct width of the seat even if much is wasted.

DROP-IN SEATS

Single chairs with drop-in seats will take a full width for two seats – unless you intend using leathercloth of the type used in car upholstery. This is usually 137cm (54in) wide, and it is best put on lengthwise across the seat. The reason for this is that leathercloth has a stockingette backing which stretches more in width than length. It is then possible to achieve a smooth taut front edge – most necessary for good looks – and to cut three seats out of one width.

So much for measuring up. Remember to allow plenty for turning . After totalling the measurements, take them to the nearest half metre over requirements. It is far better to have a little left over than to find later you are short of a centimetre or two.

Ripping off

Ripping off is the term used in the trade for removing old upholstery materials from the frames of upholstered furniture. So let's see what we can learn by stripping our Victorian spoonback chair as a starter.

The chair is in remarkably good condition considering its age. I would guess that the green leathercloth may be the original covering, so beneath it will be the original upholstery. This will be a very valuable source of information for us to study, but do we have to disturb it? Couldn't we save a great deal of work by adding new padding and covering over?

Don't be tempted to do this. Consider the state of the covering material. It's worn out, cracked and rotten, so everything beneath it must be in much the same condition, since it was put on at the same time. When upholstery reaches this age, it must all go – every bit of it – back to a clean frame so that we can start again.

Turn the chair upside down, for it is the bottom that is always removed first. Rest the arms on your trestle, with the top of the back resting on a piece of foam on the floor to protect the show-wood. The bottom of the chair will be almost level and at a convenient height.

THE TOOLS
You now need a mallet and ripping chisel, sharp knife and scissors, small pincers, your adapted side-cutting pliers and a tack-lifter.
Using the ripping chisel *(see fig.56)* Hold the chisel with the blade edge against the tack head *(a)*, and drive with your mallet. As the tack begins to lift, lower the handle of the chisel *(b)* while still driving, forcing the tack up and out. Keep your eye on the tack being

removed and not on the chisel handle. You may hit your knuckles at first and say a few bad words, but after a little careful practice you'll soon get the hang of it. You will be able to drive out the tacks without chiselling into the wood.

There are several points to note when ripping with a chisel. Work with the direction of the grain of the wood, for in this way you are less likely to split the wood and the tacks come out more cleanly. Take great care at the ends of bottom rails, where they join the legs. Great pieces can be split away if ripping is not done gently, especially on

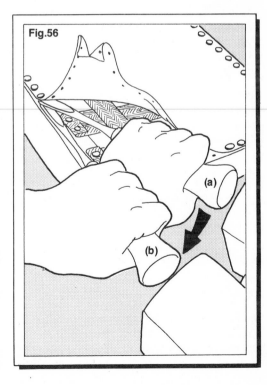

Fig.56

rails like those on your spoonback chair which are curved at the back. You can see how short the grain is as it rounds into the back legs.

In such awkward corners it is best to use pincers or your adapted side-cutting pliers. When ripping, tacks fly in all directions, so watch for the ones whose heads come off. They could fly up in your face, so remember – never hold your face directly over work that you are ripping.

HESSIAN, WEBBING AND SPRINGS

Remove the bottom canvas from your chair, noting how neatly this has been cut and fitted around the legs. Next, rip out the tacks holding the covering turned over the rails. The bottom webbing will now be exposed, so take a sharp knife and cut the twine holding the springs to the webbing, then rip off the webbing.

Have a large box handy so that you can throw all the useless bits and pieces in as you remove them. You may encounter a little brass plate that you remove with the bottom canvas. This is the maker's name. Put it in a safe place so that you can fix it back on the chair when it is refurbished.

Cut out the springs and, as you do so, note the way in which they were laced and fixed.

UPHOLSTERY, LAYER BY LAYER

Remove the outside back next. This had banding made of leathercloth and leathercloth-covered studs concealing tacks underneath. The studs can be removed with pincers or a tack-lifter. Try removing the tacks holding the covering with the ripping chisel, but take great care not to split the wood of the frame. This is mahogany and brittle with age, so I would advise you to use pliers. It will take longer, but you will be less likely to damage the woodwork.

Put your small mask on, because we've come to the most dusty part of the operation. Stand the chair on its legs on a table or trestles. You can then see how the inside back and seat covers are fastened on to the bottom rails at the back and sides. Unfastening these pieces is rather an exciting

moment, for this is when long-lost treasures come to light! There is no knowing what you may find in the back of a Victorian chair. All kinds of treasures fall down between the back and the seat, never to see the light of day until the chair is re-upholstered.

I have found a few valuable things such as brooches, rings and other jewellery, but objects such as pencils, pens, hairgrips and coins are more common. I've never found a lot of money – and that's an upholsterer's dream! Finding a chair stuffed with five pound notes has never come true for me. You may also find nasty things such as mouldy peanuts, sticky boiled sweets, spiders and even mice – but I hope this doesn't put you off!

When I tackle a piece of upholstered furniture, I like to cut away all the covering, hessians and webbing with a sharp knife before starting with the ripping chisel. This gives easier access for the chisel, and you are less likely to damage show-wood and facings. But in this first instance, I suggest you remove the upholstery layer by layer so that you can examine and learn something from the old work.

IS ANYTHING WORTH SAVING?

Now a word or two about the various stuffings and fillings and whether they are worth saving. Let us start with the sorts to throw away and burn. In the cheaper chairs you will find wood wool, which is just wood shavings – better known (jokingly) in the trade as 'best Italian hair'. Then there is brown seaweed, and where this has been used as a first stuffing the salt it contains usually causes the springs to rust through the hessian covering them. Flock may be made of old woollen clothes carded up, and 'mill puff' is a white cotton stuffing resembling tapioca pudding. When this is used it makes a real pudding of a seat – hard and ungiving.

Now for the ones that you can save and re-card. The best are the long stranded curled horsehairs and sheeps' wool. Take great care of these two stuffings when you come across them, for at the present time they are like gold dust to buy.

Treat animal fibre fillings such as these with a spray to discourage moths.

There are vegetable fibres worth saving too, among them Algerian fibre, a curly grass-like filling usually green or black in colour, and coconut fibre, also known as coir fibre. Both are very durable stuffings and can be re-carded successfully. However, if they show signs of becoming dry, brittle and short, they are best thrown out and burnt. Cotton and wool/cotton felt fillings can also be re-carded and used as top stuffings.

The only things worth saving from the upholstery of our chair will be the horsehair stuffing and the springs which are of the early type, with sometimes twice as many coils as modern springs (*see fig.57*). Note how they are finished off at top and bottom, each end bound to the last coil with wire.

Test each spring by pressing it hard between your hands and watching for any change in shape when released. This means a 'distemper' somewhere around the coils. Springs of later manufacture are best discarded and replaced with new ones, for even though they look healthy, metal fatigue will have set in, and it will not be long before they buckle or break.

THE BARE FRAME

When you have all the upholstery stripped from the frame, make sure that every tack has been removed. I can't bear to see a single tack left in – which is a good policy, for nothing is more annoying than trying to put in a new tack only to find there's an old one underneath! This causes your tack to 'curl up its toes' so to speak, hooking itself into the material or hessian and becoming very hard to remove.

The frame is now clean and bare (*see fig.58*), so examine it thoroughly for signs of woodworm. This is also the time to repair any loose joints, renew broken dowels or strengthen the seat rail by adding corner glue blocks. Even if there is no evidence of woodworm, it's as well to give the wood a brushing with a woodworm-killing fluid to

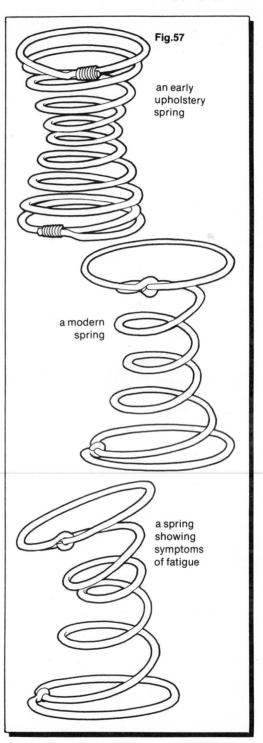

Fig.57

an early upholstery spring

a modern spring

a spring showing symptoms of fatigue

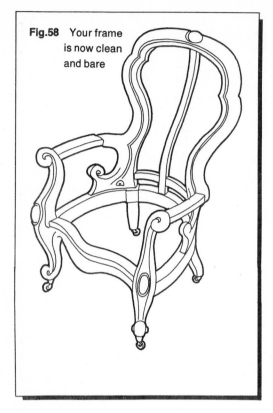

Fig.58 Your frame is now clean and bare

guard against future infestation.

Keep an eye open for graffiti on the framework. Sometimes one is lucky enough to find a date recorded, the name of the upholsterer or perhaps some amusing anecdote. I once found the following written on the wood of the front scroll of a couch – probably by an apprentice when his master was out of the way: 'This couch was upholstered by old Bodger Boakes June 1895. He likes his food and he likes a drink but he don't like us.'

I remember discovering what could have been another apprentices' lark. When removing the seat stuffing from an easy chair, I came across a paper bag hidden in the centre of the first wood wool stuffing. It contained two very hard, dried-up objects that were obviously once cheese sandwiches!

The show-wood on your chair can now be cleaned down, renovated and polished. It is so much easier to do this before it is re-upholstered. Then I suggest you put it aside for a while, because it will be best to upholster something simple to begin with, coming back to this when you become more proficient.

Starting upholstery

I have spoken to a number of folk who have enrolled for a course of upholstery at an evening institute and have been thrown in at the deep end. Instructors have invited them to bring along a piece of furniture of their own to re-upholster and, of course, they've taken something quite elaborate – like our spoonback chair. Expecting to do a first-class job on it, they have ended up in a bit of a mess, realising that they have bitten off more than they can chew. So let us be sensible and begin with something simple.

What about a dining chair? One with a

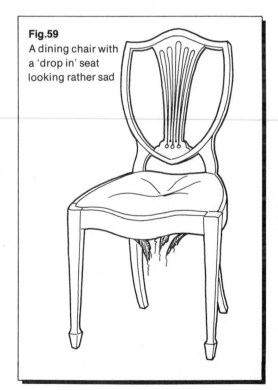

Fig.59
A dining chair with a 'drop in' seat looking rather sad

loose, drop-in seat would be ideal as a first step in upholstery *(see fig.59)*. Let us have a look at the underside. The webbing has become very slack, and it won't be long before it gives way altogether. The covering fabric is still quite good, but I would advise you to buy new covering to make a completely new job of it.

Let us imagine there are four chairs. If you measure them you will probably find that you can cover them all from just one metre of cloth, 127cm (50 in) in width.

Before you start, make sure you have everything you need: black and white webbing; tarpaulin hessian; wadding; twine; 16mm (⅝in) improved tacks for the webbing, 13mm (½in) improved for the hessian and 9mm (⅜in) fine for the coverings; some calico for undercovering; and, of course, the furnishing fabric for tight covering.

Now you can start ripping off *(see fig.60)*. I would work on all four seats together, for it is far quicker to complete each stage on all four, and one can more easily get them all to the same stage rather than working on each one separately. This will depend upon your circumstances. If the chairs are being constantly used, you may find you have to do them one at a time.

I find the best way to rip a loose seat is to hold it in the carpenter's vice *(a)*. Make sure that the part of the frame from which you are removing the upholstery is held firmly, then no damage will be done to the frame joints.

With the frame clean and bare, the next important step is to check that, when covered with new fabric, the seat will fit into the chair frame. If the cloth is thicker than the old covering, you will have to take a shaving or two off the sides of the frame. While the frame is bare, see if there is anything you can do to improve it. If the outside edges and corners of the frame are sharp, chamfer them off with a plane or rasp. The rounded wood will then be much kinder to the covering cloth. Also, take the sharp edges off the rails on the inside top edges. This will prevent cutting and wear to the webbing.

Now is the time to test the joints in case you need to knock them apart and re-glue them. There is always the temptation to say 'what the eye doesn't see . . .', and I've seen the work of many a good upholsterer ruined because he didn't take the trouble to do a simple repair to a framework when he had the chance.

RE-WEBBING THE FRAME

We can now start re-upholstering. The first thing to put on is the new webbing. This is where I always feel the human body would be better equipped with an extra hand! But we can use a substitute in the form of a cramp to hold the back rail of the frame *(b)*.

We have already discussed how to fix webbing, so we just need to know how many lengths we need and at what distance apart to put them. On this seat frame, being of medium size, three lengths from back to front and two across will suffice. At *(c)* you can see how the lengths of webbing are spaced and how they are woven under and over each other. Note that the tacks are kept to the centres of each rail and are staggered to avoid splits. On a larger seat, three lengths back to front and three across would be needed. And on a very large seat, say of a carver armchair, you may need four and four to give correct support.

TACKING ON HESSIAN

With the webbing secured, use the tarpaulin hessian to cover it. Cut off a piece about 20mm (¾in) larger than the frame size *(d)*. Fold over the front edge 20mm (¾in) and tack down so that the edge of the fold is about 1cm from the frame edge, with tacks about 30mm (about 1¼in) apart.

. Turn the frame around *(e)*, stretch the hessian tightly across and fasten down to the back rail. If you have hide strainers, use these to get it tight, then tack through the single thickness. Fix tacks at 50mm (2in) intervals, then turn over the surplus and tack it down. Space the tacks in between those underneath the fold. Do the same on the side rails, fastening one side and stretching the hessian to the other. It should then look like *(f)*.

STUFFING

The stuffing that you remove from the seat will be horsehair, and if you card this, or pull it out so that it's soft and springy, you can use it again. You need to put in what we call stuffing ties, to attach the horsehair to the hessian. At *(g)* you can see how this is done. With the aid of the largest circular needle, loops of twine are sewn through the hessian.

Take a little horsehair at a time and tuck it evenly beneath the ties in lines across the seat *(h)*, then fill up with hair in between. This ensures an even distribution of stuffing. At *(i)* another layer of hair is added. What would happen if no stuffing ties were put in? Well, after a short period of time the stuffing moves away from the front edge and centre of the seat and piles up near the back, giving it a very strange appearance.

Horsehair Horsehair varies greatly in practical value. If the strands are short and straight (what we in the trade call pig hair), it will pack down tight and have little resilience. But the longer and more curled the hair, when carded, the greater it will increase in volume. The best – long tail and mane hair – becomes two or three times larger in volume when teased.

I am telling you this to give some idea of how much stuffing is needed on a seat, for even the best carded long hair applied to a depth of 150mm (about 6in) will be reduced to about 50mm (2in) when the calico undercover is stretched over it and pulled down.

To make sure you get all your chair seats the same size, it is best to weigh the amount

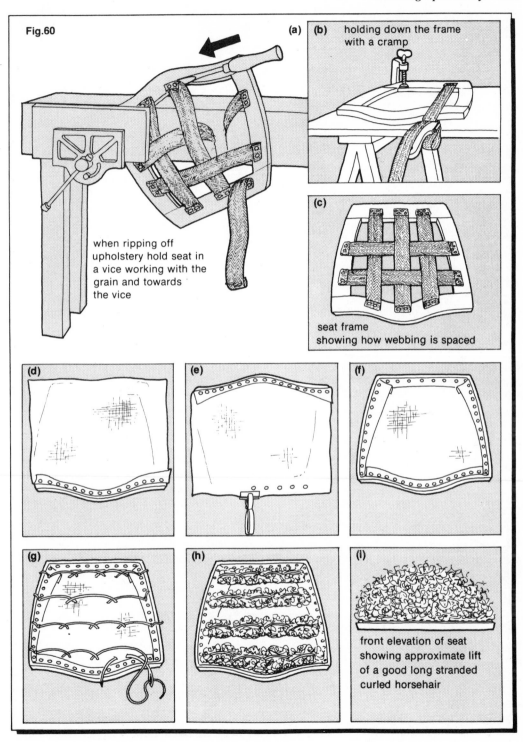

Fig.60

(a) when ripping off upholstery hold seat in a vice working with the grain and towards the vice

(b) holding down the frame with a cramp

(c) seat frame
showing how webbing is spaced

(d)

(e)

(f)

(g)

(h)

(i) front elevation of seat
showing approximate lift
of a good long stranded
curled horsehair

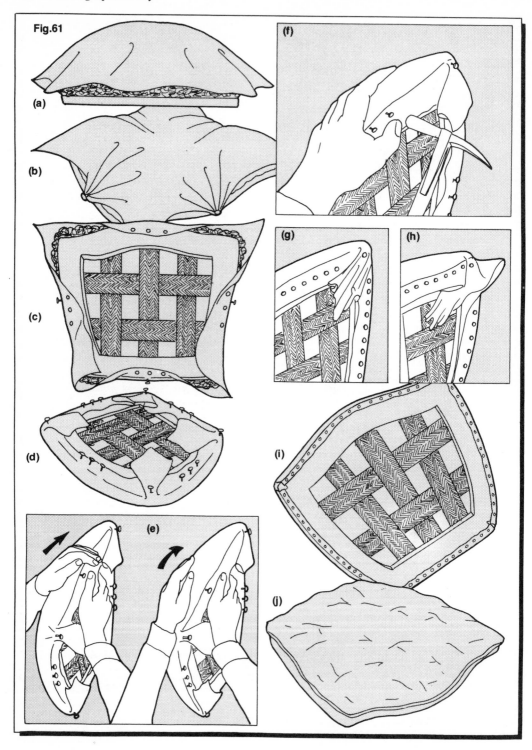

Fig.61

(a)

(b)

(c)

(d)

(e)

(f)

(g)

(h)

(i)

(j)

of stuffing you put on this first seat and keep a note of it for future reference.

UNDERCOVERING

The next stage is to pull the mass of horsehair down to a proper shape by putting on an undercover. I use medium-weight unbleached calico. Roughly measure the size required and tear it off. This is the best way unless it is very heavy calico. It is very tedious to try to follow the fine threads of calico with scissors, so just nip the first centimetre or two and then rip across; it will tear along a thread and your piece will be nice and square.

At *(a)* in *fig.61* we see the calico lying loosely over the hair, having been positioned so that there is equal material hanging down each side.

Place four temporary tacks (driven just far enough in to hold) in the centres of each side *(b)*, using 13mm (½in) fine tacks.

Turn and hold the seat on edge *(c)*, and put three temporary tacks in the centre of the underside of each rail. Then take out the first temporary tacks. This temporary tacking is very important, allowing you to adjust and position covering materials before fixing them.

Gently stretch the calico at the corners, pulling diagonally and temporarily tacking *(d)*. Watch the run of the threads at the centre of each side to make certain that you are not pulling one corner tighter than another.

Still holding the seat on edge with the back edge on the bench and the left side towards you (if you're right-handed), start again at the centre of the front edge. Take out the three temporary tacks and tuck back any hair that is hanging over the edge of the wood. The way in which you hold the frame and stretch the cloth is important, so do try to follow the instructions as closely as possible.

If you are right-handed, pull the cloth with your right hand, using your left to smooth and compress the stuffing *(e)*. Again, use only temporary tacking. After the middle

tack is placed, work away from yourself by smoothing and stretching the fabric with your left hand along the front of the seat. This action takes up any fullness and eliminates tack marks – lines which may run from the tack around and over the top of the seat. These will appear if the fabric is pulled very tight at the point where it is held by the tack while remaining looser between tacks.

A couple of strokes, then smooth and stretch from back to front, with your right hand still holding the edge of the cloth. Don't pull – merely anchor the material and take up any slack as the left hand smooths and stretches it.

On the last stroke of your left hand, bring your thumb over and use it to hold the cloth while the right hand picks up tack and hammer to secure it temporarily *(f)*. Complete this procedure on all four sides of the seat to within 70mm (2¾in) of the corners. Pull down corners again *(g)*, but this time driving one tack right home in the position shown.

Continue the stretching process right up to the corners, pleating the corners to dispose of any fullness *(h)*. Now permanently tack with 9mm (⅜in) fine tacks all round the seat *(i)*. Remove the temporary tacks and trim off surplus calico.

Your seat should now have assumed a good, even, slightly domed shape. But note how the horsehair is working through the weave of the cloth. Hair will always do this except with a hair-proof ticking used for mattresses. So we must arrest its progress with a material that it cannot penetrate – and that is cotton wool, cotton felt or wadding. I have never studied the scientific reasons, but I know from experience that as long as the wadding is thick enough no hair will penetrate this barrier.

So this is the next stage. Cut off some wadding and put on two layers to make sure. Trim this around the edges *(j)*, so that none will extend over the sides. Remember that the seat has to fit into the chair frame, so it must not be made any larger.

TOP COVERING

Now we come to the final stage – putting on the furnishing fabric. Mark the centres of each side of the seat on the edge and underneath with a soft pencil or ballpoint pen *(see fig.62)*. Measure the length and width of the seat, remembering to measure the width near the front as this is the greater distance. Allow a turning of 38mm (1½in) all round.

Just a word at this point concerning the way to cut various fabrics. Materials woven with large threads such as tweeds, hopsack, union and some tapestries are easily cut, for you can follow the threads with your scissors. But there are other materials which don't have this advantage. By the way, it is important to cut straight and to the thread with any woven cloth. Even your lowly hessian should be cut to a thread, as it is important, when tacking, to follow a thread with the row of tacks.

With some cloths that are woven with pronounced ribs across them, the task is simple, for the scissors practically guide themselves. Also, with a patterned material, you can follow the repeat of the design. Tapestries can be cut from the back where the threads show up better. The back will provide a guide when cutting lengthwise, for the tapestry pattern emerges through the back in the form of stripes of colour running the length of the cloth. These can be followed when cutting.

Velours and velvets in plain colours are the most difficult to cut straight, and I recommend the following procedure.

Fray out the end of the cloth until a full-width thread is obtained. Trim back the fringed threads and lay the material flat on the table with pile uppermost and with the edge perfectly straight. Measure the amount required from this edge and mark across with the aid of a straight-edged ruler. The marking can be done with the tips of your scissors. After cutting off, and before marking for the next cut, fray the edge again to make sure you are keeping to the threads of the weave.

There is one exception to the 'cut to the

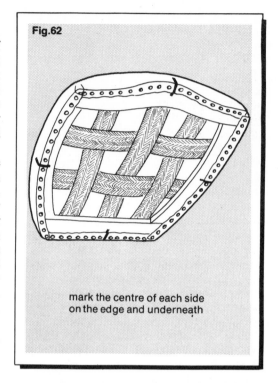

mark the centre of each side
on the edge and underneath

thread' rule. This concerns printed materials such as printed linen or union. Here you must ignore the weave and cut straight according to the pattern, which, you will find, is very often out of alignment with the direction of the threads.

Having cut the piece of material to size *(see fig.63)*, find the centres of all four sides by folding each side in half and nicking the corner of the fold so that a small vee is made in the exact centre *(a)*. Lay the cloth over the seat and adjust the position until you are satisfied that the marks on the frame correspond with the vees cut in the cloth. Temporarily tack, just as you did with the undercover, but this time take much more care to keep the weave straight back to front and side to side.

Corner pleats The corners must be neatly pleated *(b)*. Permanently fix a tack in each corner, then cut away the surplus material up to the tack. You can see at *(c)* how the two pleats on one of the corners are made. These can be permanently fixed as shown.

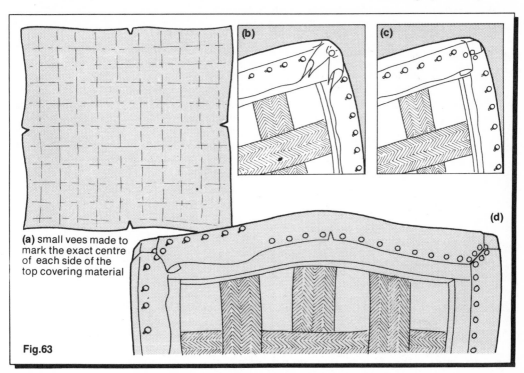

(a) small vees made to mark the exact centre of each side of the top covering material

(b)

(c)

(d)

Fig.63

Finally, at *(d)*, we see that all that remains is to turn the material under and tack neatly all round.

Wouldn't canvas over the bottom save all that 'fiddly turning the edge under' business? True, you often see seats that have hessian or black lining covering the underside, but I like to leave them open so that you can see what's happening to the webbing – and keep an eye on the woodwork for signs of the dreaded beetle!

OTHER DROP-IN SEATS

The drop-in seat we have examined is the most usual form, but before closing this chapter I want to mention some of the variations you may encounter and how their treatment differs.

Sprung seats Many modern seats have springs incorporated, usually of the zig-zag strip kind called ripple wire springs. Very little can go wrong with these springs so long as they remain well linked together laterally. Wire links or small tension springs are used

for this purpose. They do sometimes get noisy after a year or two and squeak when sat on. So, when re-upholstering, remove the springs and re-line the fixing clips with a material such as thick leathercloth.

These seats are very simple to re-upholster and require no webbing. Use a good strong hessian to cover the ripple springs, which should be tied through at several points along their length. On top of the hessian place a layer of cotton felt held by string ties just as I described for holding horsehair. Then add a layer of 25mm (1in) thick polyether foam to make a very comfortable seat.

To cut the foam, lay the seat on top of the foam sheet and cut around it with a sharp knife, keeping about 10mm (⅜in) outside the frame. With shears or scissors, chamfer the top edges of the foam, then cover with a calico undercover as already described.

Some good-class chairs made before the Second World War had small coil springs in the loose seats *(see fig.64)*. When re-

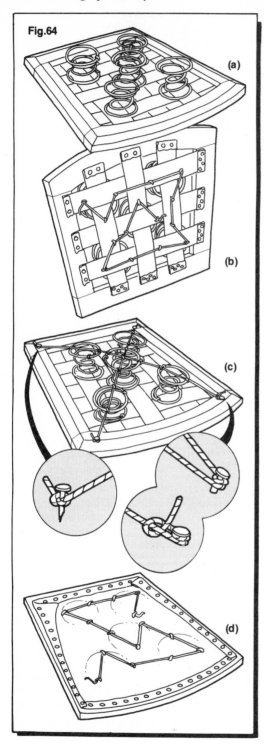

Fig.64

(a)

(b)

(c)

(d)

upholstering these, you can either dispense with the springs and re-upholster in the way I have mentioned or re-make as a sprung seat – in which case webbing must be placed under the frame. The springs, usually four or five *(a)*, will most likely need renewing. The sizes will probably be about 76-100mm (3-4in) high and 11 or 12 gauge. These are tied to the webbing *(b)* at three points on each spring's base. Your spring needle threaded with a stout No.1 twine will be used for this.

Assuming there are five springs, place the first dead centre and fix down from underneath *(b)*, knotting each tie with a half hitch. Now sew on the other springs to form a square around the centre one, midway between frame and centre spring. Make sure that the top knuckle (the bend of the spring where it is finished off and joined to the first coil) is facing towards the centre. The twine is used all in one piece, going from spring to spring, finishing off with several half hitches on the last stitch.

The springs are now pulled down with 'laid cord' *(c)* with two diagonal ties. To cut off the length required, stretch the laid cord diagonally over the springs from corner to corner of the frame, then add half the length again to allow for knotting. Tie a single knot in the end of each piece of cord through which you push a 16mm (⅝in) improved tack. Fix them to the back corners, about 25mm (1in) in from the outside edges. You can see the position of the laced springs at *(c)* and how they 'fan' out slightly.

Begin lacing by holding down a back spring to the required height, about 50mm (2in), and tying the cord with a locked loop on the back of the top coil and a clove hitch on the front of the same coil. Follow through to the centre and front springs, fastening the cord at the front corner by twisting around a tack driven in halfway. Then drive the tack fully home and tie a half hitch around the cord to make it secure. Do the same with the other cord, and, when you've finished, the centre spring should be no more than 76mm (3in) high.

Use 456g (16oz) tarpaulin hessian to

stretch over the springs, and tack it down in the same way as you did with your loose seat. Then, with stout twine, stitch the springs to the hessian in the same manner as the bottom of the springs are fixed – so that they are attached at three points around the top coil, secured by a single knot on each stitch *(d)*.

From this point the procedure is the same as for a seat without springs – and don't forget those very important stuffing ties. With this seat, you need to cover the underside with hessian or lining to hide the webbing and make a neat finish.

Loose seats of an earlier period There is one more loose seat that I would like to mention – the type found on early Victorian and Regency dining chairs *(see fig.65)*. These seats fit in between raised side rails and are prevented from slipping forward on the chair seat frame by a peg protruding from the top centre of the front rail of the chair. The peg fits into a corresponding hole in the frame of the seat. These seats are a little more complicated to upholster, as the front and sides are built up with stitched edges.

Let us examine a typical example – one which looks as if the seat is about to go through. The black, shiny material with which it is covered is fabric made of horsehair – sometimes called 'hair seating'. This is a very strong, durable material, and is, I believe, still made to this day.

The horsehair material has become a bit prickly where the front edge has become worn, so let us make this your next job. It will be an introduction to the art of edge stitching, which, in traditional upholstery, is widely used to form firm shapes to the edges of seats, arms and backs.

The job is quite straightforward at the start, and you can call on your recently gained experience to take you to the stage where you cover the new webbing with tarpaulin hessian. Once you have done that, the next step is to put some stuffing ties in with your large circular needle – not all over as you did before but along the two sides and the front, approximately 20mm (¾in) in

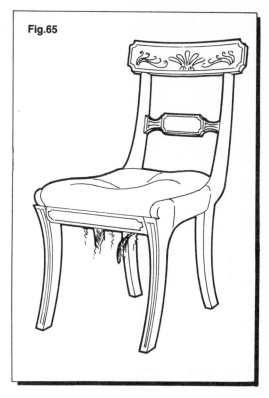

Fig.65

from the edge.

Now what about the back? As you can see, the back has a triangular section piece of wood glued on, making up the thickness of the seat, near to the finished size. You will have to build up all round to this height. But why can't the frame be made with pieces of wood on all sides, to make up the height? It certainly could be done this way, but think how hard and uncomfortable it would be – especially at the front edge.

There is another deeper, more scientific, reason for stitched edges. It allows much more movement and adds resilience to the seat *(see fig.66)*. If you look at the three sectional diagrams *(a)*, you will see more clearly what I mean. In the first, you see a seat correctly done. The second diagram shows that when it is sat on, the whole of the upholstery hinges upon the line of tacks fastening the edges. In the third, showing a seat with wooden edges, you can see that as there is no movement at the edges, a great

Fig.66

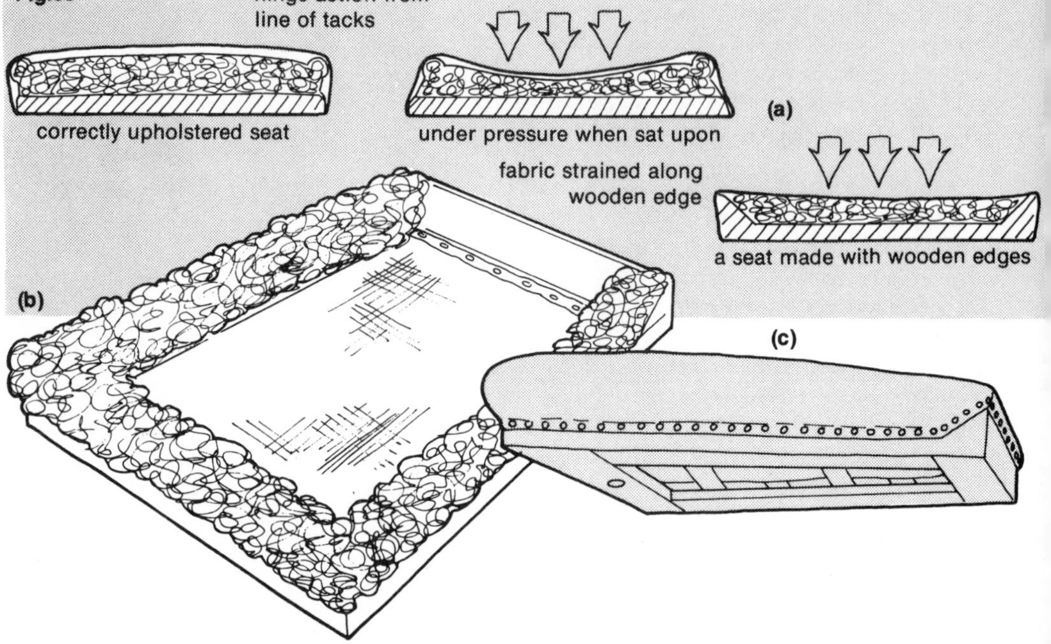

hinge action from line of tacks

correctly upholstered seat

under pressure when sat upon

fabric strained along wooden edge

a seat made with wooden edges

(a)

(b)

(c)

strain is put upon the covering. There is only one way to eliminate this strain: it is to stuff the seat solid when it becomes very hard and uncomfortable.

Assuming we saved the original horsehair so that it could be re-carded, start at the front centre of the seat and tuck in hair firmly under the stuffing ties to form a fairly solid 'sausage' about 40mm (1⅝in) in diameter. At *(b)* you see this stage complete on all three sides. Now the centre of the seat can be filled with hair. This is termed the first stuffing.

Measure and cut off a piece of 283g (10oz) hessian large enough to cover the seat. Mark the centres of each side of the seat frame and the centres of the four sides of the hessian and temporarily tack the hessian, matching the marks just as you did when covering the other loose seat. Begin permanently tacking with 9mm (⅜in) tacks, along the back, about 10mm (⅜in) down from the top of the built-up wooden edge.

Start in the centre, following the threads

along with a row of tacks. It is a great help to keep accurately to the line of a thread in the hessian, for if this is done along the front edge it ensures the exact height and shape of the seat and edges. Slight adjustments must be made at the corners, a thread or two being taken up here.

You will see at *(c)* that a small chamfer has been made along the top edges of the frame, and it is along this chamfer that the line of tacks are placed, about 20mm (¾in) apart. You can also see that the front edge is overhanging the frame by about 15mm (⅝in). The sides also overhang, but to a smaller degree. Remember, the seat must fit between the side rails of the chair!

At *(d)* you can see how to use a regulator to square up the edges and adjust the stuffing beneath the hessian. You stick the point of the regulator in and lever the horsehair towards the edge. The hessian at the corners may be pushed in with the rounded end of the regulator and manipulated into a sharp, square shape.

Tighten and pull down the ties from the slip knot to the centre stitch. This should then be fastened with a series of single knots or half hitches.

THE STITCHED EDGE

At this point it would help to devise some means of holding the seat firmly at about elbow height. I suggest making a simple stand out of any odd pieces of wood – rather like a hawk used by bricklayers for carrying small amounts of mortar. It can be temporarily screwed to the underside of the seat and then held in a carpenter's vice on the bench *(see fig.67)*.

I have made a very handy one out of a swivel screw from an old Victorian piano stool. It was round and could be raised or lowered just by spinning the seat around. By fastening a tee piece on the top for fixing to the work and by fitting the screw threaded shaft into a tight tube, it can be turned easily as the work progresses. It is possible to work without such an aid, so don't worry if you can't make a jig.

You now need the smaller 175mm (about 7in) mattress needle, threaded with No.2, medium-thickness twine, a regulator and scissors. When edge stitching, work from left to right, and put in two rows of 'blind' stitches. On the front edge, make an extra row of through stitches to form a roll edge. Describing in words the method of stitching is difficult, but I will do my best to make it clear with the help of drawings *(see fig.68)*.

Cut off 2-3m (2-3yd) of twine and thread the needle. Then with the left-hand side edge facing you, start by pushing in your needle just above the line of tacks and 30mm (about 1¼in) from the left-hand corner. The point should come through the top about 90mm (about 3½in) back from the edge *(a)*. Pull the needle through just as far as the eye *(b)*. Also in *(b)* I've indicated how one twist of the needle in an anti-clockwise direction is made to 'scoop' horsehair inside the seat with the eye end point of the needle.

At *(c)* the needle is pushed back, emerging at the far end of the side – and again just above the tacks. At *(d)* the twine is pulled

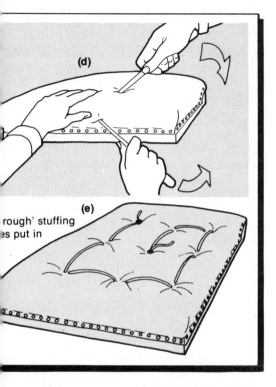

(d)

(e)

rough' stuffing
s put in

When you have finished tacking and the edges look even, straight and true, put in some more stuffing ties, this time going right through the seat and anchoring the top hessian to the webbing and hessian beneath. With a crayon or felt tip pen, mark the top hessian in the form of a square, the sides of which are 100mm (4in) from the seat edges. Take your 250mm (about 10in) double-pointed mattress needle and thread it with No.1 stout twine. Make a stitch in the left-hand back corner of the marked square 15mm (⅝in) wide, taking it through the seat. Tie loosely with a slip knot. Proceed as you see at *(e)* around the marked square, finishing with one stitch dead centre.

Unthread the needle and put it safely away. Nasty accidents can happen with these double-pointed needles – especially when they are laid down with twine dangling, ready to become entwined around foot or leg and pulling the sharp needle into a position to inflict a painful wound. I speak from bitter experience!

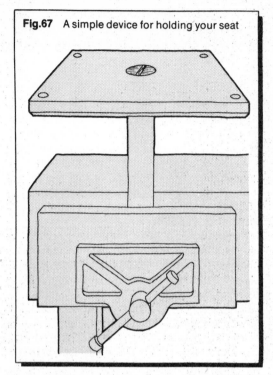

Fig.67 A simple device for holding your seat

firm the edge. Use the regulator again to work up the hair and even out the edge, then put another row of 'blind' stitches about 15mm (nearly ⅝in) above the first row. Finish the last stitch by tying a reef knot, using the end left from the first row.

It very often happens that you run out of twine before you reach the end of a row. To join on more, refer to the instructions for the half hitch on page 85, in the chapter on Fixing and Fastening. By the way, don't forget to use the lump of beeswax. When you cut off a length of twine, pull it across the wax several times. This will give it an extra dressing and it will be less likely to kink and knot up when you are stitching.

The two sides of the seat are now finished, but we must put a roll on the front edge. The method is similar to the blind stitching, but it differs in that the stitches go through to the top. Use the regulator to bring up the edge finally. Feel with your fingers to see that there are no soft or lumpy places along its length. If there are, deal with them using the regulator.

Now mark with a ruler and felt tip pen a line about 23mm (⅞in) back from the front of the edge. Draw another line on the front at the same distance down – or just above the last row of stitches – and you are ready to stitch your roll.

Make a single stitch on the right hand side *(h)*, keeping to the marked lines. Pull tight with a slip knot fastened off with a couple of half hitches. Cut off the twine leaving a 150mm (about 6in) end. The reason for this single stitch is twofold. First, it anchors the corner so that when the first stitch is put in on the left the edge is immediately tightened along its length. This is so important when making a good, even roll. And, second, there is an end on to which you can fasten the twine after the last stitch.

Begin on the left once more *(i)*, pushing the needle through the marked line on the front, about 20mm (¾in) to the right of the corner and coming through the line drawn along the top. Take the needle right out, then push it back through as near to the left-hand corner as possible. Guide it so that

through, tied with the upholsterer's slip knot and pulled tight. Begin the row of stitches by pushing the needle in 50mm (2in) to the right of the knot, at an angle *(e)*.

Do the twist with your needle as before, then return it so that it protrudes to about half its length and emerges back to the left – about 10mm (⅜in) from the starting stitch. Take the twine leading from the starting stitch and wind it three times, clockwise, around the needle *(f)*.

Pull the needle out, and the twine will follow through the twine that you have wound around the needle. Pull the whole length of twine through and tighten the stitch. Carry on stitching around the seat until you reach the other back corner. At the last stitch, jerk the twine to the left to lock it and cut it off, leaving 150mm (about 6in). Your row of stitches should look something like that seen at *(g)*.

Now you can appreciate the value of edge stitching and see how the loops of the stitches inside pull the stuffing forward to

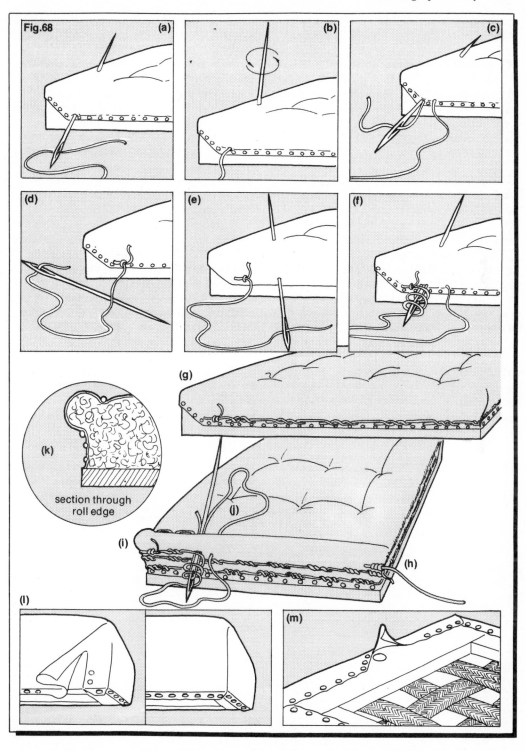

Fig.68 (a) (b) (c) (d) (e) (f) (g) (h) (i) (j)

(k) section through roll edge

(l) (m)

it comes out on the front line. Tie your upholsterer's slip knot and pull up tight.

For the next stitch, push in your needle 25mm (1in) to the right of the first stitch (j). Guide the needle so that it comes through the hessian on the line you have drawn along the top. Now pull right through and pass back through the edge, 25mm (1in) to the left so the needle enters the place where the first stitch ends.

Wind the twine around the needle three times, just as you did with the blind stitches, and pull up very tight, using the fingers of your left hand to squeeze the stitch together as you pull. Carry on to the end of the row and tie off with a reef knot, using the end you left on the right-hand stitch.

You can see at (k) how a firm, round roll is formed in this way. Here is an edge, strong enough to be sat on and remain in shape and yet not so hard as to cause discomfort to whoever sits in the chair.

Why not make a roll edge on the sides as well? On a seat like this it's not necessary, as the side edges are protected within the confines of the chair rails. But roll edges are formed all round on many kinds of chair seats – as you will learn later.

Put on the top stuffing, undercover, wadding and covering fabric in exactly the same way as you did on the dining chair seat – with the exception of the corner pleats which on this seat must be single.

At (l), you can see exactly how this is done. The material is pulled diagonally towards the corner and fixed at the front with two tacks. The surplus material is then cut away up to the tacks and the pleat folded neatly and squarely up to the corner.

With some materials, the pleat may be sewn up to make an even neater job, using the ladder stitch that I described in the chapter on Fixing and Fastening, page 90.

There is one final point. When you are neatly turning in and finishing off the material underneath the seat, don't forget to leave the hole for the peg uncovered. At (m), you can see how to cut and vee the fabric up to the hole.

More difficult upholstery

We can learn many basic skills from the smaller jobs, so let us look around for something a little more difficult than the drop-in seats. We will settle for the corner chair with the sagging seat *(see fig.69)*. This is ideal for our next job, so let's take it into the workshop and see what's to be done to put it right.

It is very nicely made in mahogany and designed to grace the corner of a room. The seat is roughly diamond shape – I say roughly because the front corner is rounded to form a serpentine shape. It has what we term a simple pincushion seat; or rather I should say 'had', for there's not much recognisable as a seat! Most of it has dropped through the frame. Most pincushion seats are simple to build, but this one has a diamond shape. The covering fabric must still run from back to front, so the difficult part of covering is that all four sides have to be stretched and tacked at a diagonal to the threads of the weave – or on the bias, as we say. However, I will lay down a few guidelines which, if you follow them closely, will help you to achieve a satisfactory finish.

Before you start with mallet and ripping chisel, wait and have a little think. This chair frame is made of mahogany, and I bet this is not the first seat it has had in its lifetime. Also, remember the wood on the back of the spoonback chair and how you removed the upholstery from that. Yes, it would be safer to use pliers and pincers, for I think you will find there is little enough wood in the rails without splitting more of it away.

I have a complaint to make concerning most chairs with pincushion seats – that the makers seldom allowed enough width in the rails to facilitate the comfortable placing of

webbing, hessian and the other upholstery materials necessary for a good seat.

Having removed all the tacks from the seat rails, put the webbing on in the usual way. Does the webbing have to run back to front, corner to corner of this diamond seat? No, the best way is to view the diamond as a square, and web from one rail straight across to the other *(see fig.70)*. Also, you can see in this illustration the spacing between the turned-over ends of the lengths of webbing and the edge of the shallow rabbet in the top of the rail. Never place the webbing up to the shoulder of the rabbet.

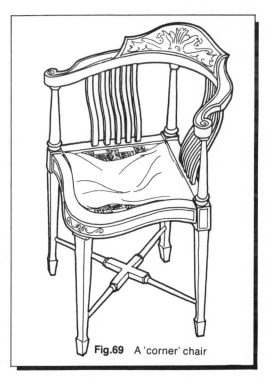

Fig.69 A 'corner' chair

This must be left clear for the final cover so that a smooth, even turning can be made.

The hessian – always use the strongest tarpaulin hessian – can also run in the same direction as the webbing. Be careful to choose tacks which will hold well in the wood but at the same time will not split the rails.

Before you go any further with the upholstery, give the woodwork a good clean with finishing cream or car cleaner. These chairs, made in the early part of this century, are exquisitely french polished, but the surface of the polish on our chair has become rather dull over the years. But you will be amazed at the lustre a good rub with cream will reveal – which will be further enhanced when followed by wax polish.

Return to the upholstery and put in several rows of stuffing ties, just as you did for top stuffing the other seats. Add a 100mm (4in) domed layer of horsehair and pull it down with a thin calico undercover. This can be tacked down without turnings, then trimmed back all round with a knife or scissors. Add a layer or two of cotton wadding and you are ready to cover with furnishing fabric.

I always think striped damask looks well on these occasional chairs, but with stripes you must be meticulous in keeping the stripes straight. This is the best way to get good results.

Cut a piece of material roughly to the size of the seat, allowing plenty and remembering that the stripes or pattern will run from back to front – or, in our case, from back corner to front corner. Also ensure that you either have your design centred or a centre stripe.

Lay the fabric over the seat. Position it and, without folding in, tack temporarily with one tack in the back corner. Stretch lightly and tack into the front corner so that the pattern or stripe is exactly centred.

Now do the same at the side corners, making sure that the pattern remains straight back to front and that the threads running across are at right angles to this.

Put in one temporary tack to hold the

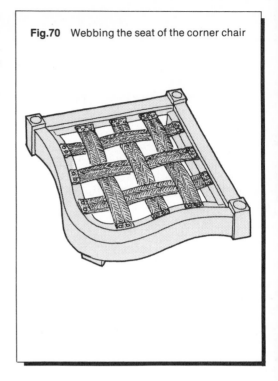

Fig.70   Webbing the seat of the corner chair

material at the centre of each rail *(see fig.71)*. Cut off the surplus material on each side, leaving about 15mm (⅝in) for turnings.

You will remember that when I described the tools and their uses I mentioned that the regulator was also useful as an extra finger. I may have puzzled you at the time, but this is the sort of job in which this tool will be of considerable assistance. When you turn in the edges of the material on this pincushion seat, you can give a bit of a stretch and hold the cloth in place with the point of the regulator while you drive in a tack.

I find that this way I am able to make a neater and more accurate job, rather than trying to hold the cloth with a finger. By the way, if you have a pin or cabriol hammer with a tapered head, now is the time to use it to avoid damaging the polished wood surround.

You must now temporarily tack the material all round, stretching and turning in as you go. Use 9mm (⅜in) fine tacks or 13mm (½in) gimp pins. Or, if you intend to

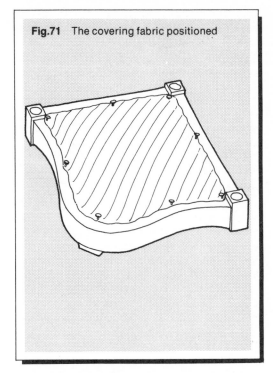

Fig.71 The covering fabric positioned

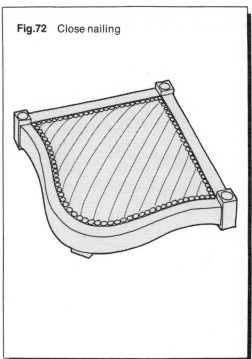

Fig.72 Close nailing

use staples, use larger tacks such as 13mm (½in) fine which can more easily be pulled out as you fix with the staple gun.

It is worth using staples to secure coverings to seats and back panels, especially on chairs where the width of the tacking rabbet is narrow. Staples have the same fixing strength as tacks and do far less damage to timber that is hard and liable to split.

Start at the back corner and work to the centres of both back rails, placing tacks at 15mm (⅝in) intervals. Fix alternately, one in the left rail and then one in the right rail, taking up any fullness to keep the cross threads of the material straight. Also keep a constant eye on the pattern, ensuring it is straight back to front.

When you reach the centre of each back rail, stop and begin the same procedure from the front corner to the centre of each front rail. Repeat this process from each side corner, and remember to drive the tacks in only to about a third of their length so that it

is easy to remove them and make adjustments as necessary.

A material with a uniform design is a great help. For instance, a tack can be put exactly through a flower, dot or stripe to the right of the centre corner, then the corresponding point can be found and tacked through on the left side – and so on.

When all the temporary tacks have been put in and you are satisfied that everything looks right, drive home all the tacks. The seat is now ready for trimming.

Some occasional chairs have upholstered back panels, and with these the same principles can be applied as with the pincushion seat – except that usually the outside back material must be fixed on first. This is so that, from the back, it appears to be framed by the polished wood. A layer of cotton wadding goes on next to prevent any hair coming through the back. In most cases no webbing is required – just tarpaulin hessian stretched tightly. Then follow stuffing ties, horsehair and wadding.

The tacks or staples can now be covered with a braid as previously described in the chapter on Fixing and Fastening, page 92. I always feel apprehensive about this job and proceed ultra-carefully to prevent latex adhesive getting splashed, spilled or dabbed on the covering fabric. If this does happen, it is virtually impossible to remove without leaving a nasty mark. The best place to start and finish the braid would be the back corner where you can make a neat mitre of the join.

Another method used for the final fixing of coverings is called close nailing *(see fig.72)*. No doubt you have seen this on chairs. It consists of a continuous row of dome-headed chair nails, hammered in so that all heads are touching. This makes an excellent finish to the edges so long as the line of nails is made perfectly even. It only needs a couple of nails slightly out of place to upset the whole effect.

When buying chair nails, don't get the cheaper sort which are brass plated on steel.

Fig.73

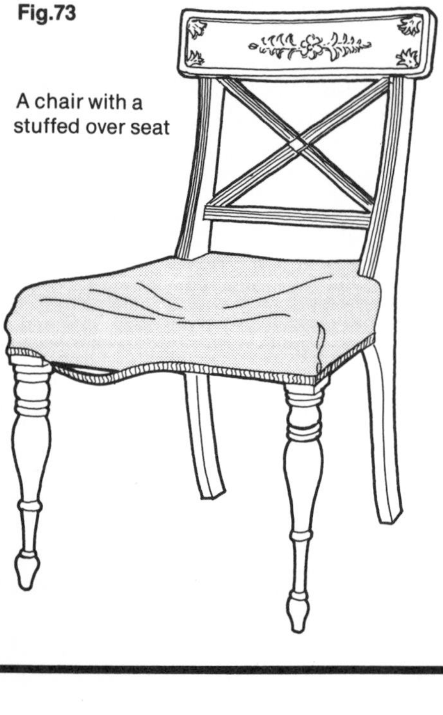

A chair with a stuffed over seat

The thin brass plating soon wears off and they begin to rust. Better-quality nails have solid brass dome heads with steel shanks. You can buy them in three finishes: polished brass, light antique and dark antique brass.

I prefer the light antique finish to the polished brass, which soon becomes dull and lacks lustre. The dark antique nails resemble gun-metal and usually have a very dark grey appearance. Of course, which of these finishes is most suitable will depend on the colour you have chosen for your furnishing fabric. ·

Chair nails do have a disadvantage in that the close row tends to perforate the wood along the grain which, on woods such as oak, may then split open along the line. The size of the chair nail most used in upholstery has a 13mm (½in) shank, with 9mm (⅜in) diameter head, but larger and smaller ones can be obtained. The trained upholsterer will close-nail just by eye, judging distance and straightness without measuring aids. But I would recommend that beginners should draw a guideline for a row of nails the correct distance from the fabric edge (the radius of the nail head). And use a very fine awl to make a start hole for each nail. This should go to a depth of about half the length of the nail's shank.

STUFFED-OVER SEATS

The next chair I want to examine has a stuffed-over seat. The term stuffed-over describes an upholstered chair seat which is built permanently on to the chair frame *(see fig.73)*. The covering is pulled over and fixed either along the sides up to facings or beads of wood or turned under and fixed beneath the seat rails.

Our seat has quite a hollow in the centre, and underneath you can see that the webbing is beginning to tear. Even so, this is a choice little Regency chair, basically in excellent condition. There are one or two worm holes in the seat rails, but the infection is not at all serious, and an injection of woodworm destroyer will ensure that there is no further trouble.

Strip it in the usual way with the ripping

chisel and mallet. If you find it difficult to remove the tacks, use pliers and pincers as this is rather a precious chair. . .!

There are no springs in this seat, so the webbing goes on top of the rails. You know all about webbing up, but as this chair has a fairly wide seat I would advise putting four lengths of webbing each way. Tarpaulin hessian covers this in just the same as in our loose seat. Then comes the first stuffing. We removed the old stitched edges very carefully – couldn't we just put them back?

It would save a lot of time, and edges which have remained in good shape can be saved and put on again, but they must always be re-covered with hessian and re-stitched. But I would rather you made up a new edge for the chair in this instance. Seeing a job right through is the only way to learn – a job that is entirely your own work and does not involve cribbing the skills of others.

So, just as with the loose seat, put in stuffing ties near the edge of the hessian, but this time all the way round, tucking horsehair under them to make rolls of stuffing on all four sides. This should be about 10mm (⅜in) higher than you intend the edge to be and should extend out, overhanging the rails by about 20mm (¾in). Push the hair under the ties so that it is very firm and even. And take some pains to get it right. Fill up the centre so that when you compress it with your hand it consolidates to about the same thickness as the edge roll.

Now for the hessian *(see fig.74)*. The 283g (10oz) is best, so cut off a piece, allowing 25mm (1in) all round to turn in. Mark the centre of each side of your chair seat and the centres of the four sides of your piece of hessian, lay over the stuffing and position at these marks with temporary tacks *(a)*. After making sure that the threads of the hessian are straight, lay back the two back corners as shown at *(a)* and cut from the corner of the hessian to within 10mm (⅜in) of the back upright. The hessian can then be turned over as at *(b)*, the surplus cut off, and the

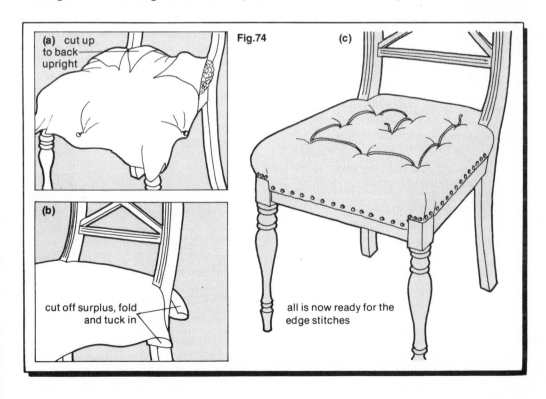

(a) cut up to back upright

(b) cut off surplus, fold and tuck in

Fig.74

(c) all is now ready for the edge stitches

remainder tucked in with the regulator.

Carry on fixing, as with the edge of the loose seat, only this time remember that the edge needs an overhang all round including the back. Work to a thread when fixing back and front, so as to keep the edges uniform in height and the back and front of the seat parallel. At the back you will have to take up a thread or two at the corners near the back uprights. This is also necessary at the front corners. At *(c)* you will see how the chair should look. And you will also notice that through stuffing ties have been put in to pull down the centre of the seat.

All is now ready for the edge stitches. Here again, follow the same procedure as before, except that this seat requires a roll edge all the way around, including the back. When you come to put the through stitches in to form the roll, begin with the front edge and don't forget the one single stitch at the right-hand corner. Continue round to the right side as far as the back upright. Then stitch the left side, doing the back last.

You know how to put on the second stuffing, calico undercover and wadding, but there are two new points to learn when you come to covering with furnishing fabric. First, when you have temporarily fixed the cover with about three or four tacks on each side and all is nicely positioned, cut the two corners into the back uprights as you did with the hessian covering the first stuffing to within 5mm (³/₁₆in) of the wood.

Take care when you cut off surplus material *(see fig.75)*. Lay the material in to see just how much you can cut away *(a)*. Tuck and turn in up to the back uprights, stretch down and temporarily tack.

The second point relates to the front corners. In my opinion these always look best and neatest when double pleated. This is how you do it *(see fig.75)*.

(b) Cut thin cardboard stiffeners and fix one with tacks around each front corner. This will keep the covering material out from the hollow of the corner and the pleats closed.

(c) Stretch and tack the corner of the material, dead centre of the seat corner.

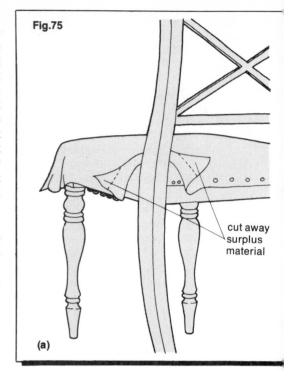

Fig.75

cut away surplus material

(a)

(d) Further stretch, tighten and tack the material.

(e) Cut away surplus material on both sides.

(f) Make and secure the pleats.

(g) If very thick, heavy material is used, cut away as much surplus fabric as possible to avoid a lumpy, uneven look.

SEATS WITH SPRINGS

Before we leave stuffed-over chair seats, a word about ones which have springs. On these the webbing is stretched on the bottom face of the seat rails and the springs are sewn on to this, as I described with the sprung loose seat. This time 125-150mm (about 5-6in) springs will be required, in 10 or 11 gauge. But the size, gauge and number of springs can be varied according to the size and shape of the seat – and also to make it harder or softer.

When I'm building a new chair seat, I try to keep the person to whom it belongs in mind, thinking of their height and approxi-

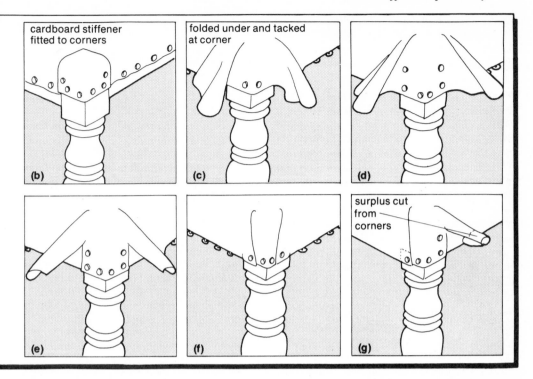

(b) cardboard stiffener fitted to corners

(c) folded under and tacked at corner

(d)

(e)

(f)

(g) surplus cut from corners

mate weight so that I can choose heavier or lighter springs accordingly.

Spring lacings should be modified from the two cord diagonal lacings of the loose seat and should lace over from back to front and side to side *(see fig.76)*. The same fanning out of the springs and the domes profile should be observed. You will also see that the laid cord is attached to the second coil down of the outside springs. This is to keep the springs straighter at the waist. If the cord is tied over the top coil it throws the centre waist of the spring off centre, and in this position it may buckle after only a short period of use. It is very important for the long life of springs to position them correctly.

The tarpaulin hessian used to cover the springs should not be pulled any tighter than the spring lacings or these will just hang loose and serve no purpose. The springs are sewn to the hessian with the usual three stitches per spring, and then the procedure is the same as for a chair which has no

Fig.76

Lacing the springs in a stuffed over seat

springs – with one exception. When you put in the through stuffing ties, these should only go in as far as the spring hessian and not right through to the webbing.

These chairs have the simplest form of stuffed over seats. More intricate work is demanded for others, such as drawing room chairs which have shaped seats with rounded or serpentine fronts. Complications occur when forming the front edge, for you will be trying to persuade a straight-woven piece of hessian to assume the wavy, serpentine shape of the edge.

The fact that hessian is loosely woven does assist this shaping, but one rule must be observed. When tacking from the front centre of the seat to either corner, the hessian must not be stretched laterally towards the corners. If this is done, the centre bulge of the serpentine front will be pulled back. To preserve the stand-out angle of this part of the edge, as each tack is put in the hessian must be gathered towards the centre to almost a pleat. This must also be done on the sides of the seat where the edge rounds towards the back uprights. The same rule applies when putting on the calico undercover and the top covering. The serpentine front edge is the most difficult to form correctly, but chairs with a bow front need the same treatment – though the hessian need not be gathered so fully.

MODERN FIRESIDE CHAIR

I would now like to move on to some modern upholstery so as to widen your knowledge and skills a little more. Let's examine what is called a fireside chair *(see fig.77)*. Just the cushioned seat and back are upholstered, and the arms and legs are of mahogany, nicely shaped. It's in a bit of a state, but it's got a very good frame – and if you look, there is the maker's name. I think we must strip all the upholstery from the chair, for the back is very soiled and it looks as if water has been leaking on to it. The cushion is of no further use, and the interior has perished.

Make a list of the things you need before you start. We need one cushion interior to

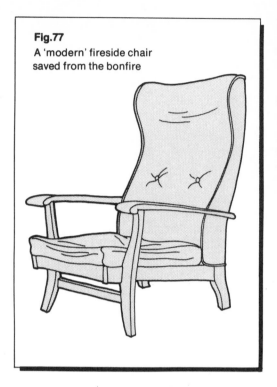

Fig.77
A 'modern' fireside chair
saved from the bonfire

begin with. Those made of rubber are best. Polyether foam interiors can be bought in various densities, but after a while they tend to lose their squareness at the edges. There are two main types of rubber foam cushion interiors: first, the more expensive ones which are made to exact sizes and are slightly domed in shape. These cannot be cut down to smaller sizes as they are made with large air pockets inside. Second, there is foam rubber of the type called blockfoam. This is virtually solid foam throughout, apart from lines of small vertical holes running through the thickness. This can also be obtained in three densities and can be cut to exact size with, of all things, a fine-toothed panel saw.

If you are using any kind of rubber foam for your cushion, it is very important to choose a covering material which is thick enough to keep out daylight. Even diffused sunlight causes deterioration of rubber.

Measure up for covering fabric, and I think you will find that 2.50m (about 2¾yd) will be ample. I think the existing springs are still perfectly good, even though the cover has worn away. Don't worry about the bare ones. I will show you how to improve the seat with a padded apron that will fit over the springs.

The side fastenings for the springs are in poor condition, but you can buy steel plates, each drilled with a double row of nine holes, which are purpose-made as replacements for spring fixings. Some of them, I'm afraid, are made of a steel which, in my opinion, is too soft. The springs wear through the metal within about two years. However, they are easily changed and replaced – especially if you use screws to fix them. So buy some spares for future use.

You will also need some 6mm (¼in) thick polyether foam; cotton felt or wadding; about 6m (just over 6½yd) of No.1 or No.2 cotton piping cord; a piece of dressmaker's chalk or ordinary blackboard chalk sharpened at the tip – and a black fibre-tipped pen will be useful for marking out your covering material.

Once the back upholstery is stripped off, we can examine the springs at this point. These are much thinner and softer in tension than those of the seat. One or two may have come adrift, but they are only secured with staples to the insides of the back uprights and some may have been pulled out. Wouldn't screw-eyes be better for attaching these springs? Yes, if you can screw them to the inside faces of the back uprights. Alternatively, take out the staples and place them down the front face of the wood, driven nearly home so that they don't cause bumps beneath the stuffing.

Talking of stuffing, when stripping we removed from the back what appears to be a bag made of calico and filled with something very soft. It was tacked over the springs. This is a first stuffing of kapok, which is a very soft light vegetable down, but I'm afraid this has been about too long and is all dust and lumps. It must be discarded.

You can please yourself whether you use new kapok for the back. Some people are allergic to it, so avoid it if you suffer from hay fever or a similar ailment. I would leave out the seat springs when you have fitted the new side plates. This will make things easier while you are upholstering.

This is where you put on your french polisher's hat once again and renovate the polished woodwork of the arms and legs. And when, after a day or two, the surfaces are hard and cannot easily be marked by handling you can start the re-upholstering.

I always view the bare frame of a modern chair or settee with some feeling of excitement, for it is easy to visualise how to accentuate or improve it. There may be modifications which could be made to make it more comfortable – or, if the chair is several years old, there may be a way of cutting and covering to bring the style more up to date. Now is the time to let your imagination loose.

It will be best to begin by upholstering the back. You can follow the original upholstery and sew up a calico bag – just two sides stitched together like a sack. The size should be 50mm (2in) wider than the back frame and about 25mm (1in) longer, top to bottom. Leave one end open through which you can stuff your kapok, cotton wadding or cotton felt. Stitch up on the machine when the stuffing is completed. This forms the first stuffing, and it must not be too thick; about a soft 50mm (2in) will be adequate.

Now tack or staple this stuffing to the back frame of the chair, fastening the sides first and keeping the seams a fraction back from the edges. Don't stretch it tightly. The idea of making the unit longer and wider is that it will not hinder the action of the springs. There will be plenty of fullness in the calico against the springs, and the calico on the front will dome out to give a good shape. Make sure that your filling is even, then put in some stuffing ties of fine twine through from front to back, to keep it all securely in place.

The next layer will be composed of cotton felt. With the chair lying on its back, measure and cut off a piece of felt to size and lay this over. With your large semi-circular needle and fine twine, fasten this layer to the

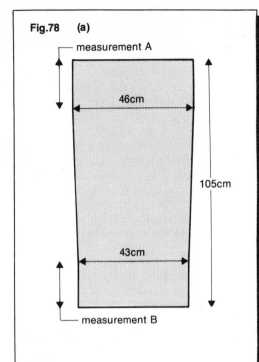

Fig.78   (a)

measurement A

46cm

105cm

43cm

measurement B

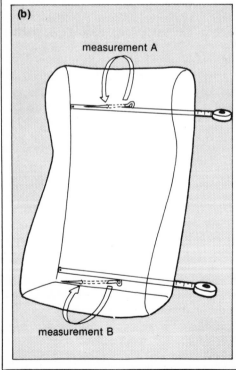

(b)

measurement A

measurement B

first stuffing with large loop stitches, like those you would use for top stuffing ties.

Place another thin layer of felt over this, then, to give a final smooth, rich feel to the surface, add a layer of 6mm (¼in) thick polyether foam. Stretch it tightly over. With this holding everything in place, you shouldn't need an undercover. The polyether sheeting, since it is very elastic, may be cut 50mm (2in) shorter than the measured width and length. It is best fixed with staples.

Covering the fireside chair You will need to thread your sewing machine with No.24 heavy cotton of a colour that will be unobtrusive against the colour of your material. A double-sided piping foot should be fitted to the machine. This is the one that can be made to slide from one side to the other, enabling you to sew piping on the right or left. For covering, let's choose a brocatelle with a pleasant pattern. Get an extra ¼m (10in) for pattern matching. This will be sufficient as there isn't a lot of matching to do. You will remember that I mentioned tapestry and the way the coloured threads forming the design are stripes running lengthwise on the reverse side. Well, with some brocatelle weaves, the stripes of colour run across the width, and this is an even greater help when cutting out.

Covering the inside back First measure the length of the inside back from under the bottom rail, up and over the top to the top rail. Allow 25mm (1in) at both ends. Make a rough drawing as at *(a)* in *fig.78* and write down the measurement on it.

The back is wider at the top than at the bottom, and it will be difficult to get an accurate measurement across the upholstered front. So measure across the frame at the back, marking the height at which you measure with a skewer pushed through the upholstery so that it shows at the front. Do this top and bottom *(b)*. Add on 40mm (about 1½in) to the width to allow for seams and the upholstery oversail.

Measure the distance from the point of the top skewer on the top fixing rail to the point where you originally measured the length.

Note this on your drawing. Do the same at the bottom. Now set out on the cloth the measurements you have on the drawing, marking with chalk. Look for a good balance in the position of the design, and make sure that the pattern is in the centre.

You may have difficulty finding the centre if you have one of those all-over patterns. So cut off the length required just to the half width of the material, as the width of the back requires no more than 63.5cm (25in).

The design on most fabrics repeats itself twice across the width, so by centering your cut on the half width you will have the pattern centred as the designer intended.

Mark the length of material with all the different cuts *(see fig.79)*. From this you will be able to see how best to lay everything out.

Would it not be much simpler to use the old covering as a template and cut to this? I don't recommend this because it is difficult to define the exact size since the edges are in a frayed condition and the cloth is sure to have stretched over the years. Also, any

cutting done slightly out of true by the previous upholsterer will most likely be accentuated if you attempt to follow the same shape.

Lay the cut piece of cloth over the back and see if it looks right. You will have to trim the two sides parallel at the top where they go over the scroll. Now return to the cutting table and take the half-width piece that is left on the roll. From this you can cut the outside back, so measure the length needed, cut it off, roll it up and put it to one side.

You now need pieces for the side facing panels or scrolls of the back. I will explain how to cut these so that the pattern will be the same on both -- not that it's possible for anyone to see both sides at once, but an expert will be very discerning, so we had better get it right!

Measure the length from the top of the scroll to the bottom of the side seat rail. Then measure the width at the widest place. Add 40mm (about 1½in) to the length and 50mm (2in) to the width to allow for

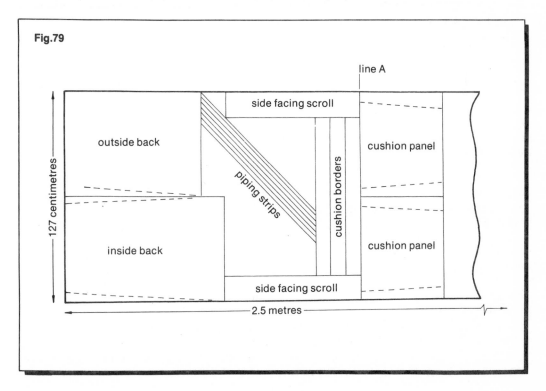

Fig.79

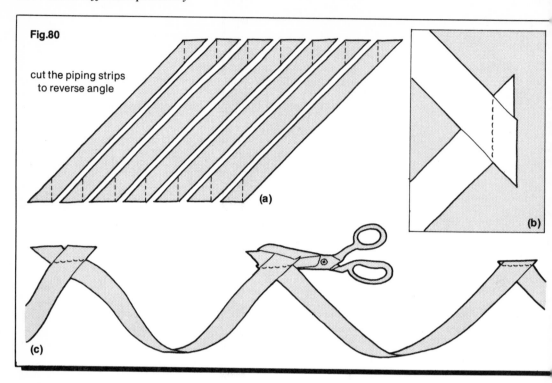

Fig.80

cut the piping strips to reverse angle

(a)

(b)

(c)

turnings. There was an odd piece left on the roll of material after you had cut the outside back. Leave this on because, as you see in the plan, it will give extra length to the strips you will be cutting to make piping. At each edge of the material mark out the pieces needed for the side facing scrolls, as in the plan, and cut out. You can cut right across the width above these pieces, along line A on the plan.

You now need some piping, but before you cut strips to make this, cut the pieces for the cushion border. Your new cushion interior is 100mm (4in) thick, but to give tension to the cover make the cushion cover border 90mm (3½in). To this measurement add 20mm (¾in) to allow for seams, so that the width of the strips to cut off is 110mm (just over 4¼in).

In the plan you can see from where the border pieces are cut. I have made no allowance in the plan for pattern matching or following through but have just shown how the cuts can be made with the minimum of waste. But on a material with a pronounced repeated pattern, the cuts drawn on the plan must be expanded to achieve the necessary follow through.

The term follow through refers to the unbroken design that continues from the front border of the cushion the length of the cushion and up the inside back. To achieve this you may even have to alter the order of cutting as well as space out the pieces.

Making up piping   Mark out the strips for the piping diagonally – roughly 45 degrees to the weave so that lengths of about 1m (about 1yd) can be obtained. The strips should be 38mm (1½in) wide when using No.1 or No.2 piping cord. Thicker or thinner cords will need correspondingly wider or narrower strips to give the required flange to the piping.

Note the direction in which the piping strips are marked on the plan. They should always be cut obliquely, from bottom left to top right of the fabric, to give a good even shape to the piping when stitched. This is

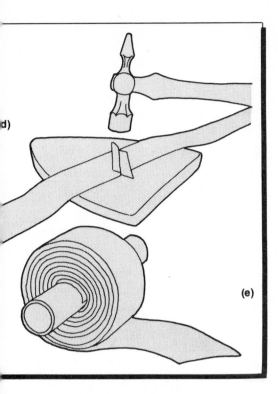

(d)

(e)

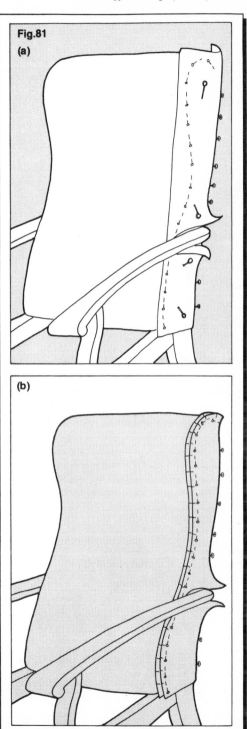

Fig.81

(a)

(b)

because in most fabrics the more robust threads run across the width. And these put up more resistance against the drag under the foot of the sewing-machine.

This rule applies if the piping is to the left of the machine foot when being made up. Anyway, try it for yourself, and you will find that piping cut in the opposite way will result in the material, when machined, being tightened around the piping cord. The piping produced will not look so neat and even.

When six or seven strips have been cut, join them to make one long length (*see fig.80*). The joins must show as little as possible – so this is what you do. The end of each strip is at an oblique angle. Cut each of these to reverse the angle (*a*), because most cloths join better along the lengthwise threads than across the width. Pile up the strips of cloth, one on top of the other, keeping them in order of cutting and all the same way.

Now stitch them together on the sewing machine (*b*). There is no need to cut the

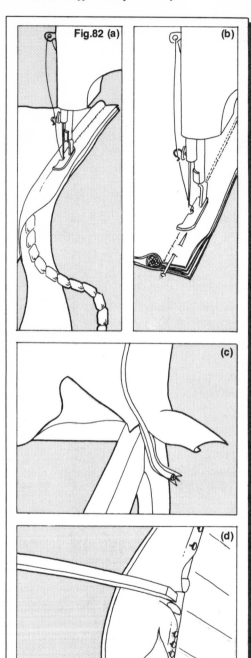

Fig.82 (a)   (b)

(c)

(d)

cottons; just carry on from one join to the next, and when they are all sewn just snip through the cottons between each join *(c)*. Trim the flanges on each join to half their width and flatten each seam by placing the piping on a clean hardwood block or piece of flat iron, then tapping with a broad-faced hammer *(d)*. Alternatively, you can press them with a hot iron and damp cloth. Roll the strip on a tube to keep it tidy and manageable *(e)*.

Back to the chair again, adjust the inside back covering to get it into the correct position, stretch it and fix top and bottom with skewers. Take one of the pieces of cloth intended for the side facing scrolls and fix it against the scroll in the required position with two or three skewers. The material should be right side out.

Pin the intended seam around the side scroll shape as at *(a)* in *fig.81*. Trim back the side facing material to the edge of the inside back material *(b)*. In this diagram you can also see how to mark, with your fibre-tipped pen, positioning lines on the seam flanges about 50mm (2in) apart. The lines on the facing scroll and the inside back edges should be exactly opposite each other. The marks at each end of the scroll should be boldly marked.

Now remove all pins and skewers and take off the two pieces of material. Lay the side facing scroll which you have shaped face to face on top of the corresponding piece that you have cut. Mark around with chalk or felt pen and cut out. Before you remove the top piece, mark the other scroll with positioning lines corresponding with those drawn on the scroll piece at the top.

Take the inside back panel and fold in half lengthwise, then put positioning marks opposite those made on the previously pinned edge. Transfer this panel to your sewing-machine together with the piping strip and piping cord *(see fig.82)*. Set the machine to a long stitch, then make up and sew the piping down each side edge *(a)*. Leave a good length of piping top and bottom.

Now fasten the two side facing scrolls

with pins, using the positioning marks you made to get them in the right place. It may seem unduly fussy to tell you which way to put in the pins, but if they are badly placed you will have difficulty removing them when you are machining.

So, with the back of the inside back panel facing you and the seam to be pinned to your right, push the pins in so that the heads are towards you. When both sides are pinned, set the machine for a smaller stitch and sew from this same side *(b)*. Follow a trifle inside the first line of stitches, holding the piping.

All you have to do now is stretch the made-up cover over the back upholstery, making sure that the seam flanges inside are lying the same way along the entire length. I like to lay them outwards around the scroll facings. This makes the piping stand up well. The only tricky part is where you have to cut and fold around the arms and seat rails. But if you stretch and temporarily tack both top and bottom, then study drawings *(c)* and *(d)*, I think you will manage to get over these difficulties. The fabric must be folded in and neatened off when finishing under the bottom rail.

Covering the outside back Find the piece you cut for covering the outside back. This can be fixed along the top by what is known as back-tacking *(see fig.83)*. After making sure that the top of the material is at the top of the chair, throw the material over the top of the back *(a)*. Centre the design and drive home three provisional tacks as shown.

Cut a strip of cardboard, tape or webbing 20mm (¾in) wide and long enough to reach across and tack against the fabric *(b)*. The tacks should be about 20mm (¾in) apart. Some 13mm (½in) fine tacks will probably do with our thickness of material. Return the fabric so that it now hangs down over the back, and if you have been careful to follow the weave while back-tacking and you have kept the line of tacks parallel with the top rail edge you should have a beautifully neat join.

Stretch the fabric and temporarily fasten beneath the bottom back rail, starting at the

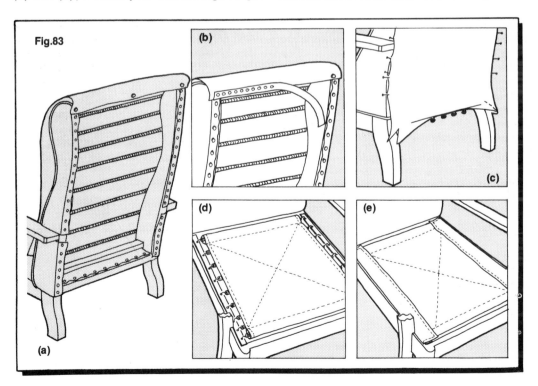

Fig.83

centre and working towards the corners. Cut into the legs *(c)*, then fold down the side seams and pin as illustrated. The material can now be turned in, neatened off and tacked permanently beneath the back bottom rail and the two side seams ladder stitched.

Making a seat quilt The next job is to make up the spring quilt I mentioned earlier, so put back the tension springs so that you can take a couple of measurements.

First, measure and note the width across the seat at the front spring, between the spring fixing plates. Likewise measure the width at the position of the back spring. It's best to make a drawing of the shape.

Second, measure the length from the back to the front springs and mark it on the drawing. Transfer these measurements to your fairly stout calico, adding 10mm (⅜in) to each side and 70mm (2¾in) to the front and back. Cut two pieces to this size and shape. Cut a piece of 6mm (¼in) polyether foam to the exact size of your drawing.

Put the two pieces of calico together and seam down each side on the sewing-machine. The lines of stitches should be 10mm (⅜in) in from the edges. Turn this open-ended bag the right side out, and lay the piece of foam inside, equi-distant from the ends. Sew a row of stitches 20mm (¾in) in from each side to hold the foam in place, then lay the quilt over the springs. Mark the calico back and front to the springs to give the exact length to which to hem. Fold over a wide hem front and back, allowing at least 31mm (1¼in) from edge to stitches.

Stitch along the two hems, finishing off neatly with returned stitches. If you want to, you can quilt the centre by drawing very light pencil lines across to form a diamond pattern which you can follow with stitches. The finished quilt should look like *(d)*.

Remove the back and front springs and thread them through the hems in the quilt. Hook on the springs and you will have a strong protective quilt which will prevent the springs from making nasty marks across the underside of the cushion.

May I suggest, as you have plenty of material, that you make two flange pieces? These can be fixed to the top edges of the side rails and will extend over the spring fixings to overlap the quilt *(e)*. These need only be hemmed on three sides, then back-tacked just clear of the outside edge of the side rails. They will give protection against wear between the cushion and the exposed metal fixings.

Making the cushion It is best to prepare the cushion interior first. The piece of block foam you purchased will have to be cut to size. I always find the best way to produce a well-fitting cushion is to make a template of the seat by laying a piece of fairly thick brown paper over the frame and marking all round. By doing this you can get the exact size and the precise shape of the back upholstery which, as you see on our chair, is slightly convex.

The cushion needs to extend over the front seat rail by about 38mm (1½in), so allow for this when cutting your template. After cutting and fitting the template to the curved shape of the back upholstery, fold it in half lengthwise and compare the curve when folded. Trim back any discrepancy to give a uniform shape, for you will want your cushion to fit whichever side is uppermost.

Lay the template on the foam block and mark around it with a felt pen, keeping 10mm (⅜in) outside the size all round. Cut along these lines with a fine-tooth panel saw, being sure to keep the saw at right angles to the surface and at a shallow angle. Put light cutting pressure to the strokes, and you will be surprised how easily and neatly it cuts.

The interior must be fastened to the cushion cover at both front edges. To do this glue strips of calico or thin binding along the edges of the foam *(see fig.84)*. Cut two strips of calico about 60mm (2⅜in) wide and long enough to go across the front of the interior. Coat them with impact adhesive mentioned previously in the chapter on Fixing and Fastening, page 91. Also coat the top and bottom edges of the front of the foam to a width of 30mm (about 1¼in) back from the edge and 30mm (about 1¼in) from the edge down the front.

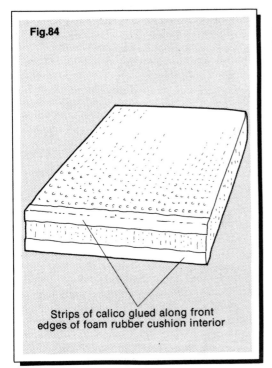

Fig.84

Strips of calico glued along front
edges of foam rubber cushion interior

edge of the template is straight with the weave and that the back edge is 10mm (⅜in) from the skewer. Place a skewer in each corner to prevent the template moving and mark around it with chalk – keeping 10mm (⅜in) larger than the template all round. Do the same for the second cushion panel on the other half width, and cut them out.

Piping can now be made around the four sides of these panels – as you did on the inside back cover – except that here you have corners to negotiate. Also, when the circuit is complete, a join in the piping must be made. So begin stitching at the centre of the right-hand side. Then you won't have a piping join on the front edge – which is something you must always avoid.

When you get within 50mm (2in) of the corner, lay the piping strip and cord along to the corner and make a small nick 10mm (⅜in) from the approaching edge (*see fig.85*). This will enable you to make a nice sharp corner as you turn the work to pipe the next side.

When you have piped all round and are approaching the place where you started, stop within 100mm (4in) of this point and disengage the work from the machine. Lay the material flat, then cut the piping cord so that the ends butt. Next, cut back the piping strip ends so that they overlap 20mm (¾in). The line of cut should be at an angle of 45 degrees, like the other joins. Stitch up the join and treat it as you did the others, making it as flat and inconspicuous as possible. Then stitch down the remaining portion of piping. The same applies to the other panel. When it is complete, turn to the border pieces.

Since we have cut off three, it would be very unlucky if we could not find one of these with a design following on from the cushion panel. If none is near enough, there is still enough material from which to cut another border piece that does follow.

When you have selected a suitable piece, stitch on the other border strips, one at each end. With a pronounced pattern, you would have to cut all the border pieces so that they match at the joins. But with our all-over

Leave for a minute or so until the adhesive becomes touch-dry, then lay the tape over the edges and press firmly. You will then have two angled, taped edges to which the cushion cover can be sewn – but more about that later. Put the interior to one side to dry while you get on with the cover.

Lay out the remainder of your covering material – and this is where you need to concentrate, for you have to get the pattern of the material on the cushion matching on from the inside back. The cushion will have a finished thickness of 90mm (3½in), so mark the height to which this will come with a skewer pushed into the inside back. Now you can see where the design is at that point. Next, turn to your material and find the nearest corresponding place in the design at the top end of the fabric, and mark this with another skewer.

This is where your template is useful again. Lay this on the material and position it so that its centrefold is in the exact centre of the half width. Also ensure that the front

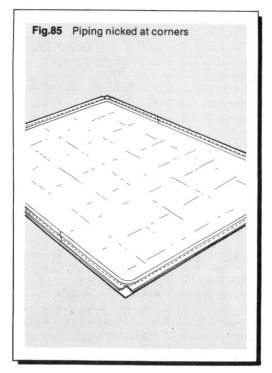

Fig.85 Piping nicked at corners

design this is not necessary. Find the exact centre of the design in the border that will be at the front and the centre of the front edge of the cushion panel and mark them.

Now place the two marks together so that you have the top of the design on the front border to the top panel, and start pinning from the centre marks. Fix the pins on the panel side, heads to the right if the panel side is facing you. When you come to a corner, make a small nick in the border edge so that you can turn the corner tightly.

There will be three joins in the border, and the two you have already stitched will occur each side of the cushion. Make the third at the centre of the back. You can stitch this when you have completed the pinning. If you cut the borders from the full width of the material, two pieces will reach completely round, so there will only be two joins.

Sew the border in exactly the same way as when attaching the inside back to the side facings. Put on the other side panel next. At the angle of each corner follow a thread up from the already sewn edge and nick the other edge of the border. Start by pinning all four corners, then, keeping the seam stretched between these pins, secure with pins each side except the back. Leave an opening to get the interior in. Leave the whole of the back edge unstitched, plus 90mm (about 3½in) at each side.

When you have finished stitching, turn the case the right side out and examine the piped edges all the way round to see that all is correct. Then turn inside out once again, for something must be done to the seam flanges or they will fray quickly. If you have a sewing-machine that does a zig-zag stitch, this is ideal to selvedge the flanges. If you don't have one, a line of stitches a fraction from the edge is the next best treatment.

The opening at the back must not be missed. In particular, if the fabric is loosely woven, the border edge should be turned over once and hemmed. Also, the piping at the mouth of the cover must have an extra line of small stitches machined along. This will tighten the piping so that it corresponds with the rest.

Don't turn the cover to the right side, because we now have to attach the foam interior *(see fig.86)*. The illustration shows the position of the front border against the cushion interior front. Note how the seam flanges are turned in to lay down the border. Securing is done with large ladder stitches, the two ends being fixed temporarily with skewers.

The stitches go through the calico strip we glued to the foam, 3mm (⅛in) down from the edge and the same distance from the piping stitches in the cover.

When this job is complete, pull the cover over itself – as if you were putting on a sock. Adjust all the seam flanges so that they lay down the border, making the piping stand up well. A fair bit of adjusting, with your hand inside the cushion, will have to be made to ensure that the interior is correctly placed. Then close the opening with skewers and ladder stitch together with small stitches. Place the cushion on the chair seat, where it should be a perfect fit. Our chair is now

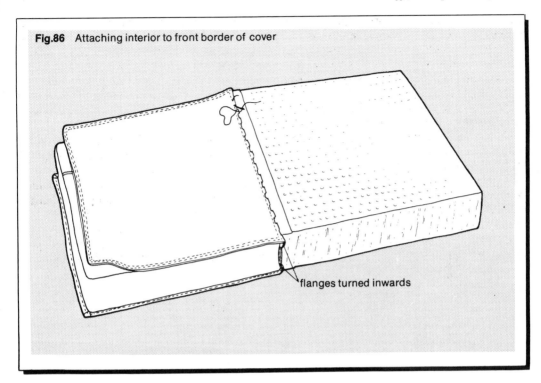

Fig.86 Attaching interior to front border of cover

flanges turned inwards

finished and ready for use again.

OTHER FIRESIDE CHAIRS

Let's consider some fireside chairs which have slight differences.

The back upholstery in many is composed of moulded rubber foam which, if perished, can be easily replaced with new plastic or rubber foam. This is a much simpler job than back upholstery. The other differences are in the spring arrangements, of which there are several.

Some makers of good fireside chairs have perfected a spider's web principle, in which the tension springs radiate out from a central ring to the seat frame. In other seats, they fan out from fixings at the four corners of the frame and are linked with small rings, short springs and metal spacers. Both of these systems are excellent and long-lasting, and they will remain in good condition despite changes of covering.

In recent years we have seen the advent of rubber webbing, which manufacturers have brought in as a substitute for metal springs. This can be used under the back upholstery as well as for seats. So long as an adequate number of webbing straps is used, it makes for a very comfortable seat. The best chairs have webbing straps with metal ends which fit into slots in the seat rails. You can make up new pieces by buying rubber webbing and fixing plates for clips.

Before cutting off the lengths, you must allow for stretching to give the required tension. The following rules apply. The straps should be 25mm shorter than the distance between frames, up to 300mm. If the length is over 300mm, they must be shorter by 20mm in every 300mm. In Imperial measure, the straps should be shorter by 1in for every 1ft; if the length is over 2ft, they must be shorter by ¾in to every 1ft. These rules may vary with the thickness of the rubber webbing.

The end clips must be very securely clamped to the webbing by squeezing them up in an engineers' metal-working vice.

Then hammer down on a piece of thick iron plate so that the metal clips grip the rubber.

In chair backs the webbing is sometimes narrower in width. This can be fixed with large-headed tacks or by two lines of staples from a staple gun.

Cushions vary in form and design, but I think our box cushion is the best for keeping its shape. Some cushions may be piped only at the sides, giving a rounded 'bible edge' to the front and back. Others are piped at the front only, accentuating the rectangle of the front border, while many modern cushions, and indeed whole chairs, have no piped seams at all – especially when the covering material is tweed or similar heavy, loosely-woven material.

There are many cushion interiors. Early fireside chairs had ready-made spring interiors stuffed with cotton felt. Polyether and rubber foam we know about, but today super-soft cushions are made with a core of plastic foam wrapped around with layers of acrylic fibre wool. These are usually buttoned through to hold them together.

Fireside chairs come in many designs. Some have wings; others have fully upholstered arms, covered arm panels or just elbow pads on top of the arms. Seat frames are sometimes covered, with padded edges made at the front of the seats. But now you have done some modern upholstery, I'm sure you will be able to tackle most jobs involving modern upholstered furniture.

Advanced upholstery

RE-UPHOLSTERING A WING EASY CHAIR

Before we start on our Victorian spoonback chair, I feel one more step is needed. And for this step I have in mind an easy chair made between about 1900 and 1910, with scroll arms, wings and a cushioned seat with a sprung edge to it *(see fig.87)*. If you look in many furniture shops now, you will see new chairs fitting this description, for the style has been revived and is becoming popular again. Your guess is as good as mine as to what lies beneath the beautifully-shaped exteriors of these new chairs, but the betting is that they don't have nearly such robust frames as their earlier counter-parts. Well, they need not have, for the seats are fitted with spring units, rubber webbing or ripple wire springs. With these, the strain on the frame is nowhere near as great as that placed on it by traditional upholstery. Don't get the idea that I'm knocking the modern upholsterer, because, for comfort, this upholstery excels. But for how long? – that is the important question.

Assuming we've found a suitable wing easy chair, let's see if we can re-cover it with a leathercloth that looks like real leather. I'm sure you will be able to do it – and with a few modifications the chair will look superb in imitation leather.

Materials needed First, measure for the leathercloth, remembering it is usually 137cm (54in) wide. Shall we retain the feather-cushioned seat? Feather-filled cushions are very comfortable, but they need constant plumping up after being sat on to keep them looking tidy. You would also have to make the cover from a matching fabric such as velvet or velour.

The alternatives to feathers are foam rubber or plastic foam. I would try making the feather cushion, since you have already made a cushion with a foam interior. It is possible to make a cushion in leathercloth, but not with a feather interior. You would have to use a firm foam, and the cushion cover has to be well ventilated to allow air to escape quickly when sat on – so it doesn't make peculiar noises! I've had some funny experiences with cushions like this. So, we will use a fabric.

You will need the usual things – webbing, springs, hessian, cotton felt or wadding,

Fig.87 A wing easy chair

twines and cords. For making piping from leathercloth, try to get some of the smooth 'paper' piping cord, which makes a smooth even piping. If you can't get this, cotton piping cord will do. This should be 4-5mm (about $1/s$in) thick.

There are several kinds of artificial leather on the market. Pvc is usually quite thick and comprises a layer of stockingette cotton fabric as a backing and a thin layer of foam with leather-grained pvc. This is now made flame-retardent and can also be obtained in a lightweight version, known as back-up cloth. It has the same colour, grain and texture and is used for outside panels, button-making and so on. A thinner leathercloth is made of polyurethane, which is very tough. It really is exciting to see the marvellous range of colours and textures now available in artificial leathers.

When you buy the leathercloth, try to get a quantity of leather-covered studs of the same colour. Bear in mind that, although it is possible to ladder stitch this cloth, joining the outside seams on the chair is best done by securing with rows of studs. You may prefer to use brass-headed chair nails, but that's up to you.

Choose a good hard-wearing fabric for the cushion. Velvet or velour are the usual materials used in conjunction with leather. The velvets made from man-made fibres are also very good and are easy to keep clean. Be prepared to pay a high price for this (luckily you need only about a metre), and make sure that it is furnishing-weight and not a thinner curtain velvet.

You will have to make a new feather-proof interior for the cushion. For this buy a metre of good quality waxed cambric. For the part of the seat beneath the cushion use a platform cloth, which is a stout cotton lining material. Get a metre of light brown to match the leather.

Just one other thing; try and get some off-cuts of 3mm ($1/s$in) plywood. Four pieces about 610 × 17mm (2 × 6in) will do, and I'll tell you what these are for later on.

I think it will be wise to strip the chair to the bare frame. True, the arm, back and wing upholstery are in good shape, but I think you should take it all off, especially now that you have decided to use leathercloth, for this needs really firm foundations, particularly at the edges. So, do the ripping, frame repairs if necessary, and renovate and repolish the front 'bun' feet and the small back legs.

When you take out the seat, note the way in which the front edge (called the spring edge) is built up. Note also the various stitched roll edges and where they occur.

Webbing the back and arms Well, there is the bare frame *(see fig.88)*. The repairs included new corner glue blocks between the bottom rails and soaking the whole frame with woodworm destroyer. So, with the materials ready and the tools laid out, start by webbing up the frame to support both the springs in the back and the arm stuffings. The drawings will help you.

When re-upholstering a frame like this, try constantly to visualise the rough height that the seat will be when it is finished – especially when working on the back upholstery. A well-shaped back will bulge out near the bottom into what we term a 'lumbar swell' which, as the name implies, should be made to fit the small of the back of a seated person.

To form this swell, larger and stronger springs are used. And to support these springs, two strips of webbing, close together, are tacked and stretched across the back frame *(a)*. This illustration shows a view of the back of the chair, and you can see the position of the webbing and roughly how far above the tacking rail it is placed. Work out the height of the seat and the position of the back swell by sitting in another chair, noting whether the height of the seat and the shape of the back are comfortable and, if not, where improvements could be made. From this test, transfer your findings to the chair frame you are working on. You will be governed a little by the position of the seat tacking rails.

Put all the lateral webbing on the outside back first, then the pieces lengthwise from top to bottom. Note how at *(a)* these are tacked top and bottom to the front side of the frame. They are not woven in and out of the cross pieces but all run behind so that when tightened they bring the cross pieces forward slightly. The reason for this is that it prevents the webbing becoming loose after some use, bulging out at the back and distorting the outside back covering. This would certainly occur if all the webbing were fixed to the back of the frame.

The other places that need webbing can be seen at *(b)*: first, on the wings, 25mm (1in) from where the wing frame joins the back and continuing at the same distance down over the arm spaces to the side tacking rails; and, second, to strengthen the inside arm hessian, one strip vertically in the centre of the space.

Springing the back and arms Don't be tempted to do the seat frame now. Leave it until later, because keeping the space open will give you good access when you are upholstering and covering the back and the arms. With easy chairs, the seat is the last upholstered part to be built in.

Sort out the back springs next. You can re-use the ones you took out if they are in good condition. They don't get the punishment that seat springs receive. The three largest springs will be fixed on the double webbing where you want the swell to be. And the smaller, softer, springs are spaced out above these *(c)*.

It is not necessary to lace the springs. It is quite satisfactory to stretch over the heavy hessian, temporarily tacking it and, through the spaces between the webbing on the outside back, adjust the springs until you are happy with their position. One way to test whether the shape is good is to place a small stool at roughly the seat height inside the frame. Pack it up as necessary. Sit on this and lean back to see if the contours of the springs fit your back. I haven't mentioned the fixing of the springs, but you know about this from previous experience.

You need new springs for the arms as the old ones are all shapes. They need to be soft – about 100-125mm (4-5in) high and 14 gauge. Harder springs will defeat the object

– which is to give buoyant support to the modest weight of one's arm. At *(d)* you can see how the arm springs are placed, fixed to the arm spring platform with a strip of webbing tacked over the base of each spring. Alternatively, use 20mm (¾in) wire staples, three or four to a spring.

There are two ways in which to pull down the springs to their correct height. At *(d)* you can see how a length of webbing is stretched over the springs from back to front. The springs are fastened with twine, four stitches per spring top. The other way is to lace them with laid cord from back to front in the manner with which you are now quite familiar.

At *(e)* you can see how the whole arm is covered with hessian so that the springs are completely boxed in. The hessian extends (sometimes as a separate piece) over the open space of the frame below the spring platform, and, again, the springs are fixed at the top with stitches through the hessian.

The two remaining spaces – those of the wing frames – must be stretched over with hessian *(f)*. This is tacked on the inside of the frame and sewn down to the webbing at the back, leaving a space between the webbing and the back upright. Its purpose will become clear later on. Also, leave the bottom unfastened.

First stuffings The most difficult first stuffing is that on the arms, so let's begin with these.

Put in some stuffing ties, in lines from back to front, along the arm – one line on each side of the 'spring box' and another along the top, then one line near the centre of the area below the springs and another near the bottom tacking rail.

Carry out each stage on both arms so that eventually you get both to the same size. Now put some short, loose loops as stuffing ties all around the wooden scroll fronts, about 20mm (¾in) in from the front. This is where you begin with your stuffing.

We have some very short horsehair, or pig hair as we call it, which came out of the chair. Let us assume we took it along to a local upholsterer and got it carded. As this hair is in very short strands it will be all the better for building up the edges, as these need to be pretty firm to support the leathercloth.

Take a good look at the chair frame and get a mental picture of the shape you want the arms to be when they are finished. The wooden arm fronts give a rough guide to the finished shape, so if you reckon on building out the stitched edges to about 50mm (2in) larger than the timber shape you won't be far out – although keeping rigidly to this distance would give a rather uninteresting curve to the scroll. You can improve this artistically by tightening in the top and bottom of the scroll line *(g)*.

Tuck some horsehair under the stuffing ties around the wooden arm fronts to make a dense, tight wall, to about 60mm (2¼in) out from the woodwork. You will remember that you have done this before on straight edges. Spend time getting both arm fronts the same shape. Horsehair is placed quite firmly under all the other stuffing ties in lines of hair along the outsides of the arms; it should decrease in thickness towards the back. Fill up the empty spaces in between with hair, and make sure that it is all even, with both arms the same shape and density.

Now cover the arms with 202 or 283g (7½ or 10oz) hessian. To get both arms the same size, with the same curve to the scroll, cut off both pieces of hessian to exactly the same size. Then, when they are put on, by noting the exact amount taken up for turnings top and bottom and by tacking the hessian to exactly the corresponding place on the frame, you will ensure that the outside periphery of each arm is the same. And that's half the battle!

Of course, the character of the scrolls can differ within these confines, so you must rely on your eye, plus a few measurements taken across the scroll at various points, to get both of them looking the same. But leave the front for the moment after fixing both ends of each scroll with single tacks and turn your attention to the backs of the arms.

You can see at *(h)* how to cut the hessian to fit into the wing uprights – into the tacking

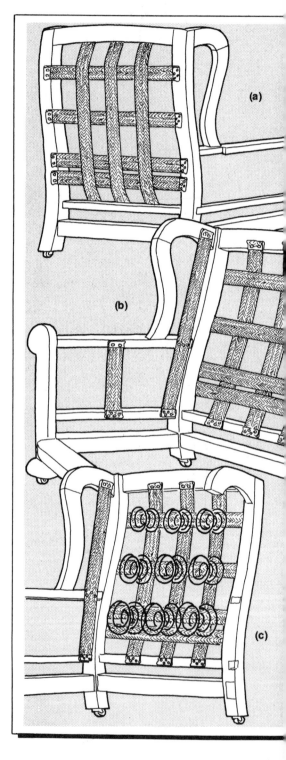

(a)

(b)

(c)

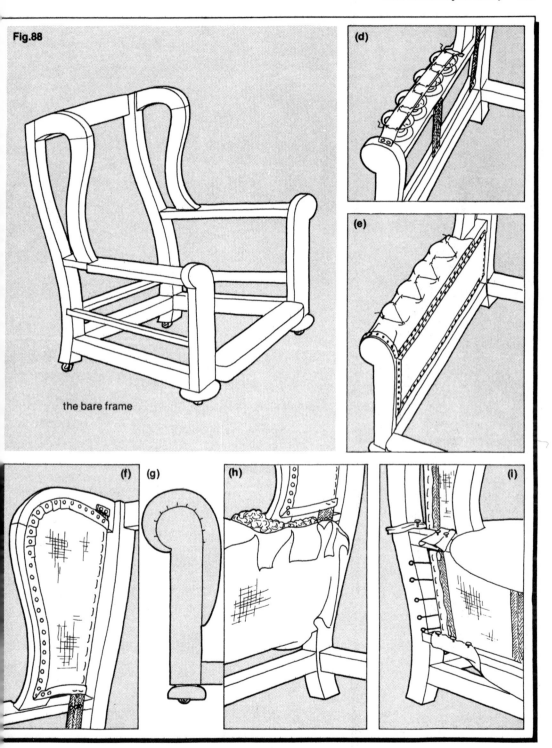

Fig.88

(d)

(e)

(f)

(g)

(h)

(i)

the bare frame

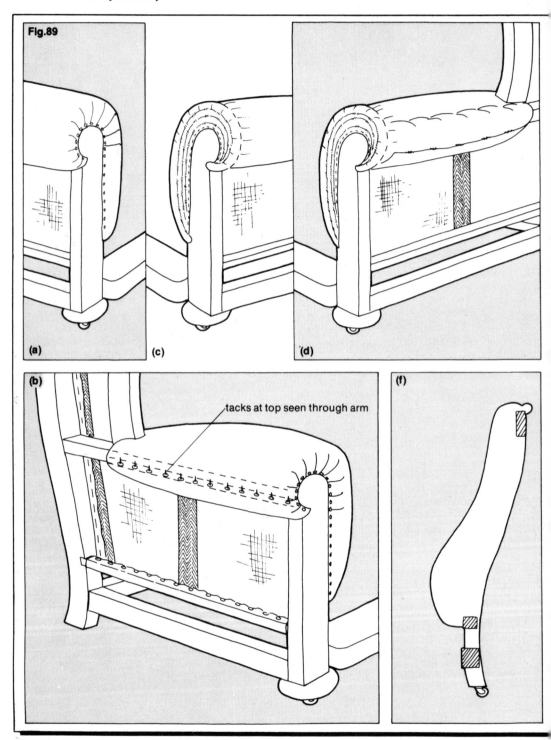

Fig.89

(a)

(b)

tacks at top seen through arm

(c)

(d)

(f)

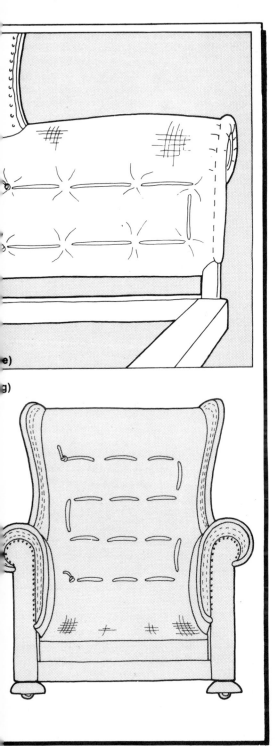

gap in the side next to the back upright and around the bottom tacking rail. Temporarily tack and skewer *(i)* and adjust until you are sure that the hessian weave is straight. Then hammer home all the tacks at the back and sew the hessian through and through with twine, fixing it to the vertical webbing next to the back upright, thus leaving the gap open.

Now return to the fronts of the arms *(see fig.89)*. Around the woodwork there should be the usual chamfer on to which you can tack. Mark with a pronounced dot the centre of radius of the top curve of the wooden scroll, then begin pleating and tacking from the top centre *(a)*. Make straight threaded pleats, all pointing in the direction of the centre dot. And do the pleating on both scrolls to get them the same. Now fasten the hessian along the tacking rail at the bottom and along the top beneath the roll-over of the arm *(b)* as well.

At *(c)* and *(d)* you see an arm stitched up with a roll edge around the scroll – a large roll along the outside and 'through' stuffing ties on the inside *(e)*. The large side roll is made without previously placed blind stitches, and its purpose is to keep the stuffing from moving down to the bottom of the arm roll and to provide a line of foundation for support and shape to the length of the arm.

A first stuffing on the inside back is the next task, so put lines of stuffing tie loops across the spring hessian. As you need a stitched roll along the top, the ties here should be as near to the top edge as possible. This is because the roll needs to over-sail the outside back. I suggest you lay the chair on its back to put on this first stuffing. And remember to put plenty of hair over the area that will form the 'lumbar swell', graduating it down in thickness as you proceed to the top of the back.

The hessian covering this will not be stretched too much vertically, but it should be tightened from side to side so that contours something like those seen at *(f)* are made. You can now see the purpose of the gaps made by the vertical webbing at the back of the wings and arms, for it is through these gaps that all the fixings for the back have to be made.

Regulate the stuffing at the top to form a pronounced lip, over-sailing the top rail – also seen at *(f)*. Put in one row of blind stitches, then stitch a roll edge. After putting in through stuffing ties *(g)*, you can move on to the wings.

The wings don't need to have an all-over stuffing at this stage. Instead, build on an edge by sewing a strip of hessian around the shape of the wing. This is tacked to form a sort of sausage containing hair on to which you can make a stitched roll edge. Leave the centre of the wing hollow; subsequently it will be filled by top stuffing. You will see what I am describing if you look at the illustration *(see fig.90)*.

At *(a)* a line is marked about 75-100mm (3-4in) in from the outside edge of the wing, to which a strip of 283g (10oz) hessian about 200mm (8in) wide is sewn. Note at *(b)* how the strip is pleated around the curve. In diagrams *(c)* to *(f)* stuffing ties and hair are put in place and the hessian is drawn over and tacked on the outside. This forms the edge, which is then stitched with one row blind and a row of edge stitches.

The edges of the wings should join up to the roll edge of the back to form a continuous lip.

The second or top stuffing Now it is time to put the top stuffing on to the arms, back and wings – and for this we need something better than the short pig hair we have been using. We will assume you have acquired an old hair mattress which can be pulled apart. Take the hair down to an upholsterer to get him to card it. The white hair from the mattress is like gold dust. It really is beautiful hair and you already know what to do, so carry on.

Just a tip or two about these particular top stuffings. First, to help with the very important task of getting both arms the same size, weigh the amounts of hair to gauge the exact amount to be used for each arm. Use a small spring balance for this job, placing the stuffing in a bag, sack or square piece of cloth which you can tie up at each of the four corners.

When the time comes, you can weigh the hair for the wings too. But stuff up the arms first and get them covered before putting on the back and wing stuffing. It is probably best to leave the wings until after the arms and back have been covered with leather.

Don't use too much top stuffing, for when covering with leathercloth you don't want the various parts to take on an inflated, bulbous look. Use just enough to fill up the indentations made by the through stuffing ties and edge valleys, plus an all-over layer of an inch or so. Cotton wadding is not essential as horsehair will not penetrate the leathercloth – but it would add richness.

A calico undercover is also optional, but whether you decide to use it or not I would recommend that you cover all parts with some of your 6mm (¼in) polyether foam. This will give a really marvellous appearance to the leather's surface. Soft leathercloth shows even the smallest lump or bump left underneath, so be very meticulous when applying all top stuffings so as to get them evenly distributed and free from tangled lumps and foreign matter.

If you do use calico for undercovering, there is just one point I would like to mention. This concerns fixing at the front of the arms around the scrolls. When covering arms with undercover or top cover, the rule is: secure at the back and stretch to the front before any stretching is done in the width. This will ensure a nice, straight, even shape.

So, secure the calico at the back after cutting into wings and corners, then stretch towards the front and fix with skewers just under the lip of the scroll roll edge *(see fig.91)*. Diagrams *(a)* and *(b)* will help you here. Stretch and secure at the top centre of the scroll, then at the outside extremity, stretching the calico tightly around the perimeter as well as pulling forward. Do the same at the bottom of the scroll, then stretch and fasten the calico all round the remainder of the scroll shape.

Do this on both arms, and only then should you tighten the calico over from

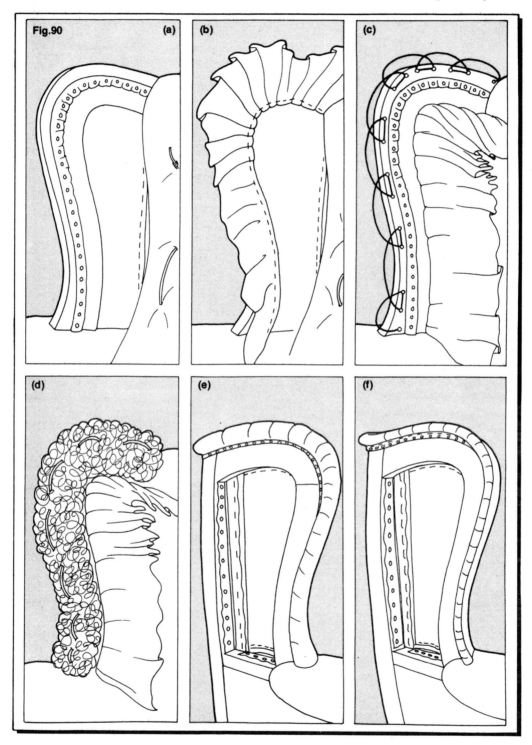

Fig.90 (a) (b) (c) (d) (e) (f)

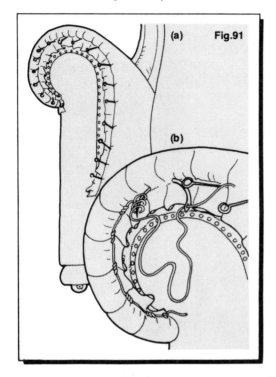

(a)   Fig.91

(b)

bottom to top. Begin at the bottom (the material passes right under the arm tacking rail and is fastened on the outside of this) and fasten at the front. Now work to the back and the same way at the top under the 'roll-over' of the arm.

Let me remind you how to stretch the fabric. Do this as you did when covering the loose seat – with strokes of your free hand while the other hand takes up the slack. Just tugging at the cloth will only cause unevenness. Much of tight cover work relies on touch, and as your free hand moves over the cloth you will be able to feel when it is correctly tensioned. So coax and caress those arms into a really good shape.

You may be wondering how the calico is fixed at the front scrolls. Do we tack it to the woodwork? You can tack it, but the better way is to sew it with blind stitches close under the lip of the roll edge. Have a look at (b) and you will see what I mean. You can use the straight double-pointed needle for this, but I would prefer you to try blind

stitching with a semi-circular needle. Your 150mm (6in) one will do, but you may need a smaller needle to sew around the tighter curve at the top of the scroll.

The same principle applies as with the straight needle. By inserting the circular needle so that the point emerges back along the row, you simulate the action of a straight needle being returned through the edge. The rule of three turns of the twine leading from the previous stitch around the needle is observed. At (b) you can see this at the end of the row of stitches.

The reason for sewing the calico into the underside of the roll edge is that it adds support to the edge. Also, with the calico fixed in this way, it will cause no impediment to the facing when it is fitted into the front of the scroll.

This method of fixing is also useful practice for future occasions, for it may well be that the next chair with scroll arms that you cover will be in woven fabric. Apart from the fact that you must make neater pleats around the edge, the same procedure applies as with your calico.

Top stuffing and undercovering the inside back presents no special problems. You will learn a lot about how to cut into the arm rails, tacking rails and wing top rails where they meet the back uprights by practising your cuts on the calico. It will not matter too much if the cuts are not in quite the right place. Fixings should be made on the back edge of the bottom tacking rail and at the sides on the front face of the back uprights, through the gap left between them and the vertical strips of webbing.

There is a crafty bit of cutting to be done at the two bottom corners. Stretch the calico and temporarily tack top to bottom to within 100mm (4in) of the corners, then turn it back on itself (see fig.92). Now cut so that a flap of material can be pulled through under the side tacking rails, a little distance out from the back upright. This gives a good tension to the base of the back covering. The other cuts are also shown in this diagram.

Covering arms, back and wings Don't try to undercover the wings but leave them until you have covered the arms and inside back with the leathercloth. So unroll the leathercloth and plan your cuts. But first let me tell you about the direction in which the cuts should run.

I mentioned previously the effect that the stockingette backing has on leathercloth – namely that you are able to stretch the material more in width than length. So you must note the places on your chair where most tension is needed, for this will be satisfied by the lengthwise application of material. For example, the leather on the arms needs to be most tightly stretched from back to front, while the tension around the arms is much less. Therefore the pieces for the arms are best cut so that the length of the material runs from back to front.

The leather for covering the back will run lengthwise from side to side, for then you will be able to create a smooth top edge and retain the curve of the swell. The front seat border and seat front should also run in this direction, but the wings may be cut with the length from top to bottom. All the outside panels can be cut with the material running in either direction – whichever way is most economical.

There is plenty of width to your leathercloth, so try to leave an entire length on one side of the piece from which you will be able to cut long strips for piping. This way there will be no need for joins. The last point to remember when measuring and cutting leathercloth is that it is going to stretch, so there is no need to allow too much for turnings. In the length of the arm, for example, I guess you will stretch the leather by more than 25mm (1in).

While drawing out a plan of the cuts and getting everything nicely sorted out, remember that if you were working on a more expensive covering material you could save on the amount required by using what are known as 'fly pieces'. These are strips of hessian, linen or similar strong cloth sewn to the bottoms of pieces cut for covering inside arms and the inside back, thus saving up to 150mm (6in) on a cut.

Now let's see how we get on working with leathercloth. Begin by covering the inside back, which I think you will find easy because it stretches so well. You can easily eliminate any fullness resulting from the convex shape of the back. I remember the early days when leathercloth was made of a coating of nitrocellulose on a tough cotton backing cloth. How we used to have to tug and pull, warm, persuade and force the material to assume the shape we needed!

Having put on a calico undercover, you are quite capable of succeeding with the leathercloth so long as you take care to cut in the right places. Get it temporarily fastened at the bottom and top, then, if you wish to refresh your memory as to the way to cut in to the various rails, look again at *fig.92*.

The four corners are the most important stretching points, for tightening from the corners will eliminate all fullness. Especial attention should be given to the top corners. Stretch up and out to give a smooth, pleat-free top edge. When you have satisfactorily fixed the inside back with temporary

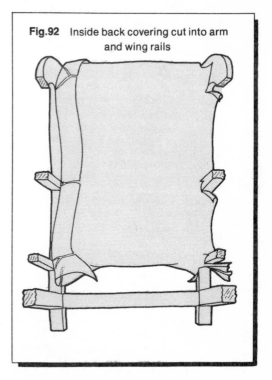

Fig.92 Inside back covering cut into arm and wing rails

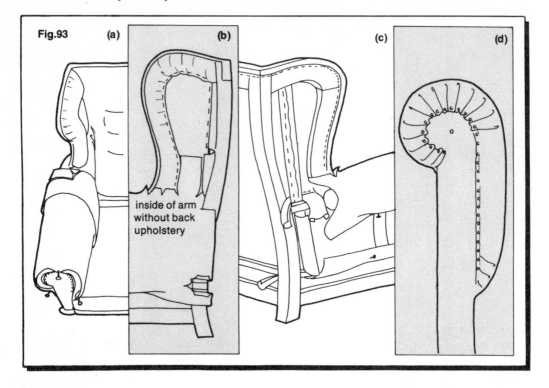

Fig.93   (a)   (b)   (c)   (d)

inside of arm
without back
upholstery

tacks, drive them home and start on the arms. I will give you a little more advice as you proceed with the work.

I will describe the work on a single arm, but you must operate on both arms together. Lay the piece of leather over the arm with the length from back to front. Position it so that there is enough to reach under the bottom tacking rail and so that it will go well under the roll of the arm. Also ensure that there is adequate back and front. Temporarily fix with three skewers at the front, pressed well in and near to the wood of the scroll *(see fig.93)*.

At *(a)* you will see how to make the tricky cut into the wing upright. Never make a cut until you have visualised just where and how the material will lie when cut. After the first cut has been made, fix temporarily at the far back of the outside of the arm, then stretch vertically down in line with this cut. Smooth the material out towards the inside back and carefully make two cuts – one at the rail along the bottom of the wing and the other at

the bottom tacking rail. Be very careful not to cut too far or the cuts will be visible.

At *(b)* and *(c)* you are shown how the bottom corner cut allows the leather to be pulled through at the back corner beneath the back tacking rail. This gives a good tension to the bottom of the arm. And it illustrates the final cuts at the wing upright and vertical webbing, made so that the covering can be taken through at the bottom of the wing and fixed there. You can now fasten all of the back edge of the arm cover permanently to the front face of the back upright.

Turn your attention to the front scroll. Having made a dot with a felt pen in the centre of the wooden scroll at the radius of the top curve, start at the outside extremity and stretch and pleat the leathercloth so that each pleat is aligned to the centre dot. Temporarily tack to the woodwork *(d)*.

Try to space the pleats evenly and take up a similar amount of material with each pleat, sharpening the folds by inserting the flat end of the regulator and drawing it up to the top of the pleats. The bottom and top of the arm can now be stretched and fixed, and then you can move on to the wings.

If you haven't already done so, put the stuffing on the wings. I don't think you need put on an undercover – just the cotton wadding over the hair and a layer of 16mm (¼in) foam stretched over them. Then get straight on with the leathercloth. A great deal of care is needed here, with very accurate 'cutting in' at the bottom of the wings where they meet the arms *(see fig.94)*.

Once you have the bottom cut and secured, stretch up to the top and cut into the top back corner. Fold the material above this so that a mitre is formed over the top at the junction of the wing and the inside back cover.

You will have to work around the 'ogee' curves of the wings several times, temporarily tacking, undoing and tacking again until the fullness is neatly pleated away. Try to get the top curves so that no pleats extend further than the outside planes of the edges. And, on the hollow curves facing the front, make cuts in from the edge of the leather so that it can be stretched tightly into the curve. As with the arm coverings, each process of stretching, tacking and cutting should be exactly duplicated on both wings. In this way you will ensure that they are the same shape as each other.

Building a spring edged seat Now we come to the job of re-building the seat. New webbing comes first, on the bottom of the rails. When the chair was stripped we noted that the webbing was quite closely woven, so I would put the pieces on about 50mm (2in) apart. Then we need six from back to front and six across from side to side. Since it is a large seat, it will need strong support for the springs, and these will be fixed in next. We have bought new ones, but we also need the shorter springs that go in the front row.

Here, this seat differs from any that we've done so far. The front four springs are independent of the rest and are not laced to the others. You will see why this is so later

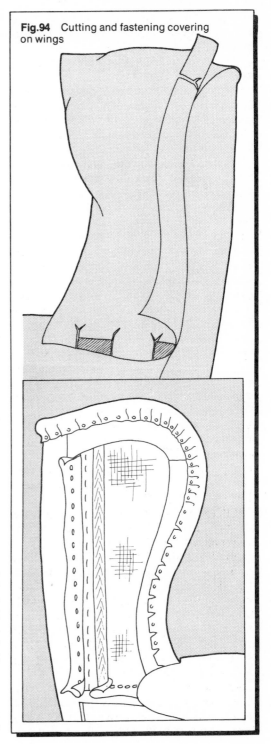

Fig.94 Cutting and fastening covering on wings

on. These springs should sit on the front rail with the knuckle of the bottom coil towards the back.

Fix these in place first. There are two ways of doing this. They may be secured with wire staples (four per spring) direct to the wide front rail of the chair, or they can be held in place by a strip of webbing tacked over the bottom coil of each spring. I have drawn this method *(see fig.95)*.

The larger main springs can be positioned in three rows of three. The front row has to lean forward to give that fanning-out effect; consequently, they must not be placed too close to the edge springs.

Because the chair is to have a platform seat to take a cushion, it needs to be reasonably flat, so the main springs must not be too high. A good guide to spring height is that they should stand, unlaced, about 25mm (1in) higher than the bottom arm tacking rails. When laced they should not be pulled down below this height, so that the tops of the springs will be kept level all over.

As the springs will be under very little tension from lacings or hessian, they should be of a stout gauge, and I would recommend No.9 gauge. The front edge springs, however, need to be laced down under considerable tension, and when pulled down into position they have to be level with the main springs. So these should, when still free, stand about 40mm (1½in) higher than the other seat springs. Their gauge is No.10.

With the springs in their proper place, we can talk about lacing and tying down, beginning with the edge springs *(a)*.

Cut off a couple of metres of laid cord and, starting with the spring on the right-hand side, tie a slip knot on to the back of the bottom coil where it overlaps the seat rail. Bring the cord up to the top of the spring and, after pulling it down to the required height, tie with a single half hitch. Now bring the cord to the front of the spring top and tie again with a half hitch *(b)*.

Hammer one of your 20mm (¾in) wire staples half-way home into the seat rail at dead centre of and below the spring. Thread the cord through the staple and pull down

the spring until its top is level, then drive the staple home and tie a half hitch around the taut cord to make it fast. Do the same with the spring on the left-hand side, but measure its height as you pull it down so that it is fixed at the exact height of the first spring. Exactly the same method applies to the two centre springs.

When we stripped the seat, we found a piece of cane fastened along the front of the spring tops, and if it is in good condition it can be used again. But if it is split or worn, use an edge wire instead. This can be made from an ordinary coil spring straightened by holding one end in the vice and unwinding it. Our piece of Malacca cane looks all right to me, so lay it along the spring tops. This has to be fixed to the springs as seen at *(b)* by whipping with twine – here I would refer you back to the chapter on Fixing and Fastening, page 88. The cane is bent at the two ends. Make sure that these ends are also well fastened to the springs.

To bring the springs forward a trifle and to help keep them there put small straps of webbing folded in half lengthwise threaded over the second or third coils from the bottom of each front spring *(c)*. These straps are pulled down and fastened with tacks in the form of inverted vees. Then, to brace the springs sideways, make a lacing with laid cord from side to side. Begin near the bottom of the left-hand spring, rising to near the top of the centre springs, and then move down to near the base of the spring on the right. The front edge finished to this stage is also shown at *(c)*.

Lace up the main springs, giving them the necessary 'fanning-out' but pulling them down very little. The cords are fastened at the front on the top of the front rail between the edge springs. Now measure the amount of tarpaulin hessian needed to cover the springs by placing your steel tape over the springs and extending beyond the back rail by 25mm (1in).

Push the tape down between the main springs and the front edge springs to a depth of 40mm (1½in) to allow length to form a well. I will tell you about this in a minute.

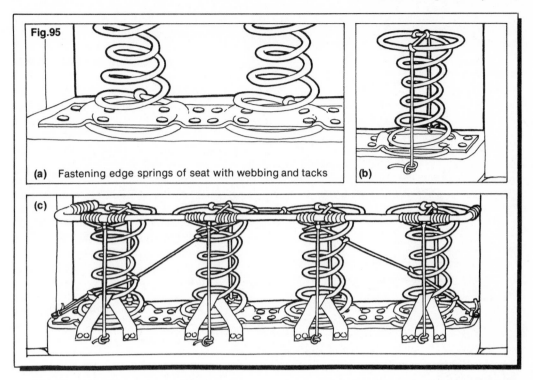

Fig.95

(a) Fastening edge springs of seat with webbing and tacks

(b)

(c)

Keep the loop of tape in and continue to take it over the edge springs. Now read off the measurements at the bottom of the front rail.

Measure the width 25mm (1in) beyond the outside of the side seat rails. Cut off the hessian and lay it over the springs, then fasten at the back on the top of the seat rail, making the usual 25mm (1in) turnover to tack through. Cut diagonally into the back corners, then come round to the front of the chair and pull the hessian over and down to the front rail. Temporarily tack it there, in about four places. Next fasten the sides also along the tops of the rails, about 10mm (⅜in) in from the outside edges.

Fasten only the main seat springs at this stage, with the usual three stitches per spring. Then release the temporary tacks at the front. This is where you form the well between the main and the edge springs – and you will now see what I meant when I spoke about the edge springs being independent.

Press the hessian in to form a 35mm (1⅜in) channel at the back of the edge springs. Take a length of laid cord and lay it along the bottom of this channel as at *(a)* in *fig.96*. Stretch it across and fasten at each end with two 16mm (⅝in) improved tacks.

Lift the loose hessian from the front and throw it back over the main springs. Now take a look at *(b)* and you will see that 'guy' cords are fixed, two between each front spring. These are threaded through the hessian around the well cord, tied with a slip knot and cut off, leaving plenty of length to pull on. When all the guys are in place, pull them tight and fasten with staples or 16mm (⅝in) improved tacks to the top of the front rail, between the front springs.

Now you can see the purpose of the well. The guy cords assume the position and purpose which, in a seat without a spring edge, would be taken by the hessian continuing to the front rail. The well and guy cords also restrain the edge springs, keeping them from being pushed back into the seat. It is therefore very important that these cords should be well fastened.

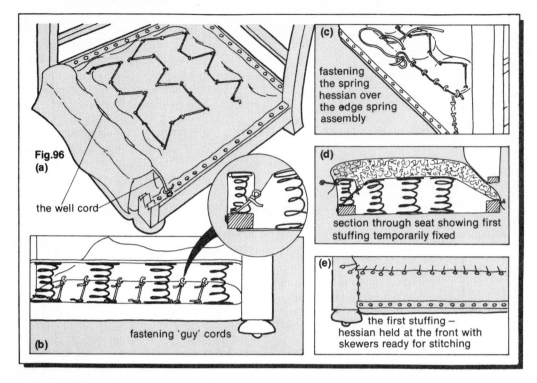

**Fig.96
(a)**

the well cord

(c) fastening
the spring
hessian over
the edge spring
assembly

(d) section through seat showing first
stuffing temporarily fixed

(b) fastening 'guy' cords

(e) the first stuffing –
hessian held at the front with
skewers ready for stitching

Bring the hessian forward again over the edge springs and fasten it at the front *(c)*. Also in this drawing you can see how to sew the hessian to the edge cane and close up the side pleats with a knot stitch (or ladder stitch if you prefer). Three stitches are needed in the tops of each edge spring to make doubly sure that they will remain in position. The seat is now ready for its first stuffing.

The first stuffing can be of horsehair, coya fibre or Algerian fibre. If we still have some pig hair left, we could use it along the front to form the roll edge. And from the old seat we took some green, grass-like fibre which has carded up well. This is Algerian fibre – a very durable substance.

With this type of seat, the stuffing tie loops to hold the roll edge hair are put in as usual, and a substantial roll of horsehair is made along the front. But do bear in mind that this only has to be a roll and that there won't be rows and rows of blind stitches building it higher. So make the thickness or depth not more than 45mm (1¾in) above the

edge cane. The well in the hessian is then filled up. Make sure you pack the stuffing in fairly tightly.

Work stuffing into the cavities between arms and seat and the back and seat from the inside and outside. Don't be too heavy-handed or the action of the springs will be hampered and the seat may become too hard.

Lay 283g (10oz) hessian over as a cover, tucking it in and pulling the edges through to the outsides of the sides and back. Here it is securely tacked on the top sides of the side and back seat rails, level with the front edges. And, at the front, where a roll is to be formed, the hessian is pulled over and temporarily held with skewers put in immediately below the edge cane.

At this stage the shape of the seat should resemble the sectional diagram *(d)*. Now, before putting in the through stuffing ties in the seat, it is best to stitch up the roll edge first. This pulls the hessian nice and tight from back to front.

Adjust, stretch and finally fix the hessian along the sides, and don't forget to tack neatly along, following a thread at the back. Adjust the hessian held by the skewers at the front, also working to a thread and folding the hessian under and re-skewering. Leave about 10mm (⅜in) of fold below the line of the skewers *(e)*.

This is what you do at the front to fix the 283g (10oz) first stuffing hessian to the tarpaulin spring hessian. With a straight needle, simply sew a row of ordinary blind stitches fairly close, following a line just below the skewers so that the hessian is fastened just beneath the edge cane.

Only one other row of blind stitches is needed. This is sewn along at the top of the edge cane. Its purpose is to bring the hair firmly to the front. Then, after regulating, a roll of about 30-45mm (1¼-1¾in) diameter can be stitched. These through stitches on the front should be only a thread or so above the last row of blind stitches so that the roll is made no higher than necessary.

At this point, draw with a felt pen a straight line across the seat 150mm (6in) back from the extreme front of the roll. This will be the site of the valley you will be making in the top cover. Your longest double-pointed needle will be needed to negotiate the thickness of the seat when putting in the through stuffing ties. And as I said before, these ties only go through to the spring hessian.

It is difficult to see up through the gaps in the webbing underneath, but do make sure when you are returning the needle to the top surface that the twine has not ensnared any of the spring coils.

Covering the seat We can now return to the cutting-out table, for the next task is to make up the seat covering *(see fig.97)*. There are two ways of doing this, and *(a)* and *(b)* show the two styles. Take your choice. The first is easier to do and is more modern, while the second is, to my mind, best suited to this chair. Let's choose the second alternative. Later on you will see that this was right because the pronounced roll edge with the piping beneath it follows the same style

that you will get when the facings are fitted at the scroll fronts.

The seat covering and border must be made up together. There will be four pieces in all – the border, the piping, the leather for the top in front of the valley and the matching lining which will cover the remainder of the seat from the valley to the back. At *(c)* you can see the seat in section and where to measure. First measure for and cut off the piece of lining. Measure for the length from 15mm (⅝in) forward of the line drawn on the hessian (the valley) to well over the back seat rail – plus 50mm (2in) to allow for the length that will be taken up when the stuffing is added. Likewise measure the width from seat rail to seat rail, adding 50mm (2in) for the extra height of the top stuffing.

Now measure the piece of leathercloth for the front of the seat, going 15mm (⅝in) behind the valley line to the line of roll edge stitches under the lip of the edge – and add 40mm (1⅝in). The width of this piece should be the same as the width of the lining.

And now the piece for the border. Measure the height from the bottom of the edge lip to 50mm (2in) below the front seat rail. This will allow enough for turnings plus the swell of the border stuffing. The width of this border piece should be enough to reach 125mm (5in) back along each side of the seat – that is, into the crevices at each side within the confines of the arms. Finally cut off a strip for piping as long as the top piece of leathercloth plus 150mm (6in).

To begin making up, lay the piece of leathercloth cut for the top wrong side up over the front part of the seat top. Centralise it, and fix it with skewers so that it overlaps the valley line by 15mm (⅝in) – placing the skewers along this line.

Pinch up and pin a pleat at both corners *(d)*, stretching the leather well out to each corner as you do so. Now take this piece to your sewing-machine and stitch up the pleats. Start to sew from the edge up to the point of the pleat, and return so that the stitches hold and do not gape or grin when the leather is stretched. Cut away the

Fig.97

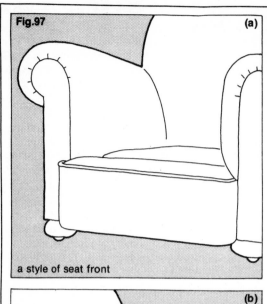

(a)

a style of seat front

(b)

an alternative style of seat front

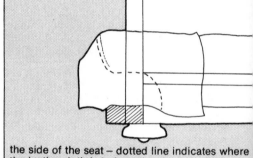

(c)

section of seat – taking measurements
for covering material

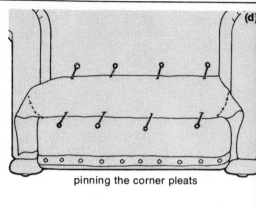

(d)

pinning the corner pleats

(e)

the side of the seat – dotted line indicates where
the leathercloth is to be cut

(f)

front of seat cover placed inside out
over a table for ease of fitting the piping

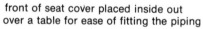

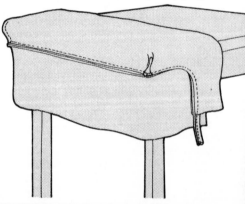

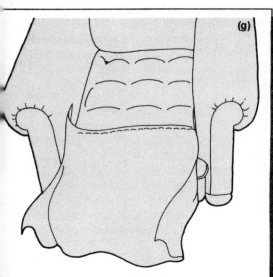

(g)

large 'through' stitches to fasten
the seat cover into the 'valley'

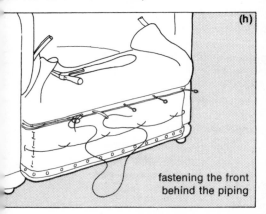

(h)

fastening the front
behind the piping

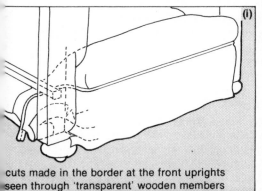

(i)

cuts made in the border at the front uprights
seen through 'transparent' wooden members

surplus leather from the pleats.

Place this piece back on the seat – and this is where you must use a bit of good judgement. After you have stretched it over and made sure that the pleats fit neatly, trim back the leather to the outside of the pleats, level with the front edge and around and into the crevices as far as the scissors will reach. Remove the leather from the seat and continue these cuts in arcs which end at the side edges about 50mm (2in) from the back edge *(e)*.

You can make each arc the same by cutting one, then using the piece that you have cut out as a template to mark the other side. The piping is made up on this bottom edge and around the arcs. Then mark the centre of this edge and the centre of the piece for the border. Pin the two pieces together, starting at the centre and securing up to the beginning of the curve of each arc.

Stitch this seam only as far as you have pinned it up, then look at *(f)*. Here you see the border and the top laid wrong side out over the corner of a table, so that the border can hang down square to the top. You can then mark and cut the ends of the border to match the piped arcs at each side – allowing enough for the seam flanges, of course. Pin up these places and stitch together.

And so to the last piece to be attached – the lining, which you can sew on after you have marked and located the centres and pinned together. When you are sewing this seam keep the leathercloth uppermost on your machine. The seam flanges should be 15mm (⅝in) wide.

Well, that is the most difficult part of the seat covering operation done. Now here is how you put it on.

Mark the centre of the valley line and nick the centre of the last seam sewn. Put the cover to one side while you make up a flat, even layer of top stuffing on the part of the seat in front of the valley line. This can be composed of a thin layer of horsehair topped with cotton felt, or it can be cotton felt only. Sew two or three layers, the last layer being laid well over the roll edge, then a layer of 6mm (¼in) foam stretched over. Try to keep the stuffing as flat as possible.

Take the cover and stretch it on over the front edge first. You will probably find that the inside out, putting-on-a-sock principle is the best way, tucking in along the side crevices as you go. When the front leathercloth top piece is correctly placed, leave the platform lining lying forward so that the flanges of the valley seam can be seen.

Find your longest double-pointed needle and thread it with well-waxed medium (No.2) twine. After stretching and fixing the valley seam at each end with skewers and thereafter securing all the way along, keeping to the line, sew a line of large stitches that will fasten right through to the spring hessian. The largest stitches should be made on the top *(g)*. These stitches should not be pulled tight, otherwise the valley will be made too deep.

If we turn to the front once more, I'll show you how to fasten the leather at the back of the piping *(h)*. Turn up the border piece and lay it back over the seat, putting a hammer on top to keep it there. Stretch the piping and seam flanges from end to end, and skewer along the entire length. Then with blind locked stitches (made with a semi-circular needle) similar to those with which you fixed the calico at the arm scrolls, put in a row of stitches which will hold the piping in under the lip of the edge.

Before you pull down the border, put some ties and stuffing along the front and fill well the crevices at each side. While you have stuffing available, do the remaining part of the seat. Pull down the border and note that you will have to cut this into the sides where it encounters the junctions of the front seat rail and the front uprights. Think carefully before cutting, and study how to do it at *(i)* first.

Tuck in the seat covering material all round, cutting the platform lining to allow for the back uprights. Then pull the material through to the outside so that it is ready to tack. Follow the usual method of temporary tacking and finishing off.

The correct place to fix the sides and back of the seat material is, again, on the top of the seat rails. You will see the wisdom of this when you are putting on the outside panels, for any thickness of materials or tacks along the outside of the bottom rails would give an uneven appearance to the leathercloth covering it.

Pull down and tack or staple the front border under the front rail, stretching it evenly. Measure the depth from piping to the bottom regularly, so as to make sure you are getting it parallel. Why the piping and border curve down in an arc after they disappear into the side crevices is because the piping and ends of the border are drawn out at each side. By stretching these parts you can successfully tension the border and piping laterally.

Leather-covered scroll facings Once the seat is finished, you can enjoy the job of making and fitting some facings for the arm scrolls *(see fig.98)*.

Mark and cut out a template of thin cardboard or stout brown paper to the shape of the scroll so that it fits neatly within the confines of the lipped edge. It should be flush with the outside edge of the front upright and reach to the bottom of the frame. From this template, mark and cut four pieces from your 3mm (⅛in) plywood, using a coping saw.

You can cut them all at once if you cramp four pieces together and mark the top piece. When they have been cut out, trim them with plane or rasp to an even shape and offer them up to the scrolls to make sure they fit. They don't need to be a tight fit. If they are 2-3mm (⅛in) smaller around the curve and inside edge, this will allow for the piping. Take two of the pieces and mark them with a 'B' to denote that they will be for the back of the facings.

Find eight wire nails with the usual round flat heads, 38-50mm (1½-2in) long. Choose two twist drills from your kit, one to make holes that the nails will push through to give a tight fit; the other should be one size smaller than the gauge of the nails.

Drill four holes in each of the two back pieces with the larger of the twist drills, in the positions shown at *(a)*. Now change the

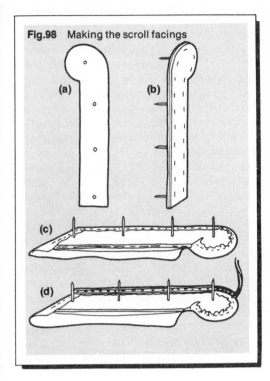

Fig.98 Making the scroll facings

(a)

(b)

(c)

(d)

around with felt pen, about 25mm (1in) larger all round, then cut to this line.

If you look at *(c)*, you will see how the covering is done. First, place the leather face down on a clean smooth surface, then the foam and the facing shape. Pull the leather over the back of the shape and fasten with 6mm (¼in) staples from the staple gun or 6mm (¼in) fine tacks. Stretch and secure top and bottom first and then what will be the inside edge. Note how at *(c)* a cut is made to within 10mm (⅜in) of the corner of the scroll curve, after which the leather can be fixed around the remaining part of the curve. The straight side, which will be the outside, is left unfastened.

There is still a final touch to add. Make up some piping and fix this all around the edge, except the outside one. If you follow *(d)* you will have a really professional finish.

Now to fasten these to the chair – and may I suggest you take great care with this operation? Position the nails in the holes already drilled in the front uprights and push in as far as you can with hand pressure. Then take a small flat hardwood block, about 76mm (3in) square, and cover it with a layer of leathercloth. Place this over the location of each nail in turn and drive the facing home, little by little, with gentle taps from a mallet.

Go carefully, because if you hammer too hard the nail heads could break through the layer of plywood and cause damage to the covering. When the facings are fully home, the unfastened sides can be tacked to the outsides of the front uprights.

Covering outside areas To put on the outside panels is a comparatively easy job, but, before you start, try to eliminate all sharp or rough corners of the framework. This is especially important when using leathercloth. Do this by cutting strips from odd pieces of 6mm (¼in) foam and stretching and fixing them over sharp corners and edges like the outside edge of the back upright and along the bottom rails. Then, all the outside surfaces need reinforcing to withstand the buffeting that the chair is bound to receive in use.

drill for the smaller one and, holding each shape in turn in the exact position on the scroll, drill through the holes already made in the ply into the front upright. Mark the backs of the pieces so that you will know which is for the left and right. Push the nails to their full extent through the holes from the front of the plywood pieces, then take the other two shapes and place them on the outside, covering the nail heads.

Fasten the two layers together with staples from a gun or 9mm (⅜in) fine tacks. Hammer them in with a piece of flat iron underneath so that the points clench over. Round off and smooth the front outside edges either with a rasp or with coarse glasspaper, after which the facings should resemble the one at *(b)*.

Next, place the shapes face down on some 6mm (¼in) foam and, pressing firmly, cut around the edges with a sharp knife. To cover the facings, once again place them face down, this time on pieces of leathercloth with the back uppermost. Mark

Covering the wings Make up a length of piping long enough to fix in a continuous strip from under the bottom of one wing, around the wing – keeping it up to the lip of the edge – across the top of the back and likewise around the other wing. This can be attached at wide intervals with staples or gimp pins. The first panels to put on are the outside wings, and for reinforcement fill up the space within the wing frame, just proud of the surface. Use horsehair covered by a layer of wadding and a layer of thin foam.

Temporarily fix the rectangular piece you have cut for one outside wing. Use a skewer at each corner, then trim to 15mm (⅝in) over the finished size which, of course, takes you up to the piping. Calipers are needed now to space out and mark the places for your leather-covered fixing studs. I think they look best spaced at about 30mm (1¼in) centres. The outside panels and the stages of covering these are illustrated *(see fig.99)*.

Turn in the leather at the top centre of the outside wing and put in the first few studs *(a)*. Then stretch and fix under the centre bottom. Next fix at both side centres, then stretch diagonally towards the corners. Turn in the remainder and fix with studs, and the wing should look something like *(b)*.

The outside arms are quite simple to do. Use 283g (10oz) hessian as reinforcement behind these. After laying something soft on the floor, such as underfelt, old carpet or a sheet of foam plastic, turn the chair on one side. In this position it will be easier to fasten the panel.

Back tack the top under the roll of the arm and below the wing, using a half-width strip of webbing and fixing both the leather and the reinforcing hessian together *(c)*. Stretch the hessian over the side frame as tightly as possible. If you like, you can place a thin layer of cotton wadding over the hessian before stretching and fixing the leathercloth.

Stretch and fix under the bottom rail first, cutting diagonally into the back leg and front 'bun' foot. Turn the front edge under and fasten with studs and finally fasten to the

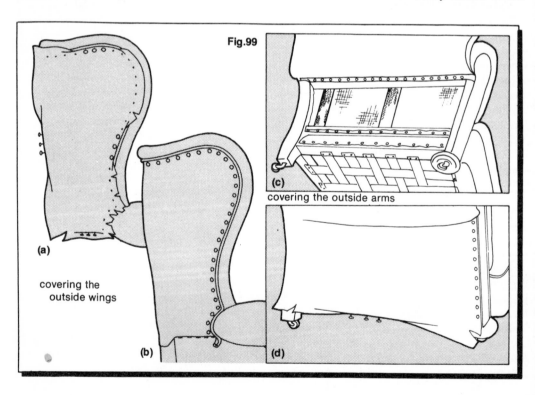

(a)

covering the
outside wings

(b)

(c)
covering the outside arms

(d)

Fig.99

back face of the back upright. Follow the same procedure with the outside back, the two sides being fixed with studs.

Finally, turn the chair upside down using a small trestle with plenty of padding on top to support the arms. Cut, fit and tack a piece of 283g (10oz) hessian or black lining over the bottom.

Making the cushion The main part of the chair is now finished, and all you have to do is make up the cushion. A cushion interior case of waxed, featherproof cambric is made first. This is just a box-shaped case formed by combining top and bottom panels with a border. This sounds simple enough, but there are three points to note. First, the size should be made 25mm (1in) larger in width and length and the border 10mm (⅜in) deeper than the size your top cover will be. No need for accuracy here, so long as it is just that little bit larger so that it will fill out the top cushion cover nicely. The length and breadth can be measured from the chair seat. The border depth of the top cover can be between 63 and 90mm (2½ and 3½in).

Second, the waxed glazed side of the cambric must be on the inside when the case is finished and turned right side out. Third, when you have sewn all the seams except for a mouth at the back, rub every line of stitches on both sides with beeswax to seal the needle holes and make the case really featherproof.

Feathers are another expensive commodity these days. There are several grades. In the lowest, the feathers are complete with centre quills. In the grade called 'cut feathers' many of the quills have been removed. The next grade up is feather down, while of course the top grade is the real down, beautifully soft, light, with ne'er a quill in sight.

The feathers in the original chair cushion seem to be of good quality, so place the old interior in the airing cupboard for a day or so to allow the feathers to fluff out. Then, knead, pat and work them about while they are still in the old case so as to dispose of most of the lumps caused by the feathers binding together.

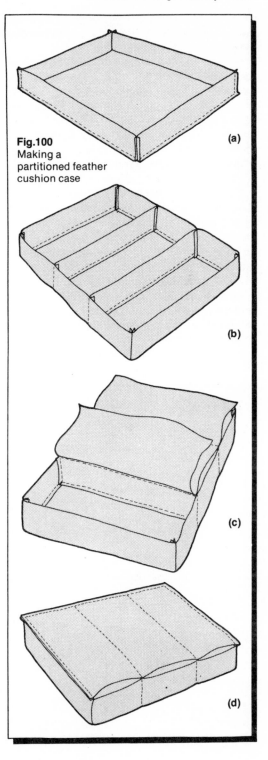

Fig.100
Making a partitioned feather cushion case

(a)

(b)

(c)

(d)

The operation of transferring the feathers from the old to the new case is best done out of doors for, as you can imagine, they can fly about and make a terrible mess. Cut the old case clean across one side, keeping the cut closed until you have placed it in the mouth of the new case. Gradually work the whole of the old case inside the new one, then slowly withdraw the old case leaving the feathers behind. If you are very lucky you will only spill a few. Then sew up the mouth on the machine.

A feather interior made in this way means that the cushion will have to be adjusted and plumped up after being sat on, as the feathers tend to move to the back of the cushion. But there is a way of making the interior so that it contains three separate sections or compartments for the feathers. Thus the feathers are confined to one of these three areas and the cushion remains in good shape without having to be constantly adjusted.

Perhaps you would like to try this better way of doing it. The construction is illustrated *(see fig.100)*.

At *(a)* the case is made up with the border sewn to one side panel. At *(b)* this part of the case is turned the right side out and two partition pieces sewn across the inside. At *(c)* the top panel is stitched to the two partitions, and at *(d)* the finished case is shown. The top panel has been stitched on from the outside leaving the ends of each section open at one side to facilitate filling. Of course, you can't employ the clean method of filling as you could with the one-section interior, so fill by hand, putting a handful at a time into each compartment to keep them equal.

When your interior is finished with the mouths sewn up and waxed, brush away the loose feathers from the outside and lay the interior in the chair seat. Then lay a sheet of brown paper on the top of this and make a template to the shape that the cushion cover should be. From this point onward, do the same as you did when you made up the cushion for the fireside chair.

Wing chair in woven cloth There are a few ways in which fixing and fastening woven cloths differs from the methods used when covering with leathercloth. First, the seat: if you wanted the same effect with a lipped edge, this would not be sewn to the border before fitting but would be fastened beneath the roll edge with a row of blind stitches in twine.

The piping is made on the top edge of the border, which is cut long enough to reach well into the crevices at each side. Lengths of twine would be attached to both ends of the border to be pulled through the crevices and attached to the side seat rail – thus pulling the border tightly across.

Ladder stitches, sewn as closely as possible to the row of machined stitches holding the piping, are used to fasten the border to the underside of the seat lip.

Second, the front arm scrolls (although wooden facing shapes can be used) are usually hand sewn direct on to the front. The piping is fixed around the scroll first, with pins or skewers, then the stuffing is put on,

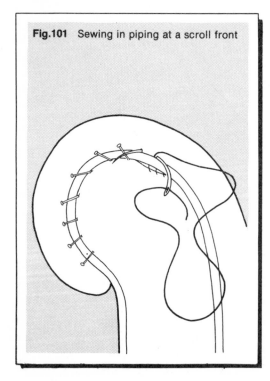

Fig.101 Sewing in piping at a scroll front

followed by the scroll covering. This is also pinned in place, using the pins or skewers already holding the piping. The method of ladder stitching when incorporating piping in the seam is illustrated *(see fig.101)*.

This is the same as the simple ladder stitch, except that each stitch is taken through the piping on the line of its stitches. This also applies when fastening the outside if piping is being used.

Third, the seams at the front of the outside arm panels and those fastening the outside back the length of the back uprights will be ladder stitched, in place of the studs used with the leathercloth.

The luxury look To add a touch more class to an easy chair which has been covered with woven fabric, chair cord can be used instead of piping. Chair cord is a silken twisted decorative cord usually about 8mm (⅜in) in diameter and should either match or contrast with the chair covering in colour.

When the intention is to trim with this cord, simply ladder stitch the seams in the places where it is to be used – namely the arm scrolls, front border, wings and maybe the top of the outside back. After this, pin the cord into position over the seams and sew on with a fine semi-circular needle. The method of attaching chair cord is illustrated *(see fig.102)*.

(a) Begin sewing with a slip knot stitch which will be concealed beneath the cord.

(b) Make a stitch sideways through the centre of the cord.

(c) Going back from this a fraction, make the next stitch of about 10mm (⅜in) beneath the cord and in the line of the ladder stitches. When it emerges, bring the needle to the opposite side of the cord.

(d) Backing again a fraction from the end of the last stitch, make a further stitch at 90 degrees through the centre of the cord.

Continue in this fashion along the length of the cord and fasten well at the end.

Another alternative to piping is ruche; the two most common kinds are the cut ruche and berry ruche.

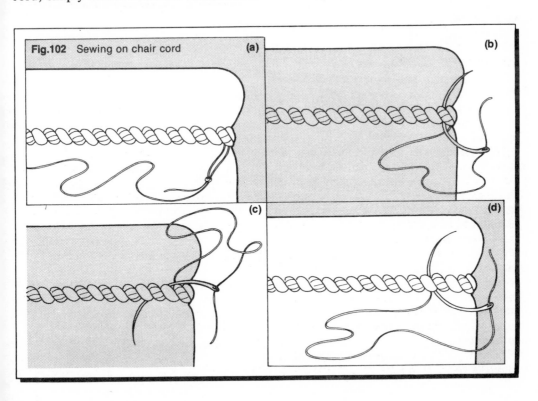

Fig.102 Sewing on chair cord

Ruche is made up ready for use with a flange so that it can be sewn into seams in exactly the same way as piping – either by machining (on cushions) or hand sewing on scrolls and the edges of outside panels.

The cut ruche gives a fringed brush-like edge, and the berry ruche forms a tubular welt of looped, uncut pile.

Some chairs need just that extra something to finish the bottom of the front, back and sides. Sometimes a wide braid is used or, more often, a fringe which is sewn on with two rows of hand stitches in the way I have illustrated *(see fig.103)*.

(a) With the first row at the top you can see that every small stitch catches a loop of the braid of the fringe at intervals of about 1cm. The needle is put through the loop and emerges above the braid so that the next stitch can be made through a loop once more – and so on.

(b) The second row of stitches is a row simply made in and out to hold in the lower part of the fringe braid.

Well, now we have completely refurbished our chair.

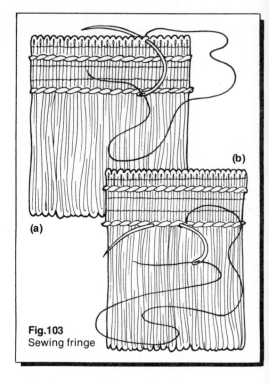

Fig.103
Sewing fringe

UPHOLSTERING THE VICTORIAN SPOONBACK CHAIR

I think the time has now arrived to work on the Victorian chair. Having dealt with a variety of ways and methods of upholstery, I think the moment has arrived to take the final step.

The frame looks much better since we have stripped and re-polished it. And one can now see the true colour of the wood.

Things you will need The material we've chosen for covering the chair is acrylic velvet, and that colour goes well with the show-wood on the chair. The material is very good quality and, although expensive, will last a long time and wear well. Though people today go mad about velvet and velour where buttoning is concerned, there are a number of fabrics which look just as good, or even better, when they are used for buttonwork.

Tapestry with a small design; plain colour damasks of good weight; brocatelles with designs which are not too defined – in fact any fairly plain good-quality cloth will look well as long as it is of furnishing weight.

Silk or satin finishes will really show up buttonwork. Velvet does too, but to my mind and eye the shading effect which this gives when put on correctly with the pile running down from top to bottom is contrary to what one would expect to see. In normal room light, the light and shade occurring on buttonwork normally show as a darker shadow around the top and into each button recess – then lighter where the material emerges beneath the recess. A pile cloth put on with the nap running down reverses this effect, because of the shading caused by the different planes of a piled surface.

I saw a new three-piece suite about four or five years ago at a house I visited. This suite, covered and buttoned in an old gold acrylic velvet cloth, looked superb, and I thought at the time that it looked far better than anything I had done in the same cloth. This puzzled me until I called recently to replace some of the buttons which had popped out. I found the secret lay in the fact that the material had been put on with the pile running sideways – even on the cushions. Whether this had been done purposely to alter the shading, or purely for reasons of economy, I don't know. I do know that the fabric put on in this way seemed to be wearing badly, and it no longer had that look about it which had caught my attention the first time I saw it.

I will run through the other items that will be needed for this job. As usual, webbing, tarpaulin hessian, 283g (10oz) hessian, springs, twine, hair stuffing, cotton wadding, 6mm (¼in) polyether foam and tacks. By now you will have built up a small stock of these sundries, but there is one new item for you to get – nylon twine for holding in the buttons. It lasts very long, as it is stronger than ordinary twine. Buy a cop of this – about the same gauge as the No.1 stout ordinary twine.

As well as the usual tools, there are two which you need specially for this job. They are the upholsterer's pin or cabriol hammer with the very small face area, which you will need when fixing close into the show-wood on the chair, and a 152-203mm (6-8in) semi-circular double-pointed needle. But you will be very lucky if you can find one!

I mentioned in the chapter on tools, page 82, that an ordinary single-pointed needle can be modified. I have done this by finding a needle that has the eye pierced a little distance from the end, thus permitting a short point to be ground at this end.

Now what about buttons? Most upholsterers make their own with small button-making machines which include a cutting press for stamping out discs of fabric and a fly press to which can be fitted dies of various sizes to make the different-sized buttons. If you bought your fabric from a furniture shop which has workshops as part of the establishment, they will probably make up the buttons for you – if you ask them nicely!

There are alternatives. Button moulds can be purchased at drapers' shops. These you cover individually by hand, as per instructions which come with the moulds. They are a bit fiddly to do, but luckily this first buttoning job doesn't need many. Another suggestion is that a button-making machine could be bought jointly by a group of enthusiasts for common use, as already suggested with the carding machine.

Buttons made with a machine are far superior to any that you can make from hand-sewn button moulds. The size of button most used in Victorian upholstery work is 14mm (just over ½in), sometimes called a No.24.

The foundation for the back First we need to build the foundation and edges for the back upholstery *(see fig.104)*. If you look at *(a)* you will see that three pieces of webbing have been placed where most strain will occur. Then cover the back frame with best tarpaulin hessian, stretching it very tightly from bottom to top so that the back retains the hollow spoon shape.

Be careful when driving all the tacks home. Hold a flat iron or something equally heavy (wrapped in some padding) against the outside back, opposite the tack you are hammering home. This will help to prevent damage to the rest of the frame.

Now look at *(b)*. Use a felt pen to mark a line which follows the outside shape of the frame but is 85mm (about 3¼in) in from the tacking rabbet. An easy way to do this is to cut off a small flat stick to the required length, then use it as a scribing distance piece.

This is to some extent reminiscent of the upholstery on the wings of the leather chair, but these edges will be of an entirely different form. Cut off a strip of 283g (10oz) hessian 180mm (7in) wide and as long as the perimeter of the back frame. Make a turning of about 10mm (⅜in) along one edge, then sew this strip up to the line you have drawn, making generous pleats around the top curve. Use a short straight double-pointed needle and go through and through with fairly small stitches, using your fine twine.

Lay the hessian back towards the centre, out of the way, and then put some stuffing tie loops of twine all round, 25mm (1in) in from the rabbet at the edge of the show-wood.

The stuffing for this chair is horsehair saved from the original stuffing, plus some of the beautiful hair from the mattress used earlier. It will be perfect for this chair. I would suggest we use the original hair for stuffing the edges, so place a goodly wedge of it around the shape of the back.

To make sure you get it right, look at the relevant drawings before you do any more.

At *(c)* you can see the back in section, looking down from the top. This gives you some idea of the size that this edge around the back needs to be. Pull the hessian over and fasten with 9mm (⅜in) fine tacks into the rabbet. Try to leave 5mm (³/₁₆in) between the edge of the hessian and the rim of the rabbet.

Although the chair back is already beautifully shaped spoonwise, it is still necessary to build a lumbar swell to fit the small of the back. I mention this now because as you continue to build the edge down towards the seat it should gradually be brought forward and deepened to form this swell. A side view of the back is shown at *(d)*.

Edge building is connected with the depth of the buttonwork, for buttonwork which is not within an evenly-shaped outer form tends to look unfinished and untidy. The edge that we are forming makes for an all-over evenness of buttonwork. The Victorian chairs you see in the 'lesser antique shop' windows in down-town areas, which have been tarted up with a thick layer of foam into which the material has been buttoned, have no character left. Their spoonbacks are no longer spoon-shaped, and the thickness of the upholstery disappears unevenly to nothing where it is fastened around the frame, forming a convex surface within the concave spoon on the back.

Having finished fastening the edge hessian, take your regulator and work up the stuffing so that, in section, the edge is formed into a right-angled triangle as at *(d)*.

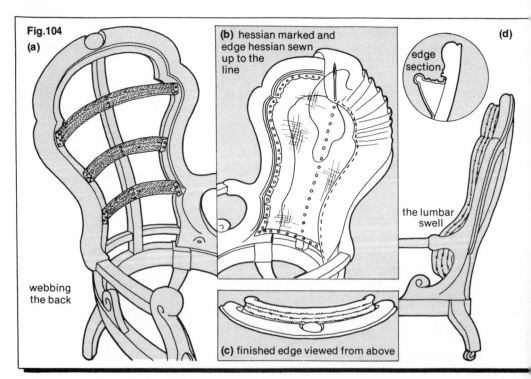

Fig.104

(a) webbing the back

(b) hessian marked and edge hessian sewn up to the line

(c) finished edge viewed from above

(d) edge section

the lumbar swell

Now to the stitching up. You need to put in two rows of blind stitches and one row of through stitches to form a small roll.

Your adapted double-point semi-circular needle is used for the first row, which must be as near to the frame as possible. Because of the concave shape of the back and the width of the show-wood surround, it is not possible to use a straight needle for these stitches. You will probably be able to use a straight needle for the next row, but for the through, roll-forming top stitches you must resort again to the semi-circular needle. The roll should be made with a diameter of about 15mm (⅝in).

Don't forget to regulate constantly the stuffing between putting in each row of stitches, ensuring that the edge is made firm and is standing out at right angles to the chair frame.

Now a warning. Watch the returning point of the needle or you will scratch the show-wood that you have polished so beautifully and with so much care.

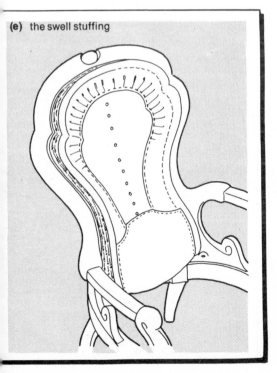

(e) the swell stuffing

In forming the edge, you have deepened it at the lower part of the sides to form the shape of the swell. The next task is to sew a piece of hessian across, from edge to edge *(e)*. This, when stuffed with hair, will complete the lumbar swell foundation. The bottom of this piece of hessian is tacked to the bottom tacking rail, and this completes the foundations for the back.

The arm pad foundations While you are edge building, I suggest that you build up the first stuffings and edges on the two small arm pads.

To hold the horsehair initially *(see fig.105)*, fix a row of stuffing tie loops down the centre of each platform with the aid of small tacks *(a)*. The hair should be put on so that it consolidates at about 35mm (1⅜in) thick. Have plenty over-sailing the edges of the platform, as the finished edges need to mushroom a little. To ensure both pads are the same size, cut pieces of 283g (10oz) hessian exactly the same size and tack them on with the same amount of turn under. Follow a thread with the rows of tacks.

When you come to stitch around the edges of the arm pads, just one row of blind stitches above the line of tacks will suffice before making the roll edge. Take care to avoid getting this upholstery lopsided. Before you stitch the roll it will be wise to put in some temporary fixing such as a row of 32mm (1¼in) wire nails down the centre of each pad. Hammer them in just far enough to hold the hessian, so that when you are stitching one side the hessian is not pulled over by the stitches, causing the other side to be reduced in height and over-sail. The nails can be removed when the edges are completed.

After stuffing ties, add top stuffing put on thinly, then layers of wadding and thin foam. Cover them with calico, and the arms are ready for the top covering in due course. I like to get the small, odd pieces like the arms done first, otherwise they seem to sit there, constantly diverting your attention from the more enjoyable job of upholstering the buttoned back.

Top stuffing for buttonwork Now continue

with the back by sewing in stuffing tie loops. Make about four or five horizontal rows across, from edge to edge. Why should you use stuffing ties if all the stuffing is to be held in with buttons? Well, remember that you are going to use the beautiful white hair for this top stuffing and that to get it to the right density, since buttonwork must be fairly firm, this carded hair would be an unmanageable bulge without the restraint of ties.

So, after the ties have been placed in lines fairly close together, pack the hair beneath them quite tightly – especially across the swell foundation. A covering of cotton felt, or a double layer of wadding to keep the hair from working out through the cover, goes on next, followed by thin polyether foam. You can stretch this over and tack it at the bottom, then fix temporarily all around the outside of the stitched edge in the way shown at *(b)*. When stretching the foam over, tuck back the excess hair so that none is left on the outside of the edges.

Some upholsterers will say that using modern foam – even a quarter of an inch of it – is cheating, and that it should not be used for re-upholstering antique or Victorian furniture. But, for myself, when I can see a way of improving the traditional work with the aid of modern materials, I'm all for using it, so long as the foundations are to the period specification.

There are three advantages in using foam in this instance. First it helps to hold the second stuffing in place, compressed nearer to the finished thickness. Second, it makes setting out the places for the buttons much easier. And, third, the foam gives a very even, rich appearance to the surface of the covering fabric.

In bygone days, before the advent of plastic foam, I can remember what a job buttoning was when there was nothing but cotton wadding to keep the hair from moving while I got the buttons in place! It was much more of a hit-and-miss operation than the way I will now describe.

Setting out buttonwork Find a very soft lead pencil, your felt tipped pen, steel measuring tape and a ruler or straight-edge.

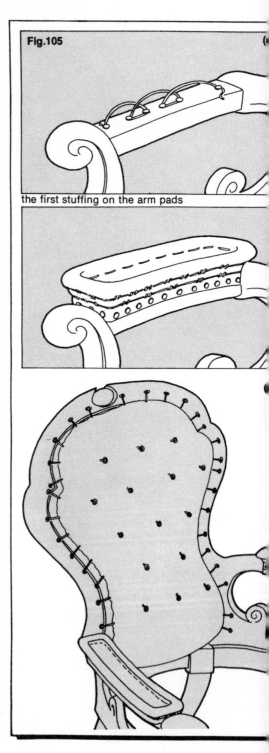

Fig.105

the first stuffing on the arm pads

diagram for setting out buttons

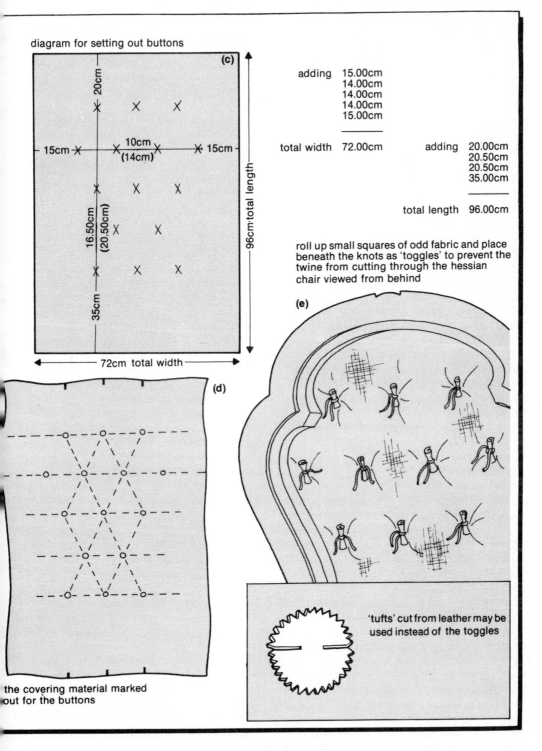

(c)

20cm

×   ×   ×

15cm ×   ×   10cm   ×   × 15cm
           (14cm)

×   ×   ×

16.50cm (20.50cm)

×   ×   ×

×   ×   ×

35cm

96cm:total length

◄— 72cm total width —►

	adding	15.00cm		
		14.00cm		
		14.00cm		
		14.00cm		
		15.00cm		
total width	72.00cm		adding	20.00cm
				20.50cm
				20.50cm
				35.00cm
			total length	96.00cm

roll up small squares of odd fabric and place beneath the knots as 'toggles' to prevent the twine from cutting through the hessian chair viewed from behind

(e)

(d)

the covering material marked out for the buttons

'tufts' cut from leather may be used instead of the toggles

At the back you will see a wooden centre upright bar, though very often this is not accurately situated in the centre. By measuring across top and bottom, mark the centres and draw a vertical line on the bar or hessian.

Next, measure for and mark a vertical centre line on the foam covering the inside back. This time use the soft pencil, for I'm always a little frightened about using felt tip or ball point pens on materials immediately behind a covering. I feel that, should they ever get wet, the pen colour could come right through.

Beginning at this centre line on the front, set out the places where you want the buttons to be, using skewers pushed into the foam.

When setting out for buttonwork, there are several points to remember. The spaces between the buttons should form diamond shapes with the length always greater than the width. Where possible, the distance from the buttons to the edges of the sides and the top should be no more than the width between the buttons – and no less than half this measurement. And the bottom row of buttons on a chair such as this should not be set too low, but should be so placed that when pulled in they terminate the top of the lumbar swell.

Where possible, all buttons should be spaced equally and in straight lines, although the top row may be slightly bowed or curved upwards to follow more nearly the line of the chair frame. And, in some cases, the width between the buttons may be reduced a little with each row down, to enable the number of buttons required in a row to be comfortably placed within the space between the converging frame sides.

When all the button positions have been spaced accurately and marked with skewers; remove these one by one, making a dot in their place with the felt pen. I have a special 'washer cutter' (a steel tube closed at one end and with a sharpened edge at the other) with which I cut holes 25mm (1in) in diameter through the foam at each dot – twisting it round and round to effect the cut.

You can make a cutter from any odd piece of steel tube about 25mm (1in) in diameter. An old piece of bicycle frame, curtain rod or thin gauge piping will do. If you have nothing like this available, just make a star cut through each mark with a sharp-pointed knife.

Deepen each hole right through the stuffing to the hessian with a large regulator or just a couple of fingers.

On the outside back of the chair, use the felt pen to mark the hessian with small crosses which correspond exactly with the button positions on the front.

We can now unroll our beautiful velvet, for this is the time to cut off and set out the cover. Make a drawing (c), showing all the button positions and the measurements between. Take a measurement by inserting the end of your steel tape into the top centre button hole in the chair back; bend the tape over and read off the measurement 20mm (¾in) beyond the top rail rabbet in the show-wood. Record this on the drawing.

Do the same at the sides where the greatest width occurs. And, at the bottom, take a measurement from deep inside the bottom centre hole, down the swell and underneath to the back face of the bottom tacking rail. To each between-button measurement on your drawing you must add an amount of material to allow for the depth to which the buttons will be pulled in. Here is a rough guide as to how much is needed for the different depths of buttonwork.

For the shallowest work, add 25mm (1in). For medium depth, add 32-40mm (1¼-1½in), for deep upholstery, 45-50mm (1¾-2in). Look at (c) once more and you will see the measurement with the added allowance bracketed. And at the side are a couple of simple sums which, when added up, give the total length and width of the piece of cloth required.

You will see that I have added on an extra 40mm (1½in) to the between-button widths, which will be best for our chair – giving a medium depth to the buttons.

Cut off a piece of velvet to the size required and lay it out on the table, face down. Mark the top of the run with a cross or a 'T'. I know this may sound rather elementary, but it would be very sad if you did your setting out on the back of the cloth only to find when you turned it over that you had done it top to bottom!

Take a piece of tailor's chalk or your soft pencil, measure and lightly mark lines across to indicate the position of the five rows of buttons. These lines should follow threads accurately, right across the piece. If you are using a pencil, press lightly or the pile will be marked on the front.

Mark the positions of the buttons which are to be in the centre of the appropriate lines on the centre of the cloth and from these measure and mark the places for the other buttons according to your diagram. Double-check that all marks have been made the correct distances apart, then, with a regulator, pierce the fabric at each mark so that the holes can be seen on the face side.

There is just one more thing to do before the setting-out is complete. Turn the material face-up, and along the bottom and top edges make small, clear marks, corresponding with the positions of the buttons in the rows nearest each edge, *(d)*.

Covering and buttoning Everything is now ready to begin the covering and buttoning, so have your buttons handy!

A double-pointed needle of medium length, threaded with a goodly length of nylon tufting twine, is now required – also some small pieces of leathercloth, thick hessian or other substantially thick material. Cut this about 50 x 50mm (2 x 2in) square, so they can be rolled and used as a tuft or toggle at the back of each button *(e)*. Your larger and smaller regulators must also be to hand.

With all back buttonwork you should begin at the centre of the bottom row, so throw the cover over the inside back. It is best to have the chair in an upright position on medium high trestles for this job.

Fold the material over on itself lengthwise, so the centre button marks just show. Insert your needle from the outside back on the bottom centre mark. As all the centre marks occur on the centre back upright bar,

this means to one side of this bar. By inserting a finger into the hole at the front, guide the point of the needle through the stuffing.

Locate the hole in the cover for the bottom centre button and pull needle and twine through. Thread on a button and return the needle and twine through the same hole in the cover, back through the stuffing so that it emerges on the other side of the centre upright bar. Pull all the twine through, fasten with a slip knot over the wood and pull up to a medium tension (so that the button is pulled about half-way in). Do not lock the slip knot, but tighten it so that it does not slip. Cut off the twine, leaving an end about 150mm (6in) long.

Insert the other two buttons in the bottom row in the same way. As there is no wooden bar behind these, insert the needle 10mm (⅜in) to one side of the position mark on the outside back. Return it 10mm (⅜in) on the other side of the mark. Tie the slip knot, and before pulling up roll up one of the small squares of odd fabric and place it behind the knot as a toggle to prevent the twine cutting through the hessian.

When pulling in the buttons now, you will need to use a little persuasion with a finger or two beneath the cover, because the foam overlaying the stuffing tends to grip the back of the cloth. If no adjustment is made, it will be pulled into the button hole, disturbing the stuffing and the set of the button.

The next row of buttons is now put in. When it is complete, make the diagonal pleats or folds between the two rows. This is how you do them *(see fig.106)*.

Lay the chair on its back and place the larger of your two regulators in from above, underneath the cover, so that the rounded flat end is pushed up to a button in the bottom row. Hold this with one hand while you use the smaller regulator in the other to tuck the material under to form the fold, bringing both regulators diagonally to a button in the second row *(a)*.

This action is repeated until all the folds fall neatly into place. Note that all the tucks or pleats in buttonwork are folded downwards. We all know what a dust trap buttoned upholstery is, and making the folds in this way prevents dust accumulating in them. And in addition they look much better this way.

Carry on up the back, row by row, until you have all the buttons placed and every fold satisfactorily made. Then the folds from the outside buttons to the edges can be temporarily made *(b)*. Turn up the cover from the bottom, exposing the swell; cut the foam from the button holes in the bottom row in straight lines, working downwards with a sharp pointed knife. Then part the wadding and hair beneath back to the hessian with a regulator.

It is here that the small marks made on the bottom edge of the cover are of value. Look at *(c)*. Hold the edge of the cover with thumb and forefinger over one of these marks; stretch down tightly and ease the material into the crevice from the button downwards, using a regulator. Fold the material at this mark, taking up about 20mm (¾in) in the fold and fasten with a skewer pushed up into the underside of the swell *(d)*.

Three cuts will have to be made to accommodate the centre upright bar, at both sides where the back frame joins the seat rails. The covering can then be pulled through and temporarily tacked at each of the edge marks. At *(e)* I indicate how the folds at the top and sides are made. Begin at the top, folding at a mark, with the opening of the pleat always facing outwards or downwards.

Fasten with one temporary tack per fold, without turning the fabric in for the time being. At the sides, make folds from the buttons adjacent to the frame at right angles to the frame at that point – except perhaps where buttons occur at a greater distance from the show-wood frame. Here you may find that the material falls into folds more easily at an oblique angle, like the diagonal pleats between the buttons. In this case ensure by measuring that the angles of the folds on both sides are the same.

It is now time to pull in all the buttons as far as they will go. Begin at the top and work

down – and go easy with the bottom row, for it may not be necessary to pull them in so far. Take them in little by little until any fullness between these buttons and the buttons forming the top of the diamond shape is taken up. They will then be sufficiently tight.

Trim off all surplus material around the frame, cutting it so as to allow 10-15mm (⅜-⅝in) for turning in. Then you can begin the finishing-off process. While your chair is in an upright position, get the most difficult part done first – which I always think is the bottom. Start from the sides and work towards the middle, stretching down and temporarily tacking several times before permanently fixing.

The sides and top come next, so lay the chair on its back. Begin from the bottom and, working up, turn in and temporarily tack as you go. Pull the pleats well in when you reach them to dispose of any fullness or unwanted creases. To eliminate as much untidy thickness of cloth as possible at the side folds, turn the cloth under first and pleat after. Use the small regulator to hold the corner of the pleat while you place the tacks.

If you are satisfied with the appearance of the upholstery when temporary fixing is complete, fasten all round with the smallest tacks – again using the pointed end of your regulator to work the cloth precisely up to the shoulder of the tacking rabbet.

It is a good idea to finish the inside back completely by trimming with braid or gimp, and it is very much easier to do this while there is no seat in the chair. The ends of the braid can be fastened well down the sides where it will be concealed by the seat upholstery. There will also be no danger of damage to the seat cover by spilled or splashed adhesive. Don't forget to stitch as well as stick so as to make doubly sure that the braid will not loosen.

Re-upholstering the seat I won't dwell too long on this part of the upholstery as I think from past experience gained from jobs such as the single chair with the stuffed-over seat, you are now quite capable of building in this seat. I will therefore just briefly run through

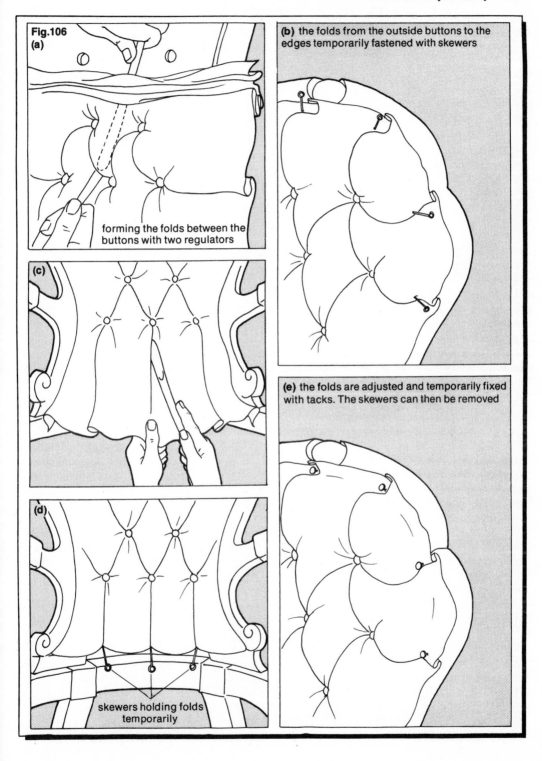

Fig.106
(a) forming the folds between the buttons with two regulators

(b) the folds from the outside buttons to the edges temporarily fastened with skewers

(c)

(d) skewers holding folds temporarily

(e) the folds are adjusted and temporarily fixed with tacks. The skewers can then be removed

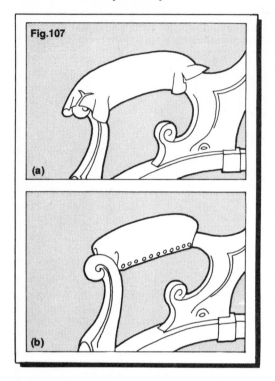

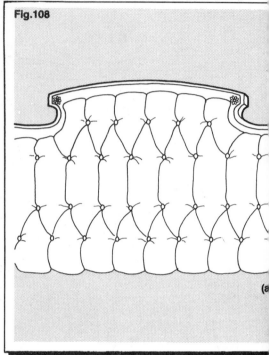

the specifications.

The webbing needs about five pieces each way about 40mm (1½in) apart, fixed on the underside of the seat rails. You will have to put in new springs 180mm (7in) high and 9 or 10 gauge. We need nine, in three rows of three. Use the usual tarpaulin hessian to cover the springs after they are laced. The first stuffing has a stitched-up edge with final rolls on the front and sides to a height of 90-100mm (3½-4in). Use horsehair for the stuffing.

The top stuffing of best hair should be laid on fairly thickly and, when confined by the calico undercover, it should form a distinct dome shape. The layers of wadding and thin polyether foam follow, then the top cover.

With this seat you have front as well as back uprights to cut in too, so take especial care and study those places at the back where the back frame joins the seat. You need some of this seat material to extend along the outside of those small carved scrolls that terminate the back show-wood.

At the front uprights, cut obliquely to within 20mm (¾in) of the wood, tucking the cloth in on both inside faces of the uprights and making straight corner pleats which will butt against the woodwork.

Covering the arms Finally, cover the arm pads *(see fig.107)*. This is a fairly easy matter, although it requires a certain amount of dexterity with the fingers. It is best to stretch the covering over the arm pads lengthwise, first from back to front, and at *(a)* you can see how to cut to the centre of the arm rail at the back and the front. Then make two small oblique cuts to form a vee to the width of the arm rail. The corners of these arm covers are single-pleated, so that the open ends of pleats are to the front and back *(b)*.

Covering the outside back The outside back covering will need some reinforcement beneath it, so stretch over some 202 or 283g (7½ or 10oz) hessian, tacking at the top and tightening to the bottom before stretching and securing at the sides. Put a layer or two

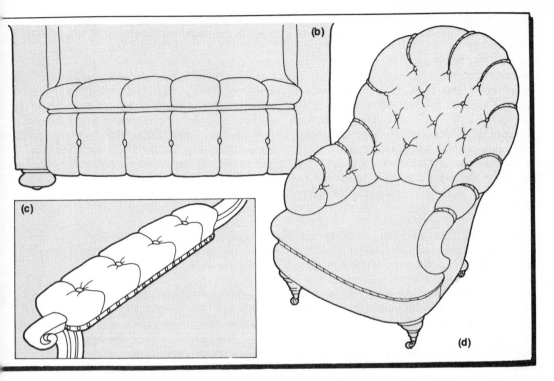

of cotton wadding over the hessian and then you can put on the velvet – temporarily at first of course. Then adjustments can be made before finally fixing.

Give all the show-wood a last rub-up before you put on the rest of the braid. And be sure to put some paper over the seat before you stick the braid around the arms. You don't want any nasty accidents now that you have nearly finished.

After all the trimming is finished, the last job is to tack on the bottom hessian – and there it is.

Variation on the theme Now, one or two questions which come to mind. First, is there another way of buttoning to produce alternative designs? Well, the diamond method is the most usual, but *(a)* in *fig.108* shows a style which incorporates straight vertical pleats between rows of buttons in diamond formation. This method was often used in carriage and early car upholstery, and it can be used on settees, couches and chairs which have rather high backs.

When you set out the measurements between the buttons at the top and bottom of the vertical pleats, the distance must be the same on the upholstery as on the back of the cloth. No extra is allowed on the cloth, so that when covering takes place the vertical pleat can be tucked well down into the upholstery and held tightly between the buttons at the top and bottom.

The front border of a chair seat buttoned with vertical pleats is shown at *(b)*. A button is placed in the centre of each pleat.

At *(c)* I've shown an arm pad similar to the ones on our chair but longer. The buttons are placed down the centre of the arm, and the material is pleated at each button across the width. Buttons for this sort of arm are usually made with a long wire nail shank instead of the usual wire loop or calico extrusion. And they are also pushed through the upholstery and hammered into the woodwork beneath. It is possible to use the ordinary button fixed with twine by bringing the twine out at each side of the arm and fixing with tacks.

On some early easy chairs, tub chairs and 'crinoline' chairs (so-called because of their iron rod and hoop construction above the wooden seat frame), the upholstery is stuffed over and there is no show-wood frame. These chairs can be trimmed with chair cord, and at *(d)* you can see such a chair and the effect given by extending cord from the buttons nearest to the edges over to the outside back. The pleats are sewn up first, then the cord fixed by twine at the bottom end, tacking or sewing at the other end and then stitching in the way I have described in the previous chapter. These corded pleats add just that final special touch to this kind of chair.

Buttoned seats Another question concerns buttoned seats. Some chairs, and a number of settees, have the seats buttoned – is there any difference in the foundation for this kind of seat? And how does one pull down the buttons underneath when you cannot get your hands between the webbing to tie the twine?

The method of building the stitched edges for a buttoned seat is slightly different, for as well as making the roll with through-stitches, the next row down is also made with stitches which go right through to the top. This row is put in last after the roll has been formed, and the result is that the seat is tightened and made a little lower behind the edge, giving more depth for the buttonwork.

It would be a most difficult task to pull down the buttons from the underside of the seat, so in cases like this, a slip knot is made on the top of the seat beneath a button. It is then pulled down from the top to the required depth, fastened off well beneath the button, and the twine cut off, leaving the ends at least 150mm (6in) long.

These ends can be disposed of by passing a long needle down through the seat beneath the button, threading both ends through the needle eye and pulling them down into the seat. The needle is then taken through and out from underneath.

It is here that I must leave you, proud of the fact that you have graduated to the stage where the mysteries and intricacies of Victorian buttonwork no longer cause you alarm. I hope my instructions will help you through many other upholstery jobs, for there is still so much to learn. Perhaps I could suggest that an ultimate goal for your endeavours might be a Chesterfield settee re-upholstered from the bare frame – fully buttoned, including the seat of course!

Index